A MIND FOR
POOL

HOW TO MASTER THE MENTAL GAME

Philip B. Capelle

First Edition
Billiards Press, Huntington Beach

A MIND FOR
POOL

HOW TO MASTER THE MENTAL GAME

By Philip B. Capelle

Published by:
Billiards Press
P.O. Box 400
Midway City, CA 92655

Sixth Printing

Printed in the United States of America.

10 9 8 7 6 5 4 3 2 1

Library of Congress Catalog Card Number: 99-94674

ISBN: 0-9649204-1-7

Praise for *A Mind For Pool*

"All sports are about being able to control the mind which enables a talented player to become a champion at any level. This book combined with **Play Your Best Pool** *covers everything any player would need to know to easily understand and enjoy the game. I highly recommend it to aspiring players who want to try to improve."*

— Allison Fisher
Three time World Nine-Ball Champion

*"*A Mind For Pool *is a perfect complement to* **Play Your Best Pool***....This one gives you a handy reference to everything about the mental side of the game. The end result is that you'll get much more out of your game—more fun and more success—after reading this book."*

— Tom Shaw
Pool & Billiard Magazine

"In fact, I find this book to be quite a writing accomplishment. ...Capelle goes on correctly interpretating attitudes, good and bad, and perceptions and mispercepions—you can hardly quarrel with a thing he says. Highly recommended once again, for intermediates on up."

— George Fels
Billiards Digest

"Phil Capelle has come up with another phenomenal jam-packed edition! **A Mind For Pool** *gives you the facts necessary for you to explode your pool game to the next level. This book is a mandatory teaching tool at the American Billiard Academy."*

— Roy Yamane
Master BCA Certified Instructor

DEDICATION

I dedicate this book to those who love pool.

ACKNOWLEDGMENTS

Part of the fun of writing and publishing a book is the opportunity to work with so many talented people. Each one of them was vital to the success of the project and they each have left their mark on the book. I wish to thank them and anyone I may have overlooked for their contributions to *A Mind For Pool*.

I thank Joe Oesterle for his enthusiasm and for his work in showing the lighter side of pool with his superb illustrations.

Alan Gadney and Carolyn Porter of One-On-One Book Production are responsible for turning the text into a very eye-catching and reader friendly book. Thank you very much for a job well done.

Mike Murad is to be thanked for his editing assistance and for his many suggestions for improving the book.

Linda Hunt cheerfully got the hard work of typing my prose off to a good start and was responsible for typing a majority of the book. Elaine Nale did a very professional job of handling corrections and revisions. Thank you both so very much.

Fellow BCA instructor Roy Yamane was kind enough to share his insights on how to succeed at league pool. Thank you, Roy.

Kelly Burton of Blazing Pages was responsible for the spine and back cover of the book and for her work on numerous promotional items. Thank you, Kelly, for all of your help.

Lastly, I would like to thank the hundreds of people that I have had the pleasure to meet on my journey in pool. I know that each one, in one way or another, provided me with some insight into the workings of the mental game of pool that appear on the pages that follow.

Table of Contents

INTRODUCTION

Once you have mastered the basics, pool largely becomes a mental game. When you reach the highest levels of the game, pool is 80-90 percent mental, as you've so often heard the pros exclaim. But what may surprise you is the relative importance of a solid mental approach to pool from the very first moment that you pick up a cue. In the beginning you need confidence that you can eventually learn to play before you can play. You also must have a great deal of patience as you deal with the frustrations of a newcomer's mistakes.

As your game develops, your mind must remain open to the changes required to advance your game to higher levels. Finally, you'll need to acquire a mindset that can enable you to reach your full potential as a competitive player.

Most of us have a gap that separates us from our full potential as a player. Our mental roadblocks are because of erroneous and destructive thoughts on various aspects of the game. Our mental mistakes show up in a variety of ways such as a resistance to change, whining about bad rolls (luck), and folding under pressure to name just a few. Our thoughts and reactions to various events that challenge us during the learning or competitive phases of pool are largely pre-programmed. *A Mind For Pool* exposes habitually erroneous thinking on all facets of the mental game and then provides you with a positive new perspective. The more road-blocks that you discover and remove, the closer your thinking will come to resembling that of a champion.

A Common Sense Approach to Pool

A Mind For Pool provides you with a logical, common sense approach to thinking pool. So don't be too disappointed at the absence of off-beat theories or magical solutions that are "guaranteed" to turn you into a world-beater overnight.

While you're reading the book, I think you'll often find yourself exclaiming that "I know that" or "that makes sense to me." Perhaps you'll be reminded of a useful pattern of thought or technique that you had forgotten or allowed to slip out of your game. Once reminded, you are ready to again reap the benefits of a previously successful train of thought. New ideas, because of their sheer logic and simplicity, may quickly become "your idea." These ideas, when implemented into your game, have the potential to significantly raise your level of play and your enjoyment of the game. In sum, the book can be either a reminder or a source of new ideas for your game.

> *Things should be made as simple as possible, but no simpler.*
> — Albert Einstein
>
> *All truth in the long run is only common sense clarified.*
> — Thomas Henry Huxley

The Little Things

The process of developing your game involves adding constantly to your storehouse of knowledge and skill. Keep adding the little things to your game and they will eventually make a big difference in your level of play. Every lesson in the book, therefore, has the potential to add something meaningful to your game. Your improvement may be in small, almost imperceptible increments. It's also possible that one new idea could serve as the catalyst for a big jump. For example, an increase in your level of concentration might, all by itself, be worth two extra games in a race to nine. Imagine what that could do for your chances of winning a Nine-Ball tournament.

Now let's suppose that you decide to have your stroke videotaped for the first time. This "little thing" could help you detect a big flaw that may have been the single most important obstacle to continued progress with your game. Yes, the little things are not really so little after all. And when you incorporate enough "little things" into your game, you can rightfully expect some big results.

> *Sometimes when I consider what tremendous consequences come from little things... I am tempted to think... there are no little things.*
> — Bruce Barton
>
> *God is in the details.*
> — Ludwig Mies van derrone

Fundamental Beliefs

When you learn to play pool, you should first become well grounded in its fundamentals. These include such basics as the grip, stance, bridge, and stroke. Your efforts to master the mental game can be similarly aided by a set of beliefs that give you the best chance for fulfilling your dreams as a pool player. The beliefs listed below can enable you to get the most out of this book—and your game. I strongly urge you to make each one a part of your "mental makeup."

- Pool should be fun.
- Your love of the game is your best motivator for accomplishment.
- There is a common sense approach to pool.
- Learning is an ongoing process—so keep an open mind.
- You are what you think about—so choose your thoughts wisely.
- A big game comes from an accumulation of the little things.
- Ask the right questions and you'll get the right answers.
- What you give to the game is what you get from it.

How to Use the Book

A Mind For Pool is divided into three parts. **YOUR GAME, PART ONE**, shows you how to get off to a good start, gain knowledge, deal with change, and evaluate your game. **COMPETITION, PART TWO**, gives you a complete course on the mental side of competitive pool. You'll learn how to play under pressure, deal with opponents, think like a player, and much more. **YOUR JOURNEY, PART THREE**, discusses your life as a pool player and how you can enjoy the game more than ever before.

Most books are meant to be read straight through from front to back. Not so with *A Mind For Pool*. You can scan the detailed Table of Contents and go directly to the chapter or section that is of immediate interest to you. As a practical matter, each section is a self'contained lesson. I would, however, encourage newcomers and those who feel that their fundamentals need work to read chapters one and two carefully before proceeding further into the book.

A Mind For Pool is designed to be your ongoing reference to the mental side of pool. As such, you should not be in a big hurry to finish the book. I think you will get the most out of it by reading one section or chapter and then taking the time necessary to incorporate the lesson(s) into your game.

Some of the most important points in the book are highlighted by a series of icons. These enable you to quickly refresh your memory on key concepts. You can also use them to skim the book or to discover sections that you'll want to then study thoroughly.

Since pool is a thinking person's game, there is no escaping the need to exercise your mind if you want to play your best pool. Throughout the book you'll be provided with a series of thought-provoking questions (☑). You may breeze lightly over the questions or you could really involve yourself in the process of self-examination. Just remember that the more you put into your game, the more you can expect to receive back in the form of a higher level of play and increased enjoyment.

While you proceed on the road to self-discovery, you will:

- Confirm the positive things you're already doing
- Recognize problem areas
- Find solutions to your problems

> *It is better to know some of the questions than all of the answers.*
> **— James Thurber**
>
> *It is a very great thing to be able to think as you like; but after all, an important question remains: what you think.*
> **— Matthew Arnold**

A number of checklists (☉) summarizes important points in the book. In many cases the lists also serve as inventory against which you can check the "assets" of your game. This can help you discover areas in which your game is deficient. The lists can also validate your strengths.

Capelle's Laws for Pool

Logical conclusions can be reached on most matters involving your pool game and your participation in the sport. These conclusions are presented at the end of each section in a series of "Capelle's Laws for Pool." I hope you'll agree that the laws represent the kind of thinking that most people would consider to be a common sense approach to pool. If you adopt these laws into your mental framework, your chances for success should be significantly enhanced. Here's an example.

 CAPELLE'S LAWS for POOL

Every shot you play can provide you with valuable information to help you improve your game.

Successful players possess a high degree of self-awareness. When they play a shot correctly, it either confirms what they already know or it teaches them something new. This information is then stored for future reference. Similarly, when they make a mistake, they do what is necessary to ensure that it is corrected and not repeated over and over again.

The laws summarize some of the most important concepts in the book. If you follow the laws, you will automatically think correctly on some of the most important matters that contribute to a rock solid approach to the mental game. Their primary value comes in helping you to streamline your thinking. By doing so you will be able to channel more of your energy into playing great pool and to enjoying the game even more.

Wisdom of History's Greatest Thinkers

A great number of life's universal truths apply equally well to pool. Fortunately enough for us, history's greatest thinkers have expressed these truths in a way that's both inspirational and memorable. Their words of wisdom will insure that you can get as much as possible from the lessons in the book. The selection process was completely at random. As a result, you'll find a wide range of cultures represented in the quotes which date back over the last 25 centuries. As you read the quotes, I'm certain you'll discover many of your favorites whose style of communication really strikes a chord with you.

> *The wisdom of the wise is an uncommon degree of common sense.*
> — **William Ralph Inge**

The quote above is one of my favorites as it so eloquently summarizes the approach of the book. Great players think in a way that makes sense. They don't possess any mystical secrets or scientific formulas about the game. Simply put, they are pool smart. They just perform correctly more of the basics and the little things that are available to us all.

The Art of Joe Oesterle

The book's cover illustrates several of the key components that go into making up a successful mental game. On the opening page of every chapter you'll find a quote from one of our great thinkers that pertains to the message of one of the sections that follows. The person quoted is also featured in an illustration that depicts the lighter side of pool. While in our pursuit of excellence, these illustrations can serve to remind us that pool is a game, first and foremost, and that games should be played for fun. The cover and all illustrations are from the talented hands of Joe Oesterle.

One picture is worth a 1,000 words.

— **Anonymous**

Without art, the crudeness of reality would make the world unbearable.

— **George Bernard Shaw**

A Final Note

Just for the record, I am completely for women being involved in pool. So I hope that no one is offended by my decision to use masculine pronouns throughout the book. When you see he, it really means he or she. Thank you.

Part I
YOUR GAME

Chapter 1
Getting Started

"The most important stage of any enterprise is the beginning."
— Plato

Developing Your Game the Right Way

There is a right way and a hard way to learning pool. The right way follows a proven game plan. This allows you to acquire the necessary skills in as short a period of time as possible given your time, talent and tenacity. The hard way lengthens the learning curve dramatically. It also reduces your chances of ever arriving at the game that you dreamed about when you first picked up a cue. The hard way is made up of much trial and error, of groping in the dark, and of putting your game together on a piecemeal basis.

It should be clear that the right way really is the only way to go if you are at all serious about progressing much beyond the ranks of a novice player. The right way is comprised of some general guidelines for progressing through the various stages of development. These guidelines are fairly rigid at the beginning because it is crucial for you to learn the basics well before moving on to the other elements. The further you progress, the more flexibility you have in establishing your plan for growth.

If you are a new player intent on learning to play a solid game, you should signal your commitment to the game by buying a starter cue. The price range for a good quality starter cue is between $50 - $150. Don't spend much more because you will be trading up to a more expensive model as soon as your game develops to where certain preferences become known. These would include the ideal weight, length, tip size and balance, to name a few.

Fundamentals First

With your starter cue in hand and with your enthusiasm running high, it's now time to get down to business. The first thing is to get your fundamentals down pat. It may comfort you to know that many of the things that will ensure your success involve no moving parts. Before worrying about the stroke you should learn to make a solid stance and bridge and to grip the cue correctly.

To become a player you must first look like a player when standing over the shot. There's really no point in going much further until your setup is correct. And because this requires no stroking motion, your set-up should not be overly difficult to master. You can check yourself in a mirror at home after you've had a qualified instructor show you how it's done. You can also use a video tape or book on pool to check your form.

Once you've learned a consistence stance, it's time to learn the stroke, which is the foundation for all that follows. A solid, accurate and dependable stroke will enable you to execute all that you will subsequently learn about the game. Without a stroke that you can trust, you will be constantly fighting to match your results to your pre-shot plans.

Stroke mechanics are covered in detail in *PLAY YOUR BEST POOL*. In addition to reading *PLAY YOUR BEST POOL*, I would strongly advise that you work with an instructor. There's no substitute for having someone who can help adjust your technique on the spot until you've got it just right.

You can figure on at least six months to a year of fairly concentrated practice to build the base for your game. This practice should include shooting a wide variety of shots over and over so that you can develop your sense of aim. There are a few products on the market that are designed to help you learn to aim as quickly and effortlessly as possible.

The final segment of the first phase consists of cueing up and down the center axis of the cue ball. This will impart follow and draw to the cue ball and it serves as your entree into the world of position play. To sum up phase one, your plan is to stand like a player, develop your stroke, learn to aim and to apply follow and draw to the cue ball.

The Knowledge Phase

Phase two could be called the knowledge phase. Now it's time to learn to play pool. Now the doors swing wide open to an unending array of skills and strategies that will keep you fascinated for your entire career. In the beginning you should concentrate on basic position play. Learn how to get shape on the next ball in an ever-widening number of situations. This will lead into what's called pattern play where you start planning ahead for two or three shots. A fair degree of competency at shotmaking, position play and pattern play will have you in good shape to play a respectable game of Eight-Ball. At this point you may also wish to start exploring the use of english.

Most players who enter phase two will soon be tempted into playing pool competitively. Your game can benefit from the various forms of competition as long as you do not neglect the basics of phase two. Unfortunately, at this point all too many players get sucked into the lure of competition and they never complete the second phase. As a result, they never fully develop into the player they could have been.

The Competition Phase

Phase three introduces you to competition. Testing and developing your game even further are the objectives as you enter this phase. Most new players are best off playing Eight-Ball for at least a year or two, if not more. Eight-Ball is the perfect game to test a developing player's skills against equal competition in an organized setting. Eight-Ball is, in fact, the mainstay of league play and of low cost tournaments that are geared to new and average players.

Many players who start out playing Eight-Ball become perfectly satisfied with it as their game of choice. More adventuresome and ambitious players will quickly add Nine-Ball to their repertoire. Nine-Ball is America's second most popular pool game and it's the one favored by serious players and the pro tours. There is no lack of competitive opportunities for the aspiring Nine-Ball player. They range from leagues and tournaments for novice players, clear through to the ranks of the most seasoned professionals. Other popular favorites of dedicated pool players include One-Pocket, Straight Pool and Bank Pool.

Postgraduate Work

Once you acquire a dependable stroke, a fairly broad range of knowledge and some seasoning, you have completed the first three phases of your education in pool. From this point forward you must make the decision to enroll in postgraduate work or to be content with the game you have. Those of you who wish to progress beyond the ranks of average players will have a number of options for furthering your game.

Your progress will hinge on many factors. These include your available time, your level of commitment, the quality of instruction you receive, your thirst for competition and your talent for the game. Most of these items are under your control. The one great constant is your innate talent for pool. Even this component probably allows for more improvement because you probably have much more talent than you may have given yourself credit for.

The mix of elements we discussed above will continue to shape your game as you progress along your journey in pool. How high you wish to ascend is largely up to you. Remember, however, that your ability to progress up the ladder will be made much easier if you take the time necessary to successfully complete the first three phases. There's simply no substitute for getting off to a good start.

CAPELLE'S LAWS for POOL

For any new player there's only one way to learn pool right: from the ground up.

Don't overspend for your first cue because you're going to be upgrading soon enough.

Desire to have things done quickly prevents their being done thoroughly.
— Confucius

Ignorance is the curse of God,
Knowledge the wing wherewith we fly to heaven.
— Shakespeare

When the ancients said a work well begun was half done, they meant to impress the importance of always endeavoring to make a good beginning.
—Polybius

The self-educated are marked by stubborn peculiarities.
—Isaac D'israeli

The journey of a 1,000 miles begins with a single step.
— Lao-tzu

My interest is in the future because I am going to spend the rest of my life there.
— Charles F. Kettering

Setting Your Goals

In the beginning you may have played pool strictly for fun. Perhaps you enjoyed banging balls occasionally with your friends. During this stage you had only the vaguest notion of how well you'd like to eventually play and what it would take to get there. Then you crossed over the big dividing line to where you wanted to definitely rise above the ranks of a novice.

Now your desire to improve will be fed by your progress. Once the improvement bug infects you, it's hard to quit as long as your improvement is being realized on a fairly regular basis. It's during this phase of the cycle that the vast majority of average or above average players acquire a significant portion of their skill at the game. At this point, a fair percentage of players continue to pursue a higher level of play while the majority enjoy the game they have while only seeking occasional incremental gains in their game.

When you start playing pool there's no telling where it may lead. Many of you will be perfectly satisfied with a game that enables you to be successful at your chosen level of competition. Some of you will continue jumping hurdles until you are a very formidable competitor. At this point the little things enter in that separate those at the top from those a notch or two below.

Your Level of Commitment

Those who seriously want to advance to some degree or another all share one thing in common: their commitment to improving their game. What you are willing to put in largely determines what you will, as a player, get back out. Let's consider three levels of commitment.

Casual player—You enjoy the game and would like to play better, but hopefully without too much practice or effort.

Serious Player—You want to improve and you have some time to practice and work at the game, which you are willing to do. You also compete regularly.

Ultra Dedicated—You will do whatever it takes to improve your game. Lessons, practice, competition and study are all part of your regular routine. Your only limitation is your God given talent.

Goal Setting

Your commitment to bettering your game is largely based on your recent progress, your available time and a deep-seated belief that the work you put in will result in measurable improvement. Once you have made a commitment to working on your game it's time to set some goals. They will give you something tangible to strive for.

Tips for Setting Goals

⊙ Your goals must be achievable (realistic).

⊙ Your goals must challenge you. They should not be too easy.

⊙ You should set a date for reaching your goals.

⊙ Use different time frames depending on the nature of the goal.

⊙ Create new goals once you've reached an existing goal.

⊙ Enjoy the process of working towards your goals.

Achieving Milestones

Your long-term goals may, in some cases, represent milestones that, when reached, cause you to stop and reflect on all that you have accomplished. After years of working on your game and competing, the result could be a win in an important championship. The victory represents the pinnacle of your career. This accomplishment could spur you to even greater heights. You could also attempt to duplicate the feat one or more times.

Your milestone victory could signal that you have accomplished all that you set out to as a competitive pool player and that it is now time to start emphasizing something else. That could, of course, be in some pool related activity. In pro sports you'll often see players turn to coaching or broadcasting when their careers are over. As a pool player, your interest could shift to teaching, running tournaments or managing a pool room.

When is enough competitive pool enough? What's your peak? What will you do when you still like to play but you've lost the edge? These are questions that can be decades away thanks to the longevity of a pool player's career. But when and if the day comes, then there will always be some other place for you in the game for once you've become a true pool person, chances are you always will be.

Why Some Players Fail

I can't recall how many times I've heard a promising young player issue a warning about how much better they'd be in six months or a year. Then time passes and nothing much happens. Why weren't their words backed up with results? Why did they fail to achieve the game they seemed so confident about? Well, there's a huge gap between saying you're going to do something and actually doing it. That's why so much credit should be given to those who actually follow through and make their bold statements or dreams a reality.

There are a number of things that could slow or even halt your progress. Most of them are within your control. But there are also some that have to do with other responsibilities that could restrict your time spent at the table.

Pitfalls to Progress

⊙ A resistance to change.

⊙ Fear of losing the game you've worked so hard for.

⊙ A mind closed to new information.

⊙ Lack of a plan.

⊙ The game turns out to be a lot tougher than you thought it was.

⊙ You reach a level of play that you are reasonably satisfied with.

⊙ You discover that you hate to practice.

⊙ Your enthusiasm for the game tapers off because your progress has slowed measurably.

⊙ Family and/or work keeps you from playing as much as you need to reach your goals.

⊙ You discover that you're not that serious after all.

⊙ You fail to be honest with yourself about what you really want from the game.

 CAPELLE 'S LAWS for POOL

Knowing what you want from the game is 90 percent of the battle.

Your love of the game is your best motivator for playing it as well as possible.

Your first commitment should be to enjoy the game.

The measure of your commitment to improving your game is a highly personal matter.

You will spend most of your time working towards a goal, so you should enjoy the process.

Set goals that are a challenge and that motivate you to improve your game.

Once you've achieved a worthwhile goal, take a few moments to savor the experience. Then reset your sights on a new goal.

Don't let the game become such an obsession that it disrupts other areas of your life.

Give the game your best shot with whatever resources that you have at your disposal.

> *The great thing in the world is not so much where we are but in what direction we are going.*
> — Oliver Wendell Holmes

> *There is a law in psychology that if you form a picture in your mind of what you would like to be, and you keep and hold that picture there long enough, you will soon become exactly as you have been thinking.*
> — William James

> *Make no little plans; they have no magic to sir men's blood.*
> —Daniel Hudson Burnham

> *The height of your accomplishments will equal the depth of your commitment.*
> — William F. Scolavino

> *If you don't know where you are going, how can you expect to get there?*
> — Basil S. Walsh

> *Choosing a goal and sticking to it changes everything.*
> — Scott Reed

> *It is never too late to be who you might have been.*
> — George Eliot

> *You see things, and you say 'why'? But I dream things that never were; and I say 'why not'?*
> — Goerge Bernard Shaw

Practicing Pool

One of the next best things to playing pool is practicing pool. Practice gives you the chance to develop and hone your skills for competition. You can implement new ideas and make discoveries that can have a lasting and positive impact on your game. And while you're working on a shooting technique or a particular shot you can see yourself improving on the spot.

 Yes, there is a lot to be said for practicing pool which, unfortunately, some otherwise serious players avoid like the plague. I would advise that you adopt a very positive attitude towards practice. Practice is something that can and should be enjoyed in its own right and, more importantly, because it will make you an even better player.

Now that you've made a commitment to practicing your game, you may find the following tips helpful for getting the most out of each session.

Getting The Most from Practice

⊙ Set some specific long-range goals for upcoming practice sessions.

⊙ Have a game plan for each practice session.

⊙ Keep a notebook of your progress and your discoveries.

⊙ Spend much of your practice time by yourself so you can work on exactly what you want to.

⊙ Politely but firmly fend off intruders.

⊙ Practice at home or when it's not too busy at the pool room or tavern.

Practice Time

How much practice is enough? That depends on your stage of development, your available time and how seriously you take the game. The amount of practice required is also related to your aptitude for the game. I advise that you not skate along on talent alone while bragging about how little you need to practice as some players seem so proud of doing. The table below provides you with the general guidelines for the hours of practice necessary to meet your goals.

Recommended Practice Time		
	Very serious	**Somewhat Serious**
Beginner	4- 7 times a week, 1-3 hours	2- 4 times a week, 1-2 hours
Intermediate	3- 5 times a week, 1-2 hours	2- 3 times a week, 1-1.5 hours
Advanced-maintenance	2- 4 times a week, 1-2 hours	1- 2 times a week, 30 minutes-1 hour

Practice Strategies

There are so many strategies that you can use in practice which ensures that there should always be something to work on that will keep your interest. For starters, try building your confidence with some relatively easy shots. Gradually raise the level of difficulty. Work on your stroke and fundamentals at the beginning of your session. This will get you tuned up and ready for shooting specific shots, progressive drills or for simulating various games.

During competition you should be able to concentrate on playing the game without worrying about your stroke. Therefore, it's a good idea to spend some time shooting while completely trusting your stroke. This can be done after working on mechanics or while practicing your favorite game.

Every player seems to have at least one or two shots that need work. One week it might be cut shots and the next it could be banks or combos. So plan on spending some time on your weaknesses. Don't, however, be too surprised if one of your stronger shots declines a little while you're emphasizing a weak point. Once you're satisfied with your progress on a soft spot, practice on your strong shot until you've got it back to previous standards. The improvement process is like a juggling act where your goal is to keep several diverse skills at a high level simultaneously.

Every player needs to spend time practicing position. Before your next practice, purchase some reinforcements for three-ring binder paper. These are used to mark the position of the balls so you can practice the same position play over and over until you've got it down pat. You can mark the target with a second object ball. If the cue ball bumps the object ball lightly, you can consider this a bulls-eye.

Game Practice

Newer players should plan on spending a good portion of their practice on Eight-Ball. Eight-Ball is a highly complex game when played properly. You can, however, still win a high percentage of games just by learning how to run-out a fairly wide open table. Start your practice by tossing out two or three balls and the eight-ball. Give yourself ball-in-hand, plan your pattern and then try to run-out. Keep adding balls as your skill rises until you can consistently run eight balls.

The next step is to add a few obstacles (your opponents group). These will add to the difficulty of getting position. Finally, practice on a full rack. Break the balls and then plot your strategy. This should include breakouts, safeties and pattern play. You may even wish to switch back and forth between the solids and stripes.

Nine-Ball is a particularly demanding game for all players, but even more so for newer players. It takes lots of knowledge and skill to keep pocketing relatively difficult shots (when compared to other pool games) and to play position for a specific ball. It takes time for any player to build their game to the point where they can run four to five balls consistently, much less an entire rack.

No matter what your level of skill, you may be surprised at how often (or not) you can run an open table in practice with ball-in-hand. You may discover that running just a few (4-5) balls consistently (70 percent) is a tougher chore than you might have imagined. Practice by spreading several balls across the length of the table in a wide variety of positions that will put your game to the test. Newer players should use no more than three balls. Advanced players can pick your number. Adjust the number of balls up-or-down depending on your level of success. You should run out about 70 percent of the time before adding another ball.

While you practice, take note of those position plays that are especially troublesome. These should be worked on until mastered. Advanced players should simulate actual game conditions as closely as possible by breaking open a full rack. Try to run out when feasible, but also make sure to practice safeties and kick shots.

Straight Pool lends itself well to solitary practice. The game teaches you to concentrate on each and every shot. One small lapse can lead to a miss. Then you must, of course, start building your house of cards, so to speak, all over again. Naturally the more balls you have run, the less pleasant the prospect of missing becomes.

Practicing with Friends

Some of your game practice should be conducted with a friend who is equally serious about improving his game. Play some cheap sets, wagering just enough to really make you concentrate on your game. Take notice of any flaws you detect in each others mechanics. Remember that the main thing is to help improve each other's game. You should also stop and ask each other advice when you come across a shot that you're not sure of.

Practice Devices

In recent years, a number of practice devices have hit the market that can help your aim and stroke. Practice cue balls with markings allow you to learn where centerball is located (this is easier said than done) and to adjust your follow, draw and english. Chalk your cue thoroughly before each shot so you can tell if you struck the cue ball exactly where you intended.

Aiming devices positioned next to the object ball enable you to quickly discover how much of the object ball needs to be cut to pocket the shot. Mirrors have been specially adapted for use on a pool table. These give you instant feedback on your stroke. Buddy Hall has also come out with the Cue Guide that can sharpen your follow-through.

CAPELLE 'S LAWS for POOL

Twenty minutes of thoughtful practice is better for your game then four hours of banging balls around.

Plan your practice carefully and practice what you plan.

A positive attitude towards practicing will pay big dividends later when you're competing at pool.

Practice may not necessarily turn you into a great player, but without it you don't even stand a chance.

Practice as long as your enthusiasm remains high, but quit the very second it starts to wane.

The time and money you spend practicing pool should be viewed as an investment that will return many years of joy.

For the things we have to learn before we can do them, we learn by doing them.
> — Aristotle

Practice is nine-tenths.
> — Ralph Waldo Emerson

There is nothing training cannot do. Nothing is above its reach.
> — Mark Twain

Practice yourself, for heaven's sake, in little things; and thence proceed to greater.
> — Epictetus

Practice is the best of all instructors.
> — Publilius Syrus

However much thou art read in theory, if thou hast no practice thou art ignorant.
> — Sa'di

The more I want to get something done, the less I call it work.
> — Richard Bach

Chapter 2
Getting Instruction

"Learn as though you would never be able to master it; hold it as though you would be in fear of losing it."

— Confucius

How to Select Your Instructor

Receiving good instruction can be a huge benefit to your game. It pays to make the extra effort to find a competent instructor. Don't settle for a fast talker who plays a halfway decent game or who makes outrageous claims about his ability to turn you into a champion. I suggest that you carefully evaluate each candidate. You may have to take a lesson from two or three instructors before you find the one that's right for you. Don't hesitate to fire a teacher because your game is too important to you to accept less than the best.

Below are a series of questions to help you evaluate potential instructors. Before you sign up with an instructor or during your orientation at the start of your first lesson you should take several minutes to go through this list. Your candidate should be more than willing to answer these questions to your complete satisfaction. If your instructor balks and adopts the all-knowing expert attitude, then they have something to hide or they are not really interested in getting to know you as an individual. These almighty guru types would rather tell you what they know than to teach you how to play next.

Questions to Ask Your Instructor

- ☑ Is he certified by the BCA?
- ☑ How long has he been playing and teaching?
- ☑ How well does he play? Can he demonstrate what he teaches?
- ☑ How did he learn to play?
- ☑ What is his philosophy of teaching?
- ☑ Does he teach a particular method, or will he adapt the proven fundamentals to your particular game?
- ☑ What is the sequence of skills that he will teach? (Fundamentals, aiming, pre-shot routine, etc.)
- ☑ What is his plan for taking you from one level to the next?
- ☑ Does he use any special teaching aides?
- ☑ Will you be given practice drills and routines to work on?
- ☑ What level of player does he enjoy working with and why?

In addition to the answers to the questions above, it's important that the chemistry be right. How you feel about the person is crucial because you will be spending a lot of time together.

During the Q & A session the instructor should also ask several questions about your game. This shows that he cares about you. It also shows that he wants to get to know you so he can put this information to work for your benefit. Below are some questions that a caring and competent instructor will ask you.

Questions from Your Instructor

☑ How long have you been playing?

☑ Have you had any other teachers?

☑ What fundamentals do you follow? Why?

☑ What special problems do you feel require immediate attention?

☑ How much practice time do you have?

☑ What are your goals?

☑ Do you have any physical problems that affect how to play?

☑ How do you learn best?

☑ What kind of cue are you playing with?

☑ Are you a competitive player?

The points that we've covered above apply to those of you who are looking for an instructor who can guide you on your journey for the next several weeks, months or even longer. Those of you who seek a solution to a specific problem in one or two lessons need not to be nearly so thorough in your evaluation. In this case all you need to know is what part of your game needs work and who is competent in this particular area.

 CAPELLE'S LAWS for POOL

Quality instruction will make a huge difference in your game, so make the necessary effort to find the right teacher for your game.

> *Treat people as if they were what they ought to be and you help them become what they are capable of becoming.*
> **—Johann Wolfgang von Goethe**
>
> *If the student fails to learn, the teacher fails to teach.*
> **— Anonymous**

> *To teach is to learn.*
>
> —Japanese proverb
>
> *The secret of teaching is to appear to have known all your life what you learned this afternoon.*
>
> — Anonymous

How to Be a Great Student

Assuming that you've gone to the trouble of finding an instructor it's now time to become a great student. Your motivation should stem largely from your passion for the game and your unwavering desire to play as well as you possibly can. The list of suggestions below should help you make the most of your time spent working with your instructor.

- ⊙ Be very enthusiastic.
- ⊙ Remain open to positive change.
- ⊙ Trust your instructor.
- ⊙ Exercise patience.
- ⊙ Stick to your game plan—don't try to rush the process.
- ⊙ Pay close attention to your instructor.
- ⊙ Ask lots of questions—learn the hows and whys.
- ⊙ Communicate immediately what does not feel right to you.
- ⊙ Practice between lessons.
- ⊙ Respect your instructor's time.

CAPELLE'S LAWS for POOL

What you fail to communicate will continue to frustrate.

> *Learn as though you would never be able to master it; hold it as though you would be in fear of losing it.*
>
> — Confucius
>
> *They know enough who know how to learn.*
>
> — Henry Adams

> *Learning is either a continuing thing or it is nothing.*
> — **Frank Tyger**
>
> *The more we study, the more we discover our ignorance.*
> — **Percy Bysshe Shelley**
>
> *He is a poor disciple who does not excel his master.*
> — **Leonardo da Vinci**
>
> *Two heads are better than one.*
> — **John Heywood**

The Cost of an Education

Not long ago the secrets and strategies of the great masters were as well concealed as a buried treasure. In the old days it took aspiring players years of experience and much trial and error to thoroughly learn the game. The learning curve was stretched out because the top players were reluctant to share trade secrets for fear their generosity might affect their livelihood.

My, how times have changed. Today we are firmly entrenched in the information age of pool. For a nominal sum you can purchase books and tapes that reveal secrets it took the old timers years to discover. Indeed, pool players looking to improve their game have never had it so good.

The cost of your tuition is truly a bargain when looked at from a business person's point of view. Let's assume that you spend $1,000 over the next five years on lessons, tapes and books. Now let's figure that you have thirty years to recover this investment in tournaments, leagues and money games. You will need to up your annual winnings by a paltry $33 to pay for your education. Anything above that is pure profit. With your improved pool game this certainly sounds reasonable enough.

Now we'll add into the equation the sheer enjoyment you'll experience from playing better pool. We're talking about the pleasure that comes from slicing a ball down the rail or from running-out on double-hill to win a tournament. These kinds of pool treasures are truly priceless.

If your goal is to make the most of your journey, plan on investing some time and money on your education. The expenditure can be easily justified both monetarily and emotionally.

CAPELLE'S LAWS for POOL

The cost of educational materials on pool is a screaming bargain when compared with the price of experience.

Old timers would have nearly killed each other for the knowledge that's now so readily available in books and tapes.

The purchase price of a book or tape can easily be recovered the next time you compete at pool.

If you think education is expensive—try ignorance.
— **Derek Bok**

I haven't heard of anybody who wants to stop living on account of the cost.
— **F. McKinney Hubbard**

Most people are willing to pay more to be amused than to be educated.
— **Robert C. Savage**

Advice: The Good and Bad

When receiving unsolicited advice on your game, it's definitely *player beware*. We're talking specifically about "help" that comes from well wishers and ego trippers whose credentials are highly suspect. You must also be on guard against falling under the spell of the witchdoctors of pool.

Advice from your close friends can be helpful as long as they are familiar with your game. They can be useful in spotting your negative tendencies before they really grab hold of your game. Your friend's advice should be limited to occasionally checking for obvious faults in your game unless they also happen to be competent instructors.

The urge to share is very powerful in some people. This can be good news for your game when advice comes from an acknowledged expert. Advice can be very damaging when it comes in the form of unsolicited tips from a well meaning, but frankly unqualified source. The prime example is the macho boyfriend who insists on teaching his girlfriend even though he grips the cue like a baseball bat.

Before you think for a split second about accepting advice, stop to consider the source. Is your adviser an excellent player or qualified instructor? If they pass this test, be polite and hear them out. You must then decide whether or not their suggestion makes sense and if it fits with your approach to the game. This decision is yours and yours alone. You have every right to reject advice no matter what the source.

There are a number of self-appointed gurus of pool who would jump at the chance to put you under their spell. These witchdoctors of pool love to ramble on to all who would listen about the mysteries of pool. If one of these types has invaded your air space, you must cut this sage off quickly before their magical cures put a curse on your game.

The best technique for fending off unwanted purveyors of the holly grail of pool is to develop a few pat lines that make your point politely, but ever so firmly. Here are a few suggestions:

⊙ "I'm working with an instructor already. We have our game plan all set. But thanks for the offering."

⊙ "I'm studying *Play Your Best Pool*." (By guess who?)

⊙ "Are you certified by the BCA?"

CAPELLE'S LAWS for POOL

There is a reasonably close correlation between the quality of a person's advice and their level of play.

The health of your game is always at stake. One bad tip could set off a negative chain reaction that could take months to recover from.

No advice is better than bad advice.

A new theory that promises to solve all of your problems is more likely to be a curse.

Be wary of the witchdoctors of pool. They teach offbeat theories that defy common sense, logic, physics and possibly all that you've learned about the game.

Wise men don't need advice. Fools don't take it.

— Benjamin Franklin

No enemy is worse than bad advice.

— Sophocles

Advice is an uncertain gift.

— Whitney Jeffery

> *The best advice yet given is that you don't have to take it.*
> — Libbie Fudim

Finding a Mentor

Excellent players who retire or semi-retire from active competition still frequent the pool room, many on a daily basis. Many of these lifelong devotees of the sport have a wealth of knowledge that can help most any player advance their game.

An experienced mentor can be found by asking around or by taking notice of some of the senior citizens in your room. You can explore the possibility of a relationship by striking up a conversation over a cup of coffee with your potential mentor. Your interest and enthusiasm for the game is often all it takes for a veteran to begin sharing their knowledge with you.

Your relationship could be limited to a few conversations from time to time. It could also blossom into a full-fledged mentor/student relationship when the chemistry is right. If a mentor takes you under their wing, be sure to follow several of the rules for being a good student. Above all else, ask good questions and listen carefully.

Over time a strong friendship may develop as your mentor takes an increasingly active role in your growth as a player. And don't make the mistake of thinking you're too good to continue learning. Even a top pro like Nick Varner, who has won numerous titles, saw the wisdom in having the legendary instructor Hal Mix accompany him to numerous tournaments.

Your mentor typically does not expect to get paid much if at all, but his compensation is strictly between the two of you. Mentors receive their payback, for the most part, from sharing their knowledge with you and from your enthusiasm and dedication to improving your game.

CAPELLE'S LAWS for POOL

Veteran pool players love to share their knowledge with new players who love pool and want to learn. It makes a wonderful combination.

Only a life in the service of others is worth living.
> — **Albert Einstein**

Make yourself necessary to somebody.
> — **Ralph Waldo Emerson**

The greatest good you can do for another is not just to share your riches but to reveal to him his own.
> — **Benjamin Disraeli**

Sharing what you have is more important than what you have.
> — **Albert M. Wells, Jr.**

Chapter 3
What You Need to Know

"A little neglect may breed great mischief...for want of a nail, the shoe was lost; for want of a shoe; the horse was lost; for want of a horse, the battle was lost; for want of the battle, the war was lost."
— **Benjamin Franklin**

Pool from the Ground Up

There are a number of highly physical games, such as football and basketball, where your peak years come in your 20s or early 30s. There is a rush to achieve optimal performance since your career is relatively short lived. Pool is much different. Your career has only just begun in pool while it is peaking or even ending in other sports.

You have a lifetime to enjoy pool, so there should be no big hurry to master the game overnight. Take it slow and steady. Understand that it takes time to learn all of the skills and strategies of the game. You will eventually arrive at your various goals in the time that it takes you to get there, no more, no less. And rest assured that, occasionally, you will experience a surge in your game that will turbo charge your desire to seek continued improvement.

Pool is learned best from the ground up. There are a few fundamentals that can lay the foundation for all that follows. Therefore, it is well worth the extra time and effort to learn how to play correctly right from the start.

Unfortunately, many players proceed with a method that is based on instinct or natural talent. While this approach may work for a chosen few, for most it is a recipe for disaster. The tendency for most newcomers to go it alone may be because the game looks deceptively easy. Poor habits can also result from lack of instruction. A newcomer may play with poor fundamentals for quite some time until the pool bug hits and they get serious about their game. By the time they finally get help, they have bad habits that take time to correct. New players simply must emphasize fundamentals, as they will considerably enhance their chances for success, which in turn will raise their enthusiasm for the game.

How much time will it take for you to beat your friends, win a tournament or help your team win a championship? That largely depends on the 4 T's: time, talent, tenacity and teaching. Tons of concentrated practice in the beginning is essential. Talent and good teaching can speed up the process. And, of course, some people just have a greater aptitude for the game.

The keys are to get good instruction, practice hard and often, and be enthusiastic about your chances for improvement. If you are new to pool, make the necessary effort to learn good habits now so that you won't have to endure the painful process of relearning the game later.

A positive attitude towards pool combined with a healthy dosage of patience will be among your best friends on your lifelong journey to excellence. Be thankful there is so much to learn, because this can help to keep your interest in pool alive.

CAPELLE'S LAWS for POOL

The first two years should be spent building a solid foundation for all that follows.

Several hours a day of concentrated play and practice in the first few years will ensure that you experience the rapid development cycle.

Be patient and learn things in their proper sequence.

Pool takes a long time to learn properly. So you should not rush the process because you will have a lifetime to enjoy the game.

Rome was not built in one day.
— **John Heywood**

Everything should be made as simple as possible, but not simpler.
— **Albert Einstein**

One thing at a time, all things in succession. That which grows slowly endures.
— **J. G. Hubbard**

A good beginning makes a good ending.
— **English proverb**

Slight not what's near through aiming at what's far.
— **Euripides**

The Three Master Skills

Pool requires the skillful blending of three primary elements: the physical game, knowledge and the mental game. All three components should be learned simultaneously right from the start. However, the emphasis on each segment changes as your game progresses.

In the beginning, learning the basics of the grip, bridge, stance and stroke as well as the nuances of aiming is of primary importance. Once you've acquired a good grasp of the physical game, you are ready to learn how to play the game. This is the time when you begin to gain a grasp of position play, pattern recognition, safeties and the other assorted skills that make up a well rounded game.

At some point early in the knowledge phase, you will probably start competing in local tournaments and leagues. This is the moment when your mental game starts developing in earnest.

THE THREE MASTER SKILLS

To summarize, in phase one your physical game is priority #1. In phase two, you begin to apply your physical skills towards playing the game as opposed to just pocketing balls. The mental game grows exponentially in importance as you begin to compete at pool, which is the start of phase three.

The Three Phases of Learning Pool

1. BEGINNERS

- **Physical:** Emphasize the physical game: pocketing balls.
- **Knowledge:** Learn the fundamentals and discover your unique shooting style.
- **Mental:** Maintain a good attitude towards the process.

2. INTERMEDIATE

- **Physical:** Further refine your stroke.
- **Knowledge:** Begin to learn about playing the game.
- **Mental:** Stay patient and enjoy your game as it progresses.

3. ADVANCED

- **Physical:** Maintain your physical game while you look for incremental improvement.
- **Knowledge:** Keep learning all you can about playing the game.
- **Mental:** Your mental game is now the top priority now as you strive to move up the competitive ladder.

CAPELLE'S LAWS for POOL

To maximize your potential you must continuously be developing both your physical and mental games while at the same time always be adding to your body of knowledge.

> *Every soul has to learn the whole lesson for itself. It must go over the whole ground. What it does not see, what it does not live, it will not know.*
>
> **— Ralph Waldo Emerson**
>
> *It is by losing himself in the objective, in inquiry, creation and craft, that a man becomes something.*
>
> **— Paul Goodman**
>
> *Skill to do comes from doing.*
>
> **— Ralph Waldo Emerson**

The Little Things Make a Big Difference

Imagine for a moment that you are an athlete preparing for the Olympics. You will be competing against the best athletes that the world has to offer. At this level of competition you can't spot the field even the tiniest advantage.

Your coach will watch your practices to make sure your body is operating like a well-oiled machine. Your personal trainer will have you in the best shape of your life. You will arrive at the host site several days in advance so you can get acclimated to the surroundings. The night before your event you will get plenty of rest. On your big day you will eat a meal that energizes you for maximum performance, and you will go through your pre-event ritual to perfection. In short, you will have as much going for you as possible so that you don't give up the slightest edge to the competition.

Playing pool at higher levels of competition is really not much different. Any important detail that you overlook could be the one that leads to defeat. How would you feel if you miscued on a crucial shot just because you forgot to bring the tip tapper? What if you ate a greasy cheeseburger that caused you to fall half-asleep during the match? These seemingly innocuous details are the kind that can take the edge off your game or lead to outright disaster.

Keep in mind that your opposition may have their house completely in order. You can't afford to unnecessarily spot them any kind of edge. If you pile on every edge that you can think of (short of sharking your opponent) you will feel a sense of confidence that comes from knowing you are completely prepared for battle.

You can also build a series of winning edges by adding as many skills to your game as possible. These could include proficiency at combinations, a powerful new break or a series of devastating safeties. Other advantages could include a detailed scouting report on your opponent and lots of practice on the table(s) to be used in competition.

I suggest that you put on your thinking cap and compose a list of every detail you can possibly imagine. These can give you an advantage or at least prevent your opponent from gaining an important edge.

CAPELLE'S LAWS for POOL

Every edge you develop gives you another way to win or to avoid losing.

Any edge may be the edge that wins a match for you.

Pile on as many edges as possible because it is comforting to know that you have as much working for you as possible.

Educated men are as superior to uneducated men as the living are to the dead.
— **Aristotle**

Little drops of water
Little grains of sand,
Make the mighty ocean
And the pleasant land
— **Julia A. Fletcher Carney**

Nothing is too small to know, and nothing is too big to attempt.
— **William Van Horne**

To be really great in little things, to be truly noble and heroic in the insipid details of everyday life, is a virtue so rare as to be worthy of canonization.
— **Harriet Beecher Stowe**

How to Really Use English

No subject seems to create more controversy in playing pool than the proper use of english. English is pool's double edged sword. Your damned if you use it and damned if you don't. Your discovery of english is both a blessing and a curse upon your game.

Every player wages their private war with english. This can lead to changing cues and shafts and to a plethora of offbeat theories on how the effects of english can be minimized if not negated altogether. This ongoing battle also turns most players into experts on the subject. That said, I'm going to proceed anyway in giving you my personal pearls of wisdom gleaned from thirty years of study. Quite naturally, I feel that they make complete common sense. I will even go so far as to promise that nearly everyone who follows these guidelines will go a long ways towards taming the beast of english once and for all.

All About Using English

⊙ English is sidespin. English is not center axis draw or follow.

⊙ Beginning players should avoid english completely until they can regularly pocket a wide variety of routine shots.

⊙ Some advanced players like to use outside english to spin balls in. This is largely a matter of personal preference.

⊙ You only need english on 15–20 percent of your shots.

⊙ Most of the time you should use no more than ½ tip of english.

⊙ On soft shots you must allow more for throw than for deflection unless the cue ball is several feet from the object ball.

⊙ On a very few shots deflection and throw actually cancel each other out. You can then aim as if you were not using any english.

⊙ On firm shots you must allow for more deflection than for throw.

⊙ When you combine english with very much draw or follow, you should severely reduce the amount of sidespin.

⊙ The further the object ball lies from the pocket, the less english you should apply.

⊙ A lively cue and a smooth stroke can allow you to hit closer to the center axis and still achieve the necessary english.

CAPELLE'S LAWS for POOL

Less experienced players use too much english. Knowledgeable players use only what's required.

When it comes to using english, too much of a good thing is definitely not a good thing.

English is a very useful tool. It is not the secret to the game.

When considering using english, the virtues of sidespin must be weighed very carefully against the evils of deflection, curve and throw.

To go beyond is as wrong as to fall short.
— Confucius

The road of excess leads to the palace of wisdom.
— William Blake

To exaggerate is to weaken.
— Jean-Francois De La Horde

Nothing in excess.
— Solon

Chapter 4
Changing Your Game

"Everything changes but change itself."

—John F. Kennedy

Breaking Bad Habits

Mechanical perfection is impossible because we are people, not machines. This implies that you are going to have to live with at least a small flaw or two in your technique. A line of distinction, however, must be drawn between your individual quirks and the bad habits that kill off your chances for playing your best pool. You must learn to live with your idiosyncrasies. After all, even the best players in the world have unique characteristics in their approach to the game. You cannot, however, live with bad habits if you wish to significantly improve your game.

The quality of your play is your best indicator of any major flaws in your technique. The balls don't lie. They are the acid test for your game. Are you missing with regularity? Does any shot cause you difficulty, such as your draw stroke? Do you dog balls under pressure? Take careful stock of your game. Try to objectively rate the quality of your basic fundamentals. Do you have any bad habits that are keeping you from taking your game to the next level?

If you've discovered a major flaw or two, the next step is to make a firm commitment to implementing the proper cure. This is easier said than done. Many players would rather accept less than their best than take a risk for fear they might play worse than they do now.

Let's assume you've decided to fix your problem area(s). Now you must select the appropriate cure and follow through with it's implementation. This will include practice exercises designed to build good new habits and techniques into your game. It helps if you have an instructor monitor your progress. You must stay patient during this adjustment phase. It has been said that it takes about 30 days to break a bad habit and replace it with something positive.

Recurring Flaws

The commonly recurring bad habit is another formidable foe to your game. This bad habit is always lurking just beneath the surface, waiting for a chance to creep back into your game. Perhaps you have a tendency to jump up prematurely. Most players do from time to time. It's not easy to stay down until your follow through is complete on 100 percent of your shots. The trouble starts when you begin to raise up on 5 percent of your shots. Then it's 10 percent and 25 percent of the time. Pretty soon you are jumping up on every shot. At this point you still may not even be aware of the problem. As you can see, a flaw that's not nipped in the bud can, left unattended, turn into a game wrecker.

You can reduce the destructive power of recurring flaws by becoming totally aware of your negative tendencies. If you are like most players, you have one or two real killers. When your play starts to slip, one of your recurring bad habits is probably to blame. Now is the time to apply a strong dose of a proven remedy. In our example above, a conscious effort to stay down until your follow through is complete and/or until you hear the object ball drop is required.

 Short-term remedies can help to quickly get your game back on track as long as the problem has been picked up soon after starting. Recurring faults, left unattended, will cause you to lose the critical edge. Worse yet, they could lead to a prolonged slump. So make double sure that the moving parts of your pool machinery are kept finely tuned and be sure to conduct regular maintenance checks on your game.

CAPELLE'S LAWS for POOL

A quirk is an individual characteristic that you can live with in your game. A bad habit is something that must be eliminated.

Every player has recurring faults which must be monitored and swiftly corrected.

A good habit is to break bad habits.

Sow an act, reap a habit; sow a habit, reap a character; sow a character, reap a destiny.
— G. D. Boardman

Habit is either the best of servants or the worst of masters.
— Nathaniel Emmons

A year from now you may wish you had started today.
— Karen Lamb

Tis harder to unlearn than to learn.
—Thomas Fuller

The best way to break a bad habit is to drop it.
— Leo Aikman

I'll turn over a new leaf.
— Cervantes

Managing Change

When you begin playing pool, you undergo a whole series of changes. Modifications are made regularly to your grip, stance, bridge and stroke as you mold a decent game for yourself. Once this time consuming process is complete, you emerge with a sense of what is your game. A hard fought battle has been won. Now you can play reasonably well.

At this point, a rather curious development takes place: a resistance to further change becomes firmly entrenched. A stubborn refusal to tamper with "your game" erects a brick wall between you and continued progress. You'd like to play better, but you hate the thought of playing just 5 percent worse for even a month or two.

Has your game has plateaued for some time now? If so, you may have reached a level you are quite satisfied with. You may also not wish to put forth any extra effort to advance your game. There's no harm is standing pat, if that's all right with you. But if you sincerely want to improve, then you must give up part of what you have for something new. You will need to take a chance that your changes will pay off in the long run. Nothing ventured, nothing gained. I can't guarantee you that your changes will work. I can assure you that if you don't try to change, then your game will remain stuck where it is.

The prospects for positive and lasting change in your game far outweigh the risks. The possibility of playing better can also fuel your enthusiasm for the game. By keeping an open mind to ideas that can elevate your game, you will build a sense of excitement that you could be playing even better tomorrow no matter how well you play today.

Your Attitude Towards Change

Implementing new techniques into your game takes a real commitment on your part. You may have to endure a period of frustration and poor play. It could take a while for your mind and body to accept the new way of doing things and for your game to jell. Patience and your belief that the new ideas are going to work are necessary in the implementation phase.

Your attitude towards change can keep you from going back to the old way of playing pool. Once the process is complete, you will be set to enjoy a higher level of play than you've ever experienced before.

You might discover, for some strange and wonderful reason, that a change in fundamentals can be smoothly and easily implemented into your game. Your level of play could take a dramatic turn for the better overnight. The possibility of sudden and substantial improvement should further whet your appetite for positive change.

 Old habits can die hard. It takes commitment and work to improve your game. Therefore, I suggest that you only tackle one or two changes at a time. Don't attempt too much at once even when you feel that your game needs a complete overhaul. Nail down each new technique (or two) before moving on to anything else that you feel needs work.

Compensating for a Change

 Changing just one thing at a time is not easy. When you make one change, however, you must often make one more change at the same time to compensate for the first one. The list below gives you some major changes in your game along with the secondary change that accompanies it. When you are about to change some part of your game not listed below, think about what else might have to change to compensate for the first one.

Two Changes at Once

MAJOR CHANGE	SECONDARY CHANGE
Moving your shooting arm to 90 degrees	Realign your stance so you are square to the target
Lowering your head	Moving your grip hand further back
Slowing down your stroke	Slowing your eye shift between the cue ball and the object ball
Loosening your grip hand	Reduce the speed of your arm swing

 CAPELLE'S LAWS for POOL

Nearly every change requires a second change to compensate for the first change.

Changing your game gives you the opportunity to improve but does not guarantee it.

Everything changes but change itself.

— **John F. Kennedy**

We change whether we like it or not.

— **Ralph Waldo Emerson**

> *When I let go of who I am, I become what I might be.*
> — Lao-tzu
>
> *When any real progress is made, we unlearn and learn anew what we thought we knew before.*
> — Henry David Thoreau
>
> *The beginning of a habit is like an invisible thread, but every time we repeat the act we strengthen the strand, add to it another filament, until it becomes a great cable and binds us irrevocably, thought and act.*
> — Orison Swett Marden

Change Breeds Enthusiasm

When your enthusiasm is running hot, you can't wait to get to the pool room. One sure method of stoking the fires of enthusiasm is a true desire to improve your game.

Knowledge is the big key to improving your game. That's why it's important to enroll yourself in a continuing course in pool. Your curriculum is available in the many fine books and tapes on the market today. Each has something to offer your game. Sift carefully through their tips and techniques for the nuggets of wisdom that are useful to you. I'll wager that when you locate an idea that is particularly suited to your needs, you'll race to the closest pool table to give it a test.

There is no one single secret to the game. Still there's probably a little voice that tells you that the next tip could be the one that unlocks the door to pool's magic kingdom. You've got a right to dream, right? Besides, it's your dream of a better game that helps keep your enthusiasm for the game alive.

Testing Ideas

Now let's assume you've discovered a new technique you are anxious to put on trial. Ask yourself if the idea is valid or if you are just hoping for something, possibly anything, that can elevate your game. Keep in mind that most new methods will work for a short period. This is the unfortunate truth no matter how little sense the idea actually makes. The reason for this is your enthusiasm for something new and the complete attention that you pay to its implementation.

The real test for any technique comes after the freshness wears off. Does the idea stand up to the harsh reality of time? What you really need are practical methods that can add lasting value to your game.

You can do without the latest concoctions of the witchdoctors of pool that offer false promises based on fiction and not fact.

The Cycle of Improvement

 Each time you make an important discovery, it perpetuates a wonderful cycle of learning and positive change. The cycle begins with your desire to improve. It ends with a positive result, which serves to ignite the process all over again.

THE CYCLE OF IMPROVEMENT

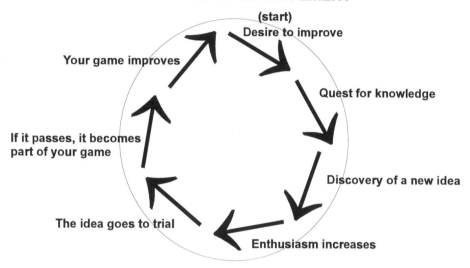

Your game improves

(start)
Desire to improve

Quest for knowledge

If it passes, it becomes part of your game

Discovery of a new idea

The idea goes to trial

Enthusiasm increases

 CAPELLE'S LAWS for POOL

When you try something new, it will usually work for a little while no matter how little sense it makes.

A continuing quest for knowledge is your best insurance against a decline in enthusiasm for the game.

It can sometimes take quite a while to learn something that is of obvious value to your game.

Zeal without knowledge is fire without light.
— **Thomas Fuller**

Thus times do shift, each thing his turn does hold;
New things succeed, as former things grow old.
— **Robert Herrick**

> *Things do not change; we change.*
>
> — Henry David Thoreau

All About Slumps

Slumps are simply an unhappy fact of life for those who play any game that depends on physical skills. To deal with slumps you must accept them as part of the game. Your game will not always be on the upswing and you can't maintain your absolute best game day after day. Your spells of excellent pool will always, sorry to say, be followed by periodic declines in performance.

Now that you accept slumps as part of the game, the next step is to remain calm and patient when your game slips a bit. This will help you to clearly and objectively diagnose the problem. Then you must adopt appropriate measures for turning your game around. Anger and frustration, which are natural bi-products of a slump, need to be replaced by a cool head and a commitment to positive action. Keep in mind that a slump does not have to be such a bad thing. A slump often carries with it a big gift for your game. Indeed, a slump can provide you with the insight(s) necessary to propel your game to a new level once the remedy has taken hold.

According to Webster's Dictionary a slump is "A decline in performance." Under this definition any time your game drops from a previous peak you are in a slump. You should differentiate between slumps of varying magnitudes. This will enable you to keep them in proper perspective, and it will help you to administer the correct cures.

Types of Slumps

MINI-SLUMPS–These occur all of the time. You may experience one or more within the course of a match. A couple of errant shots in close succession could cause you to lose confidence in your game. Most of your mistakes and poor shots stem from recurring bad habits which we discussed previously. These can be corrected on the spot as long as you know your game very well and have a remedy for each fault.

A SLUMP–Slumps can last from several days to a month or more. You must actively seek a solution for a basic slump before it threatens to take over your game for good. If you can't quickly figure out what's gone wrong, get qualified help. This kind of slump is a normal part of the game, so you can expect to experience one every year or two.

MAJOR SLUMPS –A major slump can last several months up to a year or longer. In acute cases, you may even consider quitting the game (heaven forbid). The best remedy is to prevent a major slump from occurring in the first place. Ideally you can turn things around when your game is still only in an "average" slump. Should your game hit rock bottom, don't give up. Make a commitment to rebuilding your game from the ground up. This should include the help of a qualified instructor. With any luck you will only experience a major slump a few times during your entire career, or maybe not even at all.

As a parting perspective on slumps, take a moment to consider how good you feel when your game is on the upswing. Every slump offers you the opportunity to once again experience another improvement cycle in your play. *Enjoy*!

 CAPELLE'S LAWS for POOL

Your pool career will be punctuated by a series of somewhat annoying slumps. Each one gives you the chance to feel great again about your game when it bounces back.

Knowing your game and quickly curing faults is the best way to avoid a prolonged slump.

Slump? I ain't in no slump. I just ain't hitting.
— **Yogi Berra**

When it is dark enough, you can see the stars.
— **Ralph Waldo Emerson**

The great virtue of man lies in his ability to correct his mistakes and to continually make a new man of himself.
— **Wang Yang Ming**

Whatever must happen ultimately should happen immediately.
— **Henry Kissinger**

He who can't endure the bad will not live to see the good.
— **Yiddish proverb**

Most problems precisely defined are already partially solved.
— **Harry Lorayne**

Nothing lasts forever—not even your troubles.
— **Arnold H. Glasow**

Stroke Keys Are Your Short-Term Solution

Imagine that you have a big tournament or important league match that starts an hour from now. Your game is unfortunately well below peak form. This does not give you enough time to rebuild your game or to iron out your difficulties at the practice table. So what can you do? Throw in the towel and hope for the best? Not a chance. What you need is a quick fix or a band aid that can get you through the competition.

A quick fix is not the answer to your long-term problem, but it can serve a very useful purpose. When your game is off, you may think negatively about your prospects for winning. This is only natural. A band aid remedy can help to refocus your mind on something positive. Your mind only has room for one thought at a time, so you might as well make it a good one. Make a decision to concentrate on one key thought for the whole match. Don't think of winning or losing. Just play one shot at a time while staying focused on your key thought. Instead of worrying about how bad you are playing, think about something constructive. One possible key is to anchor your bridge hand to the table until the ball has hit the pocket. Another is to concentrate on a straight follow through.

After some experimentation you will develop a whole box full of band aides. Any of these quick fixes might be very useful in getting you through a match. You may even windup winning when you least expect it.

CAPELLE'S LAWS for POOL

A quick fix should not be mistaken for your long-range program for improving your game.

A quick fix could help you win when you least expect to.

A thousand ills require a thousand cures.

— **Ovid**

There is in the worst of fortune the best of chances for a happy change.

— **Euripides**

The pessimist sees the difficulty in every opportunity; the optimist sees the opportunity in every difficulty.

— **L. P. Jacks**

Chapter 5
Secrets to Big Improvement

"The intellect has little to do on the road to discovery. There comes a leap in consciousness, call it intuition or what you will, and the solution comes, and you don't know how or why."

—Albert Einstein

The Big Secret

I'm going to wager that you are like most pool players who have been on a quest for the secret to pool. Well, your search is over. Make sure that you are comfortably seated because I'm now going to reveal the big secret. The big secret to pool is... (drum roll) that there is no big secret. That's it in a nutshell. I hope that you're not overly shocked or disappointed.

Now that you possess the big secret, your mind has been freed from the stressful search for the answer. You no longer need to waste time looking for some black magic that will transform you into a world-beater overnight. Now you can follow a much more productive course of adding a multitude of secrets to your game, one at a time, until you have constructed a rock solid game of pool.

As your game grows, you will, on occasion, discover a new secret that breaks the dam loose. Your new secret will trigger substantial and lasting improvement. When this happens, you are really benefiting from all of your previous hard work. Think about it. Suppose you started playing pool today and all you knew was the secret—what kind of game would you have? Not much is the answer. Indeed, a new secret that causes your game to jump is merely another piece of the puzzle. It is not, by itself, the answer to winning pool.

CAPELLE'S LAWS for POOL

The big secret is that there is no single big secret.

The big secret is the secret that is currently giving you great results. But this secret will not always remain the big secret to your game.

Big secrets come, and big secrets go.

There ain't no answer. There ain't gonna be any answer. There never has been an answer. That's the answer.

— **Gertrude Stein**

There are no secrets better kept than the secrets that everybody guesses.

— **George Bernard Shaw**

Chain Reactions

You are constantly receiving input from a variety of sources. Each piece of information goes into making up the sum total of your game at any given moment. No piece exists in a vacuum. Each one has the potential to trigger your game on a run of good or poor play that may last several games, weeks or even longer. I call this phenomenon where one thing can lead to another the chain reaction theory of pool.

When the input is positive, naturally, you want to build on it and develop some momentum to your game. When you receive a negative input, ideally you can quickly brush it off before it winds up costing you a match or, worse yet, leads to a prolonged slump.

Let's take a look at how this theory operates in practice. You just miscued on a draw shot during a match despite having a perfectly conditioned tip that just needed chalk.

⊙ **Positive reaction:** I've got to follow a strict routine of chalking up before every shot. My stroke feels pretty good so this mistake should be no cause for concern.

⊙ **Negative chain reaction:**

- Maybe I'm losing my draw stroke which…
- Causes you to tighten up on your next draw shot which…
- Leads to another miscue which…
- You compensate for by elevating your bridge to only 1/2 tip below center on draw shots which…
- Drastically reduces the effectiveness of your draw stroke which…
- Disrupts your position play which…
- Costs you a match to a player you know you should beat which…
- Robs you of your confidence which…
- Decreases your enjoyment of the game which…

To be continued…

Let's analyze the situation for a moment. Notice how one innocent little mistake has opened the flood-gates to what could windup escalating into a season-wrecking, possibly even career-threatening slump. A streak of poor play has to start somewhere. Often it's with a small and innocent looking mistake that grabs hold of your game and spawns a whole series of negative reactions.

The quicker that you can respond to any negative, the better will be your chances of maintaining a higher level of play. Remember, however, that even an unwelcomed downturn in your game does not have to be fatal. Let's pick up our story where we left off.

Continued:

- Causes you to do some real soul searching about your game which . . .
- Makes you determined to solve this problem which . . .
- Leads you to seek a qualified instructor who . . .
- Identifies a long standing fundamental flaw in your stroke which . . .
- You correct after several practice sessions which . . .
- Restores your enthusiasm for the game which . . .
- Motivates you to enter a tournament where . . .
- You play your best pool ever in life . . .

Our story has a happy ending just like in Hollywood. So can yours. As long as you play pool you will be subject to cycles of good play and poor play. After all, we're human beings, not machines, playing a game that requires pinpoint accuracy and phenomenal touch. Nevertheless, you can limit your off moments and extend your spells of good play by keeping in mind that every shot you play has an impact on your game. Learn from your mistakes as quickly a possible. By limiting their negative effects, you can get your game back on track as quickly as possible.

Chain Reactions in Action

⊙ **Straighter stroke** = make more shots = confidence grows = play more aggressively = run-out more often = beat better players...

⊙ **Better safeties** = less reliance on run-outs = takes pressure off game = shoot better = get more ball-in-hands = win more games...

⊙ **Bank shots improve** = can pass on some thin cuts = increases positional options = takes pressure off some position plays...

⊙ **Break better** = increases confidence = run-out more often = win more matches....

CAPELLE'S LAWS for POOL

No single shot exists in isolation. Every shot, every piece of information may be the one that sets off a chain reaction for the better or worse.

A little neglect may breed great mischief . . . for want of a nail, the shoe was lost; for want of a shoe, the horse was lost; for want of a horse, the battle was lost; for want of a battle, the war was lost.

— Benjamin Franklin

When you make a mistake, admit it. If you don't, you only make matters worse.

— Ward Cleaver

The present contains nothing more than the past, and what is found in the effect was already in the cause.

— Henri Bergson

Quantum Leap

There's nothing quite like the excitement that comes from experiencing a quantum leap in your game. Perhaps you have struggled with your stroke and then, seemingly out of nowhere, a new secret appears and you can't miss. Your game takes a noticeable and lasting change for the better.

You can increase your chances for a quantum leap by maintaining an open mind towards pool. If you truly love playing pool, have a sincere desire to improve and are open to positive change, then you are giving yourself every possible chance for the leap to appear. This sounds logical enough, doesn't it?

Many players think they would like to play better but are doing nothing to stimulate progress in their game. Instead their games reach a plateau well below their potential. Perhaps it would help to remember this invaluable phrase I learned from Fred Kalmus, a guru to several major corporations: "If you always do what you've always done, you'll always get what you've always got." In other words, don't expect your game to improve by doing the same thing over and over again.

Priming for a Leap

You can prime the pump for a quantum leap by conducting an analysis of your game. By acknowledging your weaknesses you have taken an important first step towards improving your game. Don't be disappointed if the solution does not appear right away. Learn to trust in the process. Your subconscious mind will be at work searching for the answer. You may perhaps have read some passage on the stroke five times, and it failed to register in your mind. But then, on the sixth reading, BINGO! A key phrase finally clicks and your stroke takes on a new fluidity and consistency.

It's possible you will be exposed to the same message from a variety of sources before it's conveyed in a manner that sticks with you. For example, someone could advise that you imagine your bridge hand as the Rock of Gibraltar and this could, in an instant, solve your problem of jumping up prematurely.

Again, I advise you to conduct an object evaluation of your game. Pinpoint your weaknesses and put the subconscious mind to work. Some components of your game to consider would include: correcting a fundamental flaw(s) in your bridge, grip, stance or stroke, mastering the principles of position play, learning to play one shot at a time and your safety play.

Believing in Your Progress

Now let's imagine that you're experiencing a quantum leap in your game. For several days or weeks (or maybe even a few hours), you've been playing better than ever before. You know the difference and it's also obvious to those who know your game. Now comes the moment of truth. You may wonder if your new game is for real. Perhaps a well meaning friend may counsel you to enjoy your "hot streak" while you can because they never last. Their advice would be well founded if your improved play was only attributable to a Band-Aid type remedy that typically only produces short-term results.

With a quantum leap, things are different. Now you have a rock solid reason for your improvement, one that should serve to raise your game permanently to a new level. This should, in turn, give you the belief that your improved play is for real.

The normal learning curve takes years as you continuously accumulate the knowledge required to elevate your game, inch by inch, to higher levels. Along the way, however, will come those special moments when your game leapfrogs overnight.

Perhaps you have experienced a quantum leap in your game. If so, try to recall when and how it took place. Can you remember the thrill when your game soared to new highs? It's important for you to believe that if it happened once, it can happen again.

I find it useful to remember Satori, which comes from Zen. It means instant awakening. In a flash, what was difficult becomes easy. Some part of your game you may have struggled with for years is no longer a problem. You may wonder why you didn't figure it out months or even years ago. Don't waste any time, however, worrying about the past. Now that the solution to your problem area is crystal clear, accept it and believe totally in your newly discovered skill.

Buddy Hall's Big Leap

With an open mind to positive change you can experience Satori at any time. Just ask Buddy Hall. He experienced a quantum leap in his game overnight, thanks to many years of dedication and an insight that put the final piece of the puzzle in place. Buddy's sudden rise to a world class player is vividly described in W. W. Woody's excellent biography: *Buddy Hall: Rags to Rifleman, Then What?* The passage below is one of my all-time favorites on pool. I am pleased to share it with you, thanks to the kindness of Huckleberry Publishing Company.

> When Buddy wasn't playing 9-ball, he was thinking about it, **even in his sleep**. One night, he was lying in bed holding his bridge hand up looking at it. He experimented, making different configurations of a bridge, and fell asleep thinking about it. He had a dream, and in the dream, he saw himself playing perfect pool using his new bridge. From that bridge, his targets were crystal clear and his stroke was smooth and authoritative. He realized that he could see how every shot should be hit, and he concluded: *If I know how each shot must be hit, then not to hit it that way, is just stupid! There's no reason for me to ever miss another ball. My stroke is straight, and I can hit where I'm aiming.* **Why not do it Every time?**
>
> Buddy literally went to sleep playing one speed, and woke up with his game elevated to a higher level—**overnight**.
>
> Beginning there and then, Buddy played 9-ball on a level that *he himself had never seen,* and he consistently played that way **every day, for a period of *FOUR YEARS*.**

CAPELLE'S LAWS for POOL

At any time all of your hard work could result in a quantum leap forward in your game. When it happens, be prepared to accept your higher level of play.

Like a dam ready to burst, your game may experience a quantum leap as a result of a new secret that helps you to unleash the full power of the 1,000's of secrets that you've already accumulated.

We live moment by moment. At any moment you could reach a turning point that could change your game forever. You must always remain open to the possibility.

The intellect has little to do on the road to discovery. There comes a leap in consciousness, call it intuition or what you will, and the solution comes to you, and you don't know how or why.

— Albert Einstein

This hitteth the nail on the head.

— John Heywood

Look at a stone cutter hammering away at his rock, perhaps a hundred times without as much as a crack showing in it. Yet at the hundred-and first blow it will split in two, and I know it was not the last blow that did it, but all that had gone before.

— Jacob A. Riis

Chapter 6
Your Game

" I have a dream."

— Martin Luther King, Jr.

Writing Your Story

You've no doubt read about the life and times of famous athletes and some of the great champions of pool. I'm sure it was of interest to discover how they got started, how they learned to play, about their great matches and their exploits on the road of life. While being entertained by their colorful stories you may also have been a bit envious of their lives.

Now if you stop for a moment and reminisce about your life in pool, I bet you'll realize that your journey has also been quite memorable. Now let's project another 5, 10, 20 years or more into the future. At that time, what new experiences would you like to have added to your story? How would you like the biography of your life in pool to read? I will give you some suggestions to get the process started as you lounge comfortably in your favorite easy chair.

- ☑ When and how did you start playing?
- ☑ How did you learn to play pool?
- ☑ Have you worked with any instructors?
- ☑ What has been your most important lesson?
- ☑ What were your "golden years" of pool when the game was especially enjoyable? Why?
- ☑ What are some of your most important and satisfying wins?
- ☑ What were some of your toughest losses?
- ☑ Who were some of your toughest opponents?
- ☑ Recall in detail a number of your most memorable shots.
- ☑ How long have you been playing?
- ☑ What have been some of your favorite places to play?
- ☑ Who are some of your favorite pool people? Why?
- ☑ What are a few of the funniest things you have ever seen or experienced in a pool room?
- ☑ Who are some of the real characters that you've encountered?
- ☑ If you were to write some colorful stories about your doings, what would they say?
- ☑ Do you have any fond memories of road trips?

Pool lends itself to the creation of colorful stories and characters simply due to the nature of the sport. So I am sure that upon some serious reflection you'll realize that your life in pool may be every bit as fun and entertaining as your heroes that you love reading about.

CAPELLE'S LAWS for POOL

When you take the time to visualize your life in as rich detail and emotion as possible, you will have taken a giant step towards a most fulfilling and enjoyable journey in pool.

You are probably a much more interesting and colorful character than you have given yourself credit for.

I always say, keep a diary and someday it'll keep you.
— Mae West

Memory is the diary we all carry along with us.
— Oscar Wilde

I never travel without my diary. One should always have something sensational to read in the train.
— Oscar Wilde

Your Most Prized Possession

Your most prized possession as a pool player is your game. Your game goes with your everywhere and it largely determines how you feel about your pool playing experience. Your game is the sum total of everything you know and everything you can do on a pool table.

If you are like the vast majority of pool players, then your perception of how you play and how you really play are not in total accord. Most pool players slightly overestimate their ability. There's no harm in being off a little in either direction.

Big problems can arise, however, when you are either much better or worse than you think you are. When you underestimate your game, you will shy away from tougher competition that could elevate your game. When you severely overestimate your game, you will constantly be butting up against much better players. This could cause you to develop a losing mentality. In addition, you won't get enough table time to work on your game.

Your status and reputation in the pool world are attached to your game. Some of the highest complements a pool player can receive are "got a ton of heart," "has no dog," "tough to beat," "plays all the games well" and "he's a great money player." The biggest dividing line in pool is between lesser skilled enthusiasts and those who are referred to as "a player." Every serious pool player longs for the day when his peers award him with this label of respect.

How Others Rate Your Game

- ⊙ People you can or can't beat.
- ⊙ Your best game (your "A" game).
- ⊙ Your typical game.
- ⊙ Your worst game when you are dead out of stroke.
- ⊙ How well you play under pressure.
- ⊙ How well you play for fun.
- ⊙ Who you give and get spots from and how much.
- ⊙ Your strongest game and how well you play it.
- ⊙ The parts of your game that are particularly strong or weak.
- ⊙ Your sportsmanship and sense of fair play.
- ⊙ The speed at which you play.
- ⊙ Your ability to play with a lead.
- ⊙ Your ability to come from behind.

CAPELLE'S LAWS for POOL

There is your practice game, your "home-room" game and your road game. When all three are about equal, then you have truly arrived as a pool player.

Always be a first rate version of yourself, instead of a second rate version of somebody else.
— **Judy Garland**

I'm a salami writer. I try to write good salami, but salami is salami.
— **Stephen King**

The only person you should ever compete with is yourself. You can't hope for a fairer match.
— **Todd Ruthman**

Measure wealth not by the things you have, but by the things you have for which you would not take money.
— **Anonymus**

Your Basic Nature

Your approach to playing pool should, for the most part, coincide with how you do things away from the table. When you play pool opposite to your basic nature, nine times out of ten your game will suffer. This is especially true when you play under pressure.

If you are a fast player, you need to maintain a steady pace to play your best. And if you are a quiet person, you certainly don't want your friends bugging you when you are in a serious game. The questions below will help you to understand what kind of pool player you are. Your self-awareness should help you to play more consistently in line with your basic nature.

Your Approach to Pool

- ☑ Do you play by feel, or do you focus on mechanics?
- ☑ Are you a talker, or do you prefer to be left alone?
- ☑ Is your stroke slow and rhythmic, or quick and decisive?
- ☑ Do you favor an aggressive or conservative style of play?
- ☑ Are you a fast, slow or medium paced player?
- ☑ Do you make decisions instinctively, or after careful analysis?
- ☑ Are you more concerned with results or with pleasing the crowd?

 By sticking to your basic nature, you will maximize your results the majority of the time. However, keep in mind that pool offers many exceptions to the rule. At times you should go for a shot even if you are conservative by nature. The situation may call for an aggressive shot. Sometimes it's fun to break out of your mold and try something different. You might discover that you enjoy playing pool aggressively even though you are mostly conservative in other areas of your life.

Your pool personality is usually in close alignment with your basic nature. Aggressive people play aggressively, and vice versa. Introverts keep their mouths shut while extroverts tend to babble on to all who would listen. The bottom line to your pool personality is this: do you feel comfortable playing your role and does your game benefit of suffer? The answer to the first part of the question is at least partially centered around your reputation in the pool room. Do your peers respect you, or do they dread playing you because of your antics? And do you care? You should.

CAPELLE'S LAWS for POOL

When you go against your basic nature as a pool player, then your game will normally suffer 9 times out of 10.

There are exceptions to nearly everything in pool. Sometimes your best course of action is to do the opposite of what you normally would in a given situation.

To play your best pool, your pool personality must be aligned at least reasonably close to your true nature.

Trust the instinct to the end, though you can render no reason.
— **Ralph Waldo Emerson**

We each need to let our intuition guide us, and then be willing to follow that guidance directly and fearlessly.
— **Shakti Gawain**

What does reason demand a man? A very easy thing — to live in accord with his own nature.
— **Lucius Annaeus Seneca**

It's not what I do, but the way I do it.
It's not what I say, but the way I say it.

— **Mae West**

If I try to be like him, who will be like me?
— **Yiddish Proverb**

Mastering Pool

Mastering pool requires an extremely high degree of proficiency in virtually every category of skill. At the "A" level, a player can have no glaring weaknesses. As you move down the competitive spectrum, you will find players that rate highly in a few segments and not so well in others. An average player could be an excellent shotmaker, but know little about position play.

Advancing your game demands that you further develop your competence in the areas in which your game is already strong. You must also categorize your weak points and go about systematically improving each one. And of course, you should be constantly adding to your base of knowledge. While this is all going on, you must also be developing your mental game and your heart so that you can compete successfully against tougher and tougher competition.

The upkeep on a top caliber pool game can be rather time consuming. The exceptions are those maddeningly gifted souls who seem to hardly lose a beat, even after weeks or months of inactivity. Most of us mere mortals must, however, accept the responsibility for keeping up our game with regular play and practice or run the risk of suffering a measurable drop. Maintaining and advancing your pool game does, however, give you a wonderful opportunity to build your self-discipline.

 CAPELLE'S LAWS for POOL

At the higher levels of competition you must have no glaring weaknesses in the critical areas of skill.

You must play to your strengths and minimize the impact of your weaknesses.

The better your game becomes, the more responsibility you must assume for its upkeep.

Shotmaking showoffs and winners seldom come in the same package.

Two roads diverged in a wood, and I–
I took the one less traveled by,
And that has made all the difference.
— **Robert Frost**

Unto whomsoever much is given, of him shall much be required.
— **Bible, Luke 12:48**

To keep demands as much skill as to win.
— **Geoffrey Chaucer**

The tragedy of life is not that man loses, but that he almost wins.
— **Heywood Broun**

The Keys to Consistency

This whole business of consistency is enough to drive a pool player simply mad. How can you be in dead stroke one day and play three levels lower the next? It all really boils down to the quality of your fundamentals and your mental approach to playing pool. When you have these components in fine working order, your game will become something you can count on day after day, month after month.

A Consistent Stroke

The roots of consistency lie in your stroke. Knowing that you can't perfect the stroke is the first step towards becoming a consistent player. Your goal should instead be to develop a stroke that consistently delivers very acceptable results and that requires very little maintenance. When this kind of stroke is off, it is not far from being back in the groove again. A consistent stroke will enable your good days to be great, and your bad days to be reasonably good. There are a few basics that can help you to develop the kind of dependable action that you may have only dreamed about.

Key to a Consistent Stroke

- Develop a fundamentally sound stroke to begin with or make the necessary changes to your stroke.

- Almost every pool player has 1 - 3 flaws that creep into their game periodically. Develop an acute awareness of what are your most commonly recurring faults.

- Know what your stroke feels like when it is "on."

- Develop a sixth sense that tells you when your stroke is starting to fall out of the groove. The quicker you can detect a slide coming, the quicker you can reverse the trend and get back on your game.

The following illustration gives you some additional insight into this issue of consistency. Imagine that your stroke swings back and forth, alternating between being in stroke and out-of-stroke. Notice how the average player spends a lot of time out of stroke, especially in contrast to the excellent player. You can become a very consistent player by developing a solid stroke and by gaining a heightened sense of awareness that tells you when your stroke is starting to sputter. This will allow you to quickly make the necessary corrections.

STROKE CONSISTENCY

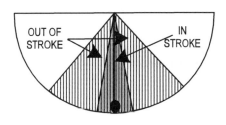

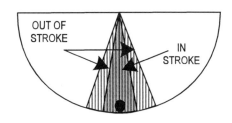

AVERAGE PLAYER   EXCELLENT PLAYER

A Consistent Mental Game

To gain the kind of monotonous consistency that can drive your opponents mad you also need to think like a pool player. Pool, by its very nature, creates an unending series of mental peaks and valleys. These fluctuations would seem to contradict the possibility of your being able to achieve a consistent mental game. Actually it is easier to maintain consistency with your mental game than with your stroke. It is always easier to know what to do than to actually do it. This is part of the reason why top players can still perform extremely well when not in dead stroke.

The mental game requires a number of highly developed skills. These skills largely involve the proper interpretation of a constant stream of information that passes through your mind as you are playing. With proper training your mind can take in the data, process it effectively, and present you with the best course of action. When your mind is properly tuned, you can quickly adapt to tables, make the correct decisions on position and safeties, and you can rapidly dismiss the antics of your opponent as useless input.

In sum, when you combine a dependable stroke with a rock solid mental game, you'll become a very consistent pool player. With a consistent game, you have a standard of play you can count on. You will also have a better understanding of what truly is "your game." This self-knowledge can help you to more easily gauge the appropriate level of competition for your game. You will also have a better sense of what you need to do to improve your game still further.

CAPELLE'S LAWS for POOL

The pendulum is always swinging from out-of-stroke to in-stroke to out-of-stroke. Your consistency is determined by the magnitude of your swings. Naturally, the smaller, the better.

The consistency of your stroke is directly related to the quality of your fundamentals.

When a great player's game is bad, it is still just short of phenomenal. This is attributable to a high degree of consistency in the mental game.

Ninety percent of this game is half-mental.

— Yogi Berra

> *All intelligent thoughts have already been thought; what is necessary is only to try to think them again.*
> — **Johann Wolfgang von Goethe**
>
> *Inconsistency is the only thing in which men are consistent.*
> — **Horace Smith**

Let the Trend be Your Friend

Your long-term growth as a pool player will feature a series of peaks and valleys. Ideally each peak will exceed the previous high watermark. The process is really one of two steps forward, one back. When you experience a short-term decline, you must realize that it's only a temporary correction within an overall positive trend. Your progression, if charted, would reveal a striking resemblance to a bull market in the stock market.

Our analogy to the stock market is illustrated below. Notice the trend of your overall level of play as it traces out a series of higher highs and higher lows. Observe how your physical game gyrates more widely than your overall game. The reason for this is that your everexpanding storehouse of knowledge helps you to keep steadily improving. It also cushions the effect of any temporary lapses in your physical game.

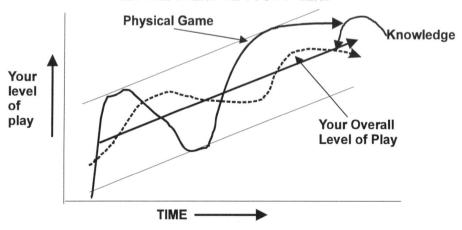

LET THE TREND BE YOUR FRIEND

Physical Game

Knowledge

Your level of play

Your Overall Level of Play

TIME

CAPELLE'S LAWS for POOL

Your game never stays exactly the same when you are learning to play. Don't let this shake your confidence or dampen your enthusiasm as long as the long-term trend is up.

> *Growth is the only evidence of life.*
> — **John Henry Cardinal Newman**
>
> *Progress, therefore, is not an accident, but a necessity... It is a part of nature.*
> — **Herbert Spencer**
>
> *Nothing is permanent but change.*
> — **Heraclitus**

How You Play Versus Your Results

You could enter into a match on top of your game. You are ready to run racks and torture your opponent. And yet, once the match is underway, you windup spending most of your time watching your opponent win game after game as a result of his sterling play and/or your lack opportunities to shoot. You can make nary a mistake and still get creamed. That, my friends, is because of the sometimes brutal nature of our sport. One man's feast definitely creates another's famine.

You can be denied an equal number of chances at reasonably plausible shots. Because of this your results may sometimes bear little resemblance to the actual quality of your game. Pool is simply not like golf were you get the exact same opportunity as your opponent.

While winning should be your objective in most matches, you can see that the final result is oftentimes out of your control due to the fickle nature of the pool gods. Of course, the breaks can also go in your favor, which could allow your fine play to help you to steamroller your next opponent.

In the long-run your results are strictly a function of the quality of your play. In the short-run it can be a completely different story. In order to keep your sanity and your enthusiasm for the game, I suggest you adopt a somewhat fatalistic attitude about your results in competition. On any given day, the quality of your game and the results that you obtain can be worlds apart. If you play long enough, it will all even out. In the long-run your game and how you play are really all that matters.

CAPELLE'S LAWS for POOL

In the short-run your game and your results will not often be very closely correlated. In the long-run, they are completely related.

Everything we do has a result. But that which is right and prudent does not always lead to good, nor the contrary to what is bad.

— Johann Wolfgang von Goethe

It is only by risking our persons from one hour to another that we live at all. And often enough our faith beforehand in an uncertified result is the only thing that makes the result come true.

— William James

Dealing with Missed Shots

No matter how well you perform the various skills that go into making up a well rounded pool game, the bottom line remains the same: you've got to consistently put the ball in the pocket.

There are valid reasons for missing balls, which have to do with areas of skill that you may have not as yet fully developed. And regardless of how well you play, you will still miss shots sometimes that have a reasonably high degree of difficulty

Cures for Missed Shots

WHY YOU MISS	CURE
Your stroke mechanics are faulty	Improve stroke
Your aim is off target	Practice aiming
Both your stroke and aim are off	Both of the above
You are careless	Work on your shooting routine
You choked	Work on your mental game
The shot was difficult	O.K. as long as you miss close

The first step in reducing missed shots is to pinpoint the reason(s) why they happen. Then you need to apply the appropriate cure. When you no longer have any reasons for missing balls, then you won't miss nearly as much.

You'll discover most of your misses result from a temporary lack of confidence. You must avoid having one miss quickly lead to another as this can cause you to doubt your ability. A downward spiral can result. When you miss, ask yourself why. Then make the necessary adjustments and move on. Put the miss behind you. As your game improves even further, your misses will appear as infrequent and isolated events. Most of your errant shots will result from a temporary lapse in concentration or because the shot was just plain difficult.

While you are competing, learn to expect a few bad shots every match. When they pop up from time to time they won't throw you completely off course. Also realize that no single shot will, in most cases, cost you a match.

One final word on missing balls: try not to fall into the habit of making excuses for your missed shots. Excuses never change the outcome, although they may ease the pain of losing somewhat. Besides, when you tell others your excuses, they know that you are only shifting the responsibility from yourself to someone or something else.

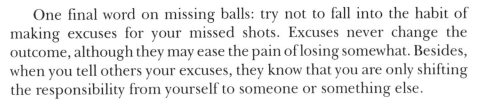

CAPELLE'S LAWS for POOL

When you have eliminated all of the reasons why you usually miss balls, then you won't be sitting nearly as much of the time.

The quicker you can recover from a poor shot, the greater will be your chances of minimizing its impact on the match.

If you can discover the humor in your poor shots, you will lessen your chances of these "accidents" from happening on a regular basis.

Every great mistake has a halfway moment, a split second when it can be recalled and perhaps remedied.
— **Pearl S. Buck**

Ninety-nine percent of the failures come from people who have the habit of making excuses.
— **George Washington Carver**

Do not blame anybody for your mistakes and failures.
— **Bernard M. Baruch**

> *How to succeed: try hard enough. How to fail: try too hard.*
> — **Malcolm Forbes**

Chapter 7
Knowledge is Pool Power

"All men desire knowledge naturally."

— **Aristotle**

Learning from Watching the Best

One of the greatest joys of the game is to occasionally spend an evening watching top players. Your journey should, therefore, take you whenever possible to where the action's at. You will have a chance to watch first-class pool and to learn even more about the game. What could be better?

The men's and women's pro tours hold tournaments in a number of major metropolitan areas throughout the year. You can locate their schedules by subscribing to any of the national pool publications (see the appendix). Several regional tours (see the appendix) feature leading semi-pros and local champions as well as an occasional appearance by a top touring pro. You can familiarize yourself with the names of the top talent in the country by checking out the rankings in the top pool publications.

You might find it worth the effort to locate the hot spots for tournament activity in your region. With a little detective work you can quickly locate some excellent pool watching. The yellow pages list the major pool rooms. Give them a call and ask the houseman about their regular tournaments or special events where "A" players will be competing. The houseman will fill you in on their events, and he may also point you towards other happenings around town. Another excellent source for action is the better players in your home pool room. They make it their business to know what's going on in your area.

A good seat is a must for watching pool. I advise that you arrive 20–30 minutes before the action starts so you can nail down an excellent vantage point. I've followed this strategy for years, and I've been consistently rewarded with great seats for viewing the best players in the world. If you can't nab tableside seats, then go for seating on an incline so you can observe the players without having to bob and weave for a view between the heads of spectators in front of you. I've belabored this point about seating because a good seat is mandatory and because seating arrangements at many venues can be notoriously poor.

Before you leave home grab a notepad. Record any nuggets on position play, safeties or anything else that can help your game. Once you're seated, it's time to adopt some proven strategies that can maximize your enjoyment and ability to learn from watching the best.

How to Watch Pool

⊙ Watch each player's warm-up routines. You'll often be treated to some amazing shot making as their stroke may be at its freewheeling best.

⊙ Evaluate each player's mechanics. Do they use a textbook stroke and stance? Are there any unusual moves or techniques? What can you incorporate into your game, such as a methodical pre-shot routine?

⊙ Think along with the players as they plot their position and strategy. What shot would you play? Then observe their choice and their results. Did you learn anything?

⊙ Top players usually possess a great break. Take note of where they position the cue ball, their mechanics and how the cue ball reacts after contact.

⊙ The break is also one of the most fun shots to watch as the players gyrate and plead for the balls to obey their wishes.

⊙ Safeties are not too glamorous to some people, but they win games. So be sure to observe carefully when and how they are played. Safety battles can create great drama as the players fight for control of the table. Ask yourself how each confrontation was resolved.

⊙ Escaping from a tough hook is a major challenge. You can learn much about the kicking game from watching this facet with special care.

⊙ Take time to simply watch the players play. Take notice of the ebb and the flow of the match and how the momentum changes hands. Watch the changing expressions on the players' faces and the crowds' reaction to the good shots and the blunders.

⊙ Go with a fellow pool nut, and you can triple your enjoyment by discussing the shots and strategies.

 CAPELLE'S LAWS for POOL

Watching good players is one of the most enjoyable and least expensive means of learning the game.

You can observe a lot just by watching.

— **Yogi Berra**

> *He is a great observor, and he loo*
> *Quite through the deeds of men."*
> — **Shakespeare**
>
> *A fool sees not the same tree that a wise man sees.*
> — **William Blake**
>
> *People seldom improve when they have no other model but*
> *themselves to copy.*
> — **Oliver Goldsmith**
>
> *Nothing is so infectious as example.*
> — **Francois de la Rochefoucauld**

Pool on the Tube

Professional pool has experienced substantial growth recently in the number of hours of air-time annually. This growth is attributable to the advent of cable TV, the success of the women's tour (WPBA) and to the growing popularity of the sport.

Pool on TV is enjoyable to watch as you get to witness two top players locked in head to head combat, each one totally focused on winning the match. You can employ many of the techniques from the previous section on watching pool. It's even more fun to watch in the company of a fellow pool fanatic. In the privacy of your living room you can both become much more vocal as you don't need to worry about disturbing the players. You should also pop a tape in the VCR and record the match. When you play it back, be sure to make liberal usage of the controls for slow motion and for freezing the action. You can learn much about the pros' shooting styles and about cue ball control and other elements of the game.

The commentator's can teach you much about the game, as there is almost always a very knowledgeable and articulate player in the announcer's booth. The commentators also devote ample time to the mental side of playing top caliber pressure pool under the bright lights of TV.

Several visual elements help to make televised pool very helpful to your game. The overhead view of the table on some shots eliminates distortion. Overhead views allow you to see exactly how the cue ball does what it does as the geometry of the game comes fully alive. The commentators will often enhance this view with a telestrator as they try to predict the players' upcoming shot. TV also gives you a close look at the players' faces as they concentrate ferociously over every shot. It's fun to try to determine if their look is revealing confidence or fear.

You may have to scour your local listings for televised pool as the matches are not normally featured in the listings for sports. The pool publications also announce the date and time of upcoming events. If you miss the initial telecast, don't worry, as most of the matches are repeated several times.

CAPELLE'S LAWS for POOL

Televised pool is very entertaining, and it can be a big help to your game.

O! Woe is me,
*   Have seen what I have seen, see what I see!*
                                                    — Shakespeare

All television is educational television. The question is: what is it teaching?
                                                    — Nicholas Johnson

Genius . . . is the capacity to see ten things where the ordinary man sees one.
                                                    — Ezra Pound

---

Tips on Video Taping Your Game

Your perception of your stance or stroke and reality may be worlds apart. Your picture perfect follow through may be closer to resembling Jack-in-the-Box. While denial may comfort you in other areas of your life, there is no place for it when the health of your game is at stake.

I strongly advise that you have your game videotaped periodically just to make sure everything is in working order. When you are reviewing the results, don't be shocked or surprised at what you see. More than likely you'll find yourself exclaiming something such as, "I didn't know I twisted my arm on my follow-through." Don't feel too bad because nearly every player has at least one or two minor flaws that have gone undetected. The good news is that now you know about a problem that, when corrected, will help you play better.

There are three main positions to use when looking for problems in your fundamentals. We'll discuss several things to check out on each position.

Videotaping Your Game

☑ **Position # 1:** From the side at a 90 degree angle to your cue and directly opposite your shooting arm.

- Does your elbow remain stationary during the backstroke and up until contact?
- Are your practice strokes smooth and rhythmic?
- Is your stroke smooth?
- Does your elbow drop after contact?
- Does your body stay still?
- Do you follow through completely?
- Is your cue relatively level on the follow through?
- How long is your bridge?
- Is your cue level at address?

☑ **Position # 2:** Looking straight down your cue from directly in front.

- Is your head positioned squarely over the cue?
- Is your dominant eye or nose directly over the cue?
- How far is your head above the cue?
- Does your cue tip extend straight down the line on the follow through?

☑ **Position # 3:** Directly behind you and a little above cue level.

- Does your shooting arm hang down at or close to a 90 degree angle to the floor?
- Is your cue as close to parallel with the table as possible?
- Is your wrist cocked in or out? It shouldn't be.
- Does your arm swing straight back or does your stroke have a loop?
- Does your arm swing straight down the line on the follow through?
- Does your grip appear loose and relaxed or are you using a death grip?
- Does your stroke look free and relaxed?
- Does your elbow drop on the follow through? It should.

Taping Your Competitive Game

The videotaping tips discussed above are to be employed with the help of a friend or instructor during a practice session or lesson. It can also be helpful to have someone tape your game while you are in competition. Your game may shine in practice or in low-pressure situations. Under the gun of a pressure packed competition, however, a number of faults could pop up.

Some things to watch for include:

- ☑ Do you take enough time selecting the best shot?
- ☑ Do you follow your shooting routine?
- ☑ Is your stroke still smooth, relaxed and complete?
- ☑ Do you stay down on each shot?
- ☑ Does your facial expression reveal confidence or fear?

CAPELLE'S LAWS for POOL

When you view yourself on video tape, you may be shocked at what you see. This shock therapy can, however, do wonders for your game.

> *Nothing is easier than self-deceit.*
> — **Demosthenes**
>
> *Self-knowledge is the beginning of self improvement.*
> — **Spanish proverb**
>
> *A single event can awaken within us a stranger totally unknown to us.*
> — **Antoine de Saint-Exupery**

Getting the Most from Books and Tapes

Pool instructional books and tapes can be among your very best allies in developing your game. The following tips are designed to help you extract maximum value from each medium.

How to study pool books:

⊙ Use books as a reference. Look for help on a specific part of your game.

⊙ Skip around the book to whatever interests you.

⊙ Use a yellow highlighter to mark important passages.

⊙ Draw a star next to extremely valuable information.

⊙ Write notes in the margin.

⊙ Take notes.

⊙ Proceed through the book at your own speed.

⊙ Work on one or two things from the book at a time.

⊙ Use what you need, and discard what you don't agree with.

⊙ Take the book with you to your practice sessions.

How to study video tapes:

⊙ Watch only as much as you can digest and put to work immediately.

⊙ Use slow motion.

⊙ Stop and rerun the tape to clear up anything you didn't understand on the first viewing.

⊙ Keep a time contents of each section.

⊙ Write down things you want to work on at the table.

⊙ Put a tape player in your home pool room.

CAPELLE'S LAWS for POOL

Pool instructional books are not meant to be read like a page turning novel.

Pool instructional videos are not supposed to be viewed in one sitting like a feature film.

Master books, but do not let them master you. Read to live, not live to read.

—Edward Bulwer-Lytton

> *That is a good book which is opened with expectation and closed with profit.*
> — A. Bronson Alcott
>
> *Books had instant replay long before televised sports.*
> — Bern Williams

Memory Power

Successful pool is largely a matter of gaining sufficient knowledge, storing it in your memory and then being able to recall what you need when you need it. The many pool games and the zillions of possible layouts ensure that you'll never be exposed to the exact same challenges twice in a lifetime. Because of this, you must be able to recall similar shots and patterns and to modify your understanding to fit the particular situation.

The first step is to learn and retain as much as possible. This comes from lots of concentrated play and practice. Your eye for a shot or situation is developed from thousands of repetitions. The closer the repetitions, the easier it becomes for your mind to link them together so you can master a given shot. It is very important for you to pay close attention on each and every shot. Did you play it correctly? If so, how did you do it? What can you retain and put to use again in a similar circumstance? If you don't remember what you did right, it makes it that much more difficult to repeat the shot (or one very similar) the next time you encounter it. With enough reinforcement pool becomes largely instinctual. When you see a shot or situation, you'll automatically know what to do. And as long as you keep playing regularly, you'll retain your pool knowledge, refine it and be continually adding to it.

According to the experts, once you've learned something it's always in your memory. It may not seem that way when you don't play for awhile. However, all it usually takes is ample table time to refresh your memory even after a lengthy layoff. And when you have learned the game really well, it can sometimes return in surprisingly short order.

Some shots can be played entirely from rote while others require that you use your imagination and adapt what you know to the shot at hand. The cycle for any shot or situation is as follows:

THE CYCLE OF MEMORY

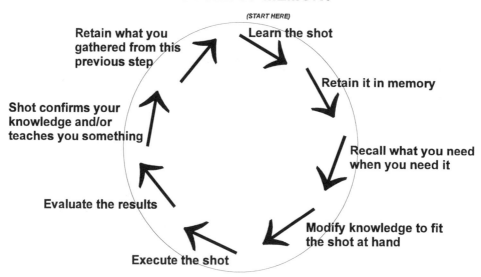

(START HERE)

Retain what you gathered from this previous step

Learn the shot

Retain it in memory

Recall what you need when you need it

Shot confirms your knowledge and/or teaches you something

Modify knowledge to fit the shot at hand

Evaluate the results

Execute the shot

The cycle may seem a little complex but it's really not as long as you plan the shot intelligently and then pay attention to your results.

CAPELLE'S LAWS for POOL

Your game is only going to be as strong as your ability to memorize tons of information and your skill at recalling what you need when you need it and effectively putting it to use.

The true art of memory is the art of attention.
— **Samuel Johnson**

A man's real possession is his memory. In nothing else is he rich, in nothing else is he poor.
— **Alexander Smith**

Memory is the thing you forget with.
— **Alexander Chase**

A great deal of learning can be packed into an empty head.
— **Karl Kraus**

Chapter 8
Evaluating Your Game

"It is obvious that there are causes, and many of them. These are discovered when we begin asking: why did this happen."

— Aristotle

Seven Definitions of Your Game

The quality of your game is open to a broad range of interpretations This is because your level of play definitely changes over time and from one circumstance to another. This is important to realize because it can keep you from becoming overly negative when your game is off. Knowing your different "speeds" can help you manage your expectations and to compete successfully.

The table below presents seven definitions of "your game." Each one is followed by a benefit that can be yours once you recognize how your game rates under each category.

Your Many Games

1. Your competitive game.
- **Benefit:** You know you have a top speed that you can access by flipping the "on" switch.

2. The status of your game right now.
- **Benefit:** This helps you to be your realistic about your chances of competing successfully.

3. You're "average" game.
- **Benefit:** This lets you know when your game has dropped and needs work. It also tells you when you're playing better than average, which is to be enjoyed.

4. Your game when it's at its best. You would like to believe this is your true game.
- **Benefit:** Your best game gives you maximum pleasure as well as hope for a breakthrough to a new level.

5. The game you played when you were at your peak.
- **Benefit: This gives you pleasant memories.** And it's still possible to taste your former magic occasionally, if not on a regular basis once again.

6. The game you normally have, but that is absent do to a prolonged slump.
- **Benefit:** This gives you hope for better days again. It can also help you to realize that most slumps are temporary.

7. The game you're capable of playing, but haven't reached yet.
- **Benefit:** This gives you enthusiasm. You believe in yourself and your potential.

When reminiscing about your long-lost best game you'll find yourself saying things like, "I used to play the seven better than I do now." Do you think you can play up to your old game again? What would it take?

CAPELLE'S LAWS for POOL

Your true game is the one that most closely matches reality with your perception of reality.

When you think you play worse than you really do, then you'll windup playing at a lower-level, which then becomes your true game.

Most people tend to slightly overestimate their game. A far worse mistake, however, is to doubt yourself by believing that you are much worse than you really are.

Somehow we learn who we really are and then live with that decision.

— **Eleanor Roosevelt**

Self-understanding rather than self-condemnation is the way to inner peace and mature conscience.

— **Joshua Loth Liebman**

Grading Your Current Level of Play

At any given moment you are acutely aware of how well you're playing. You know if you're really on your game, playing okay, or are mired in a slump. This awareness of your game can be useful in developing confidence, dictating strategy or in prompting you to seek a solution when your game has gone sour.

Your Game on a Scale of 1 to 10

10 — Career best. Super dead stroke.

9 — Excellent. You're in dead stroke.

8 — Very good. Your game and your stroke are very much in tune.

7 — Above average. You're playing pretty good.

6 — Average. Your playing okay, but it takes some effort.

5 — Your game is fair. You are grinding for your results.

4 — Below average. Despite your efforts, you just don't quite have it.

3 — Way below average. Your stroke feels awkward and your play is suffering.

2 — You're in a slump. You have problems that must be fixed before you'll play well again.

1 — Major slump. Rock bottom. You can hardly make a ball, and your confidence is shot.

The table above gives you a method of quickly identifying the current status of your game. There are three distinct categories: above average, (8 to 10); average (5 to 7); below average (1 to 4). Below are some recommendations for how to deal successfully with each category of play.

8 to 10: Go with the flow. Emphasize strategy and shot selection. Let your confidence really grow. Don't spend time or energy worrying about your stroke or whether or not you're going to make each shot. Enjoy the game. This is what you've worked for.

5 to 7: In this range your game is about average. It takes some work to get the desired results. Your stroke is okay, but you have to fiddle with it some to make it work. Your results are reasonably acceptable given the quality of your game. Stay patient, keep your concentration up, and keep looking for the little something that can raise your game into the upper zones.

1 to 4: Your game is definitely off. You need to evaluate your fundamentals and go about implementing the necessary cures. While in this phase, keep the faith in yourself and your ability to play well. Get to work on your game and believe that you can get your best game back again.

 CAPELLE'S LAWS for POOL

A realistic assessment of your game can help you to gain more enjoyment when you're playing well or to start you back on the road to recovery when your game is in the pits.

We don't know who we are until we see what we can do.
— **Martha Grimes**

Self-knowledge is the beginning of self-improvement.
—**Baltasar Gracian**

> *There is no reality except the one contained within us.*
> — **Herman Hesse**

You Versus the Competition

How well do you play? How do you stack up against the competition in your region and within the nation as a whole? These questions are not so easily answered as there's no universally accepted method of handicapping pool players. Pool does not result in concrete scores like bowling and golf. Still there are some proven steps that can give you a close estimate of your true level of play.

Tournament Ranking

Tournaments are held on a regular basis all across the country. Within a given region or pool room there are well-established systems in place that rate every players' games. Their accuracy is based on:

⊙   A knowledgeable administrator.

⊙   Regular participants whose games become known.

⊙   The integrity of the players and tournament directors.

⊙   Enough different grades so the players can be ranked very accurately.

The ten scale is one system that is gaining in favor. A nine would give an eight a small handicap in a Nine-Ball race. An eight would give a four a big spot. Again, the system relies on regular play. Unfortunately systems like these do not necessarily travel very well. An eight in Phoenix may be a six in Tulsa or vice versa.

Another common scale is the A B C system. These grades can be broken down even further by attaching a + or — to the letter. This gives you nine levels from C- to A+. This system is used in tournaments and as a gauge for making a money game.

How You Match-Up

You can gain a good approximation of your game on the local or regional scene by playing several players whose games are very well known. If you beat a C+ convincingly but lose consistently to an A-, the results clearly say you are in the "B" range. Additional play against a "B" might help you to then refine your ranking to B- if you lose, or B+ if you win regularly. After enough pool against a variety of competitors with well-established games, you'll discover where you rank in the pecking order.

The handicaps that you give and receive are also a good indicator of your game. I've found that the following spots tend to equally distinguish between A, B, and C players.

- A's can give C's the 6,7,8 in Nine-Ball
- A's can give B's the 7,8 in Nine-Ball
- B's can give C's the 7 in Nine-Ball

Unfortunately the A B C system also does not accurately reflect the abilities of players from one region to another or even crosstown. I know one local room where a low "A" is really more like a high "C." In talking with a newsletter editor in Florida, he swore that high "C's" were like low "A's" elsewhere.

League Handicapping

There are some attempts being made to standardize the handicapping of pool players. The American Poolplayers Association uses a 2-7 system for Eight-Ball. The ratings are based on carefully recording each players' missed shots. The system accurately reflects the games of beginners clear through those of above average players.

Personal Bests

Another way to measure your game is via your personal bests in one area that you can measure with accuracy: the number of racks you've run at Eight-Ball or Nine-Ball. You simply can't run too many racks consecutively without a fairly well developed game. Most tour pros have, at some point in their career, strung 7-10 or more racks of Nine-Ball. If you've ever run four or more racks of Nine-Ball at least a half-dozen times and you can consistently run-out, you are probably an "A" player or possibly a "B+" who can get very hot on occasion. If you can run out every now and then and have a high run of perhaps two or three racks," you're probably a "C+" to "B-" or thereabouts.

Using your personal bests is admittedly a somewhat crude approximation of your game. It does, however, show you what you are capable of. If you can consistently come close to your personal records, then it adds some validity to your using them as a measure of your skill.

CAPELLE'S LAWS for POOL

The best way to find out how well you play is to compete against a number of players near your level whose games are very well known.

Certain rating systems can work great within a region, but they do not travel very well.

Your personal bests are an accurate indicator of your game only if you've come close to matching them on several other occasions.

I will not be concerned at other men's not knowing me; I will be concerned at my own want of ability.
— **Confucius**

Life's greatest adventure is in doing one's level best.
— **Arthur E. Morgan**

The ultimate high: A man's abilities equaling his opinion of 'em.
— **Malcom Forbes**

Your High Run: The Straight Pool Test

Back in the days when Straight Pool was king, a player's skill was largely measured by how many balls he had run. There were two basic categories of runs: runs in competition and all other high-runs. Championship games were typically played to 150 points. Once a game ended, a player would put his cue away and the run would end unfinished. Several great Straight Pool champions have, in fact, run 150 balls and out.

The point limit puts a cap on how many balls can be run in competition. Practice and exhibition runs are not subject to any limitations. As a consequence, all of the great Straight Pool champions have run well in excess of 200 balls. Willie Mosconi is credited with the record high run of 525. However, this is an area of some dispute as the late Mike Eufemia of New York City ran 625 in practice. His run took about five hours.

Your high-run gives you a precise target to shoot for. There is a lot of satisfaction from running 20 balls for the first time, then 30, 40 and so on. Your new high-runs are also a reasonably accurate indication of your growth as a player. There's just no way you can get hot and luck your way into a run that is substantially above your current level of skill. If 25 is your best, you could run 30 or 40, but there's almost no way your next record run will jump clear to, let's say, 60 or beyond. Occasionally you'll experience a breakout of several balls to a new high. Once done, this could set your standard for some time to come. Don't let that disappoint you too much. If your personal best is 40, you should be happy running 20—30 balls regularly.

The better you play Straight Pool, the more you open yourself up to a huge jump in your all-time high-run. If you can run 50 consistently, there's no reason why you won't someday put two 50's back-to-back and cross the magical 100 barrier. And once you can run 100 regularly, you could experience a day when nothing goes wrong, you are in dead stroke and your all-time best soars to 200 or more.

The quality of your best runs are subject to the conditions. A long-run on a table with tight pockets under humid conditions that keep the balls from easily spreading on break shots is tough for even the best of players. A run under competitive pressure also carries with it a greater measure of prestige.

A 30 ball run under very demanding conditions could be equal in difficulty to a 40 or even 50 ball run on a table with big pockets. That said, I'm going to propose a rating scale to help you discover your rating as a pool player. The scale enables you to determine your level of play based on your all-time high-run. I'm going to assume that your run was accomplished on a table of average difficulty. The chart also assumes that you have played enough Straight Pool so that your ranking is closely in line with your ability at Eight-Ball, Nine-Ball or One-Pocket.

Straight Pool Ranking System

YOUR LEVEL OF PLAY	YOUR HIGH RUN
A+	150+
A	100
A-	75
B+	55
B	45
B-	35
C+	25
C	20
C-	15

CAPELLE'S LAWS for POOL

Once you really get into Straight Pool, the more balls you run, the more you want to run.

Your high run at Straight Pool is a reasonably valid indicator of your game, assuming that you've played the game enough.

When you can run 50 balls consistently, most anything is possible.

The reward of a thing well done, is to have done it.
> — Ralph Waldo Emerson

I am easily satisfied with the very best.
> — Winston Churchill

The facts, all we want are the facts.
> — Jack Webb

Facts are stubborn things; and whatever may be our wishes, our inclinations, or the dictates of our passions, they cannot alter the state of facts and evidence.
> — John Adams

Balancing Your Game

Every player's game is a unique blend of skills. In addition, every player has a certain style of play they feel gives them their best results. When you combine skills and style, you get the sum total of how a player goes about playing pool.

The skill components are not equally developed or favored by most players. Every player tends to favor one element or another when given a choice. When position can be achieved by using either draw or follow, a player who feels better using draw will do so. The same goes with cut shots versus banks. Similarly, some players tend to play aggressively while others favor a more conservative approach.

When you exercise your preferences, you naturally go with your strengths and you shy away from your weaknesses. This is called playing your game.

Going with your strengths is smart pool, but only up to a point. If you avoid follow shots even when they are clearly the better choice because you prefer draw, you may be side stepping a weakness in your game. When you over use a strength to avoid a glaring weakness, your game will suffer.

When you place a heavy emphasis on your shotmaking, you will turn into a better shotmaker. You could then develop into an aggressive and confident player who loves to go for all the tough shots. At some point, however, you will start shooting unwise shots that will cost you games and matches. You may also neglect to fine tune your position play. When you overdo any component of your game to an extreme, your game becomes out of balance. Your biggest strengths turn into your biggest weaknesses.

The scale below illustrates the concept of balance. It shows there is an acceptable range within which to exercise your personal preferences. Once you venture outside of that the zone, then your game will suffer.

BALANCING YOUR GAME

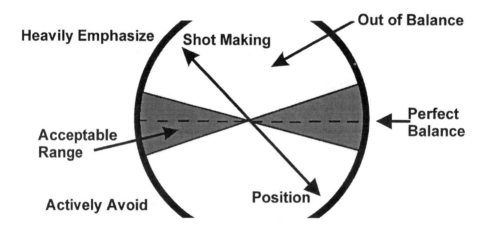

In our example, you can see that when shotmaking is heavily favored, position play suffers. The following list gives you several components of the game and styles of play. Take a few moments to evaluate your game against the list. Pinpoint any areas where you are particularly weak or any strengths that you are perhaps overemphasizing.

Balancing Your Game

SKILL OR STYLE	THE OPPOSITE
offense	defense
shotmaking	position
draw	follow
break for power	break for control
bank shots	cut shots
english	center axis
kick shots	jump shots
soft stroke	hard stroke
aggressive play	conservative play
freewheeling	grinding
fast play	slow play

CAPELLE'S LAWS for POOL

Overreliance on a strength can turn it into a weakness.

Avoiding weaknesses keeps your game from growing.

Happiness is found in the golden middle of two extremes.
— **Aristotle**

The secret of life is balance, and the absence of balance is life's destruction.
— **Hazrat Inayat Khau**

Physics and an Eye for Pool

Frozen to the rail 90-degree cut shots and masses are among the amazing shots that help make pool such an awesome game. These shots seemingly defy physics but are only pushing the far end of the spectrum of possible shots, otherwise they simply couldn't be made.

As a practical matter, it can help your game tremendously if you acquaint yourself with the physics of pool. I'm certainly not talking about complex equations, but rather about the way your eye tells you what is possible or not based on your experience. You need a highly trained eye that can distinguish between what's impossible, what's possible and what's highly probable given your unique set of skills and the realities of pool.

As a test, do you know what a 90-degree cut shot looks like? Unless the object ball is frozen to the rail, do you know how extremely difficult is a 90-degree cut shot (or for that matter an 80-degree cut shot)? While you can make razor thin cuts, they push hard on the spectrum of possibilities. After some practice you may discover that 60-degree or 70-degree cut shots stretch the limits of your ability. This type of analysis could be carried out for banks, draw shots and for any other shot.

 Once you know what you can and can't do based on the physics of pool and your level of skill, you will begin to see a dramatic improvement in your decision-making. When you know your boundaries of probable success, you also have a point of reference from which you can expand your skills. Let's assume that you have trouble with cut shots over 50-degrees. This gives you a place from which you can seek improvement.

I suggest you put your knowledge of pool's physics to the test at a practice session. The items on the list below will help you create your exam. Hole reinforcements (the kind used in three-ring binders) can help you mark the position of the cue ball and object ball. Now you can shoot the exact same shots over and over again. By doing so, you will learn much about what you can and can't do.

Testing Your Knowledge of Pool's Physics

☑ What is your maximum cut angle?

☑ How far can you draw the cue ball?

☑ At what cut angle can you no longer bring the cue ball back with draw?

☑ How far does the cue ball travel down the tangent line on cut shots at various speeds?

☑ How much english can be used before your ball pocketing really suffers?

☑ Do you know what shots have a high probability of scratching?

☑ Can you regulate the rolling distance on follow shots with great precision?

☑ Do you know when a bank shot can't be made because of a double kiss?

☑ At what distance can you no longer jump the cue ball over an obstructing object ball?

☑ Are you well versed in the effects of english as the cue ball strikes the cushion?

CAPELLE'S LAWS for POOL

The laws of physics are always at play even when the action of the balls would indicate otherwise.

The physics of pool will work in your favor once your eye for what's possible matches the reality of what you are capable of.

When you question what the balls do, it is because you are lacking knowledge in the physics of pool. The balls never lie.

It is obvious that there are causes, and many of them. These are discovered when we begin asking: why did this happen.
— **Aristotle**

The whole of science is nothing more than a refinement of everyday thinking.
— **Albert Einstein**

To every action there is always opposed an equal reaction.
— **Sir Isaac Newton**

There is no royal road to geometry.
— **Euclid**

Science is the knowledge of consequences, and dependence of one fact upon another.
— **Thomas Hobbes**

The work of science is to substitute facts for appearances and demonstrations for impressions.
— **John Ruskin**

Physics is experience, arranged in economical order.
— **Ernst Mach**

When to Buy a New Cue

A well-made production cue should be more than adequate for your game when you first start to play pool. Your first cue should fall within the normal range of the measurements as dictated by the major cue makers. The three most important specifications cover length, weight and tip. A generic cue would be roughly 58 inches long, weigh 20 ounces and have a 13-mm tip.

You will probably outgrow your first cue within a year or two. If your stroke turns out to be somewhat soft, you may now get better results with a 21-ounce cue. A 19-ounce cue could be more suitable to those who favor a firm stroke. An extremely low head position will cause you to place your grip hand further back on the cue. This head position could require that you now use a longer cue. If you develop an extended follow-through, you may now prefer a shaft with a pro taper.

Once you get the feeling your cue is no longer right for you, it's time to start testing other models. Try your friend's cues. Ask your house pro or instructor for advice or visit your favorite billiard supply store. By now you should have a pretty good idea of what specifications are best for your game. Remember, however, that the most important criteria for your second cue is how it feels in your hands and how you play with it. What you want is a cue that delivers the perfect "hit."

It's quite possible that you'll stick with your second cue for several years. Still it won't hurt to test some new wood every so often. This should confirm that your cue is still the one for you. Your test could also signal that another change is in order. At this point, a word of caution is in order: every cue plays a little differently. It takes time to keep adjusting your game to new cues. Also keep in mind that your ability and not the cue is the most important factor in determining your level of play. By hopping from cue to cue, you could cost yourself money and time. You may also windup ignoring the real reason why your game is not what you would like it to be.

By the time you're ready to purchase your third cue, your game will have settled in to the point were your preferences are now very well established. At this point, your preferred specifications will have narrowed to a fine edge. You may also have developed preferences for joints, woods and ferrules. And, of course, you will be well-schooled on tips and how to maintain them to perfection. Your third cue is one that you'll likely stay with for a long time, so now is the time to spend big on the decorative handiwork if you are the kind of person that values appearance as well as utility. Keep in mind that this cue could also be a very worthwhile investment.

CAPELLE'S LAWS for POOL

Your $2,000 custom cue will only play as well as your $5 tip, so make sure that tip maintenance is a top priority.

Upgrading to a new cue better suited to your evolving pool game can do wonders for your game.

Give us the tools, and we will finish the job.
— **Winston Churchill**

The tools to him who has the ability to handle them.
— **French proverb**

Man is a tool-using animal...without tools he is nothing, with tools he is all.
— **Thomas Carlyle**

The Eye of an Eagle

Pool is an aiming game, which certainly comes as no surprise. What may amaze you however, is the small size of the target on shots when the object ball is more than a couple of feet from the pocket. When the object ball is only two feet from the pocket, you have roughly a 1/8" wide target.

Instead of stressing out about the challenge of hitting such a small target, you should marvel at your ability to pocket balls in the first place. The precision necessary to play pool is absolutely astounding. And yet we are up to the task much more often than not, thanks to our incredible innate abilities.

The very best players in the world for the most part have fantastic vision. They can be readily compared with baseball great Ted Williams who could easily pick up the spin on a pitched ball. Perhaps you are also blessed with the eyes of an eagle. If not, you should take whatever means are at your disposal to improve your vision as much as possible.

You can test your vision by taking this simple eye examination. Set up a long, thin cut-shot with the object ball just off the middle diamond on the opposite end rail. Now get into your shooting stance. Can you see the object ball clearly, or is there a fuzz around the edge? If so, your eyesight could be causing you to miss some shots. Now set up the same shot, only this time move the object ball a foot closer to the cue ball. Is it still fuzzy? Keep moving the object ball closer until the fuzz surrounding it completely disappears. This gives your maximum range for aiming with complete accuracy.

Another indicator of your vision and your skill at aiming is the quality of your thin cut shots. Are you still able to cut the paint off the ball, or are you now banking balls that you used to cut in? If you failed either of these eye tests or if you have any doubts about your vision, I suggest you consult with your eye care professional.

Those who wear glasses may be subject to a problem which can greatly hamper your game, particularly if you get down low over the cue. If you wear glasses you may have a tendency of scrunching up your facial muscles. The purpose is to raise your glasses so you can see underneath the top rim. What this does is create unwanted tension. It also puts a funny look on your face. I know, because I suffered with these problems for ages until I finally wised up and purchased some glasses with high rims. Now I wouldn't think of playing without them.

CAPELLE'S LAWS for POOL

Pool is largely a game of aiming, so your vision should be as sharp as possible.

People only see what they are prepared to see.
— **Ralph Waldo Emerson**

Our sight is the most perfect and most delightful of all our senses. It fills the mind with the largest of ideas, converses with its object at the greatest distance, and continues the longest in action without being tired or satiated with its proper enjoyments.
— **Joseph Addison**

No object is mysterious. The mystery is your eye.
— **Elizabeth Bowen**

Your Winning Percentage

Once you've developed into an average player or better, you can win or lose as often as you care to. This can be accomplished simply by choosing your level of competition. You can win for hours on a challenge table against novices, or you may get promptly eliminated from a tournament comprised of semi-pro players. It's your decision.

Now I'm sure that everyone of you prefers winning to losing except for those with masochistic tendencies. However, when your winning percentage becomes abnormally high, winning can become too much of a good thing. If your winning percentage hovers above 80 to 90 percent, then you are missing out on the satisfaction that comes from beating worthy competition. Your education also will suffer, as you will fail to learn the valuable lessons that come from playing better players. In short, if your competition is too easy, your game won't grow.

Strangely enough, there are also those players who suffer from delusions of grandeur or who, for some peculiar reason, enjoy getting beat on. I'm not going to mince words here: these players are known to their peers as suckers, fish, marks and losers. If your winning percentage resides well under 25 - 30 percent, you have just been given your wake-up call. It is time now to improve your game, get an objective opinion on how well you really play or to find a level of competition that's more in line with your true abilities. If you are a money player, then you may also need to sharpen up your negotiating skills. Those of you who have taken losing for granted may discover that winning 40 to 50 percent of the time or more is not such a bad thing after all.

The table below illustrates the win/lose spectrum. It ranges from 10 to 100 percent. If I had to make an educated guess, I'd say most players who gain maximum satisfaction from playing pool win between 50 percent and 70 percent of the time. In a pro tournament the field, as a whole, wins 50 percent of the time. In every match there is obviously a winner and a loser. The top-10 ranked pros probably win 70 to 75 percent of their matches while competing against an army of highly talented opponents.

The Win/ Lose Spectrum

⊙ **100 percent**: you are among the world's greatest locksmiths. What fun can this be? Why not just get a job and punch a time clock?

⊙ **70 percent**: winning is important, but it's not everything. You like to have to put forth an honest effort against a tough opponent.

⊙ **50 percent**: you are the true definition of a sportsman.

⊙ **30 percent:** you could be paying your dues to learn the game or you just get a kick out of playing really tough competition. You like to win, but it's not a top priority.

⊙ **10 percent:** you are among the world's biggest suckers, sorry to say. Why go on torturing yourself? Change is definitely in order.

Now that you know the significance of your winning percentage, it's time for some self-analysis. Answer the following questions as objectively as possible. Are you okay with your responses, or is it time to rethink what winning and pool really mean to you?

☑ Why do you play pool?

☑ How important is winning to you?

☑ Would you rather win than compete?

☑ Do you feel your game is growing as a result of your current level of competition?

☑ How bad do you dislike losing?

☑ Do you learn from losses and/or superior opponents?

☑ Do you play for glory or because you truly love the game?

CAPELLE'S LAWS for POOL

Your winning percentage reveals many things about you. It is an indicator of your desire for competition, your sportsmanship, your emotional makeup and your love of money.

When the One Great Scorer comes to write against your name—He marks—not that you won or lost—but how you played the game.

— Grantland Rice

It is in the blood of genius to love play for its own sake, and whether one uses one's skill on thrones or women, swords or pens, gold or fame, the game is the thing.

—Gelett Burgess

Part 2
COMPETITION

Chapter 9
Basics of Competition

"The only thing we have to fear is fear itself."
—Franklin D. Roosevelt

Entering the Real World of Pool

Many of you will get your start in pool on your home table. At some point beating your family and friends will no longer stir your competitive juices. Then you are ready to emerge into the real world of the pool room. You are primed to cross the great divide from a champion fun player to a pool room rookie.

Your first step can be a real eye opener. Right off the bat you'll notice a sharp drop in your winning percentage. This is to be expected. You should seek your own level of competition as quickly as possible. This can minimize the trauma of losing to vastly more experienced players. Ideally, you will still taste victory often enough to feed your confidence and enthusiasm for the game.

Make it a point to play people a level or two above you on a fairly regular basis. This will speed your education and spur your desire for improvement. Tell yourself things like "in six months I'm going to beat player X at Nine-Ball" and mean it.

Throughout the book I've advised you to be patient. Perhaps it is more important for you to emphasize patience at this stage of your career more than any other. What you don't want is to get completely blown away by the realities of the pool world when you are just getting your toes into the water. So please remain patient. You will improve at your own speed with enough practice and experience.

CAPELLE'S LAWS for POOL

When you cross over from the home table to the real world of competitive pool, your journey as a bona fide pool player will have only begun. Enjoy.

All growth is a leap into the dark, a spontaneous, unpremeditated act without benefit of experience.

— Henry Miller

Things are always their best in their beginning.

— Blaise Pascal

Choosing a Format for Your Game

On your journey you will experience a mind boggling array of competitive formats. These could run the gamut from single game matches at Eight-Ball to race to 11 (or 13), double elimination Nine-Ball events. Each format has its good points and bad points. Like shoes, no one format fits the games of all of its competitors. Once you become familiar with which format(s) are best suited to your game, you will have taken a big step towards enjoying and winning at competitive pool.

Tournaments

Most new or average players enjoy Eight-Ball tournaments in which each match consists of a single game. Better players always have an advantage, but under this format anybody with a little skill and a couple of good breaks can win. This leads to two basic rules of thumb. 1) Less skilled players prefer short matches that permit luck to enter heavily into the contest. 2) Better players would rather play longer matches that minimize the luck factor.

Consider our table for a moment. In a single game match, the 70 percent favorite will win 70 percent of the time over the very long-run. If we extend the set to a 2 out of 3, his winning percentage jumps to 78.4 percent! Notice how an underdog with a 20 percent chance of winning a single game suffers a drop in his odds to only 10.4 percent in a 2 out of 3 set. The longer the match, the better the chances of the superior player.

ODDS ON WINNING		
	1 Game	**Race to 2**
	90%	97.2%
	80%	89.6%
	70%	78.4%
Your Chances of Winning:	60%	64.8%
	40%	45.2%
	50%	50.0%
	30%	21.6%
	20%	10.4%
	10%	2.8%

Longer matches are the true test of skill. They also allow you to loosen up a little and to let your stroke out. In addition, you have more time to overcome a bad start. A long set can help negate poor play, bad rolls, your opponents' fine play or any combination of these factors.

Most players favor the double elimination format for tournament play. As the name implies, you must lose two matches before you're history. Great comebacks have been launched from the one-loss side. Once you get on a roll in the loser's bracket, the steady diet of matches can enable you to get further and further into stroke.

The formula for paying out prize money can play a big role in helping you to decide which tournament to enter. A tournament is top heavy when it pays very few of the entrants with the lion's share going to first and possibly second place. This structure is favored by better players who feel they have an excellent chance of winning or finishing near the top. The self-interest of the best players may work against them as many lessor players may shy away from competing in a top-heavy tournament. Ironically, it is the "donations" of the average players that go a long way toward bolstering the winner's share.

Paying more places is a good way of encouraging developing players to enter a tournament—many of them will feel very satisfied with an "in the money" finish, even if it only returns their entry fee and possibly a small profit. Tournament directors may, therefore, be wise to take a little off first and second place money and distribute it to perhaps a half dozen or so more players so that they can taste success by finishing in the cash.

Money Games

Money players have much more flexibility in choosing the optimal format. The most basic format is to pay after every game. The contest continues until either or both players call it quits. It can be particularly annoying to the player who is behind (stuck) if his opponent quits winners. In fact, this can be a bone of great contention. You can avoid this problem by setting a time limit before you start playing. The player who is ahead may also negotiate for a time to quit so that the loser at least has a chance to come back.

A variation of per game play is what's called a "freeze-out" or "X" number of games ahead of your opponent. For example, you could play 5 ahead, 10 ahead, or whatever other number you both agree upon. Using this format, a match can be over in a flash. More than likely, however, it will result in a back and forth tug-of-war, especially when the opponents are equally matched. Under this format, matches have been known to last for several hours or even longer.

In recent years, more and more serious money games are now using races to "X" number of games. The big advantage to this format is that you know about how long a match will last. There is less need to pace yourself than when playing a "freeze-out." The big negative is that you could win more games than your opponent over the course of two or more sets and still break even or lose. Let's say you played two sets and you and your opponent win one each. The scores were 9-2 and 8-9. You out-scored your opponent 17-11 and broke even. So much for the extra yardage as they say in football.

No matter what type of competition you favor, choose your format wisely. And when it comes to a friendly wager, be firm in your negotiations. The format you both agree upon may often have as much bearing on the outcome as any other single factor.

CAPELLE'S LAWS for POOL

Choosing your competitive format wisely will greatly enhance your chances for success.

Variety is the spice of life that gives it all its flavor.
> — **William Cowper**

Cui bono? (to whose advantage)
> — **Cicero**

It's them that take advantage that get advantage in this world.
> — **George Eliot**

Tournaments = Low Risk, High Reward

Tournaments offer a legitimate means of wagering (your entry fee) on your skill. Tournaments provide everything from a training ground for newcomers clear through to competitions between top pros and world champions. There are tournaments for every level of skill and entry fees that are low enough to accommodate anyone's pocketbook.

Your entry fee represents your total financial risk in a tournament. This is completely unlike playing a money game where your losses are unlimited. Once you've paid your entry, your mind is then free to concentrate solely on playing your best pool.

I'd advise that you play in tournaments where the fields range from a little below to a couple of notches above your level of play. You will savor victory occasionally, learn from better players and gain maximum satisfaction from your tournament experience.

At times you'll want to test your game against the very top players in your area. This can serve as a valuable learning experience, and it could result in a confidence boosting victory. In addition, it gives you a relatively inexpensive means of matching skills with players who would require that you play for much higher stakes in a money game. To those of you (hopefully, no one) who chose to habitually pick on vastly inferior competition as an ego booster and a moneymaker, all I can say is it's time to grow up and learn what the game is really all about.

Experiencing Tournament Competition

In the moments before a tournament begins, you may feel a sense of excitement and anticipation about the unknown that lies ahead. How will you play? Who will you play? Will the pool "god of rolls" be with you? Will you cash in or reach the finals, possibly for the first time? All of these questions and more may quickly run through you mind. And soon thereafter each will be answered by the competition.

The winners bracket of a double elimination tournament offers the smoothest road to the finals. As you progress through this bracket, your game and your confidence must rise to peak levels so you can success-fully meet the challenge of tougher opposition. But don't lose heart should a loss deposit you into the one-loss side. Part of winning at pool is to learn how to put a positive spin on things just like a consummate politician. So after your first loss, tell yourself that you're going to get to play more pool and that the extra play will help to put you in dead stroke. This certainly sounds better than adopting a defeatist attitude that many of your opponents on the losers' side may be carrying with them.

The reality of the competition can be cruel. Even world champions have experienced two-and-out (elimination without winning a match). On the other hand, you must also be prepared to handle success. The tournament may have started out as a lark, or as a means of gaining experience. But at some point in your career, you will find yourself progressing on a beeline towards the finals. Your first big win may be in sight. You may be an experienced winner at the "C" or "B" level who is tasting success against a tougher field and for more prize money than you've ever played for previously.

At some moment, you will feel the pressure that comes with advancing well through the brackets. Can you handle the pressure, the tougher competition, the spotlight, the dollars at stake and the thought of winning? Of course you can, but maybe not the first time or two that you find yourself in this position as these are uncharted waters.

To some people, winning comes naturally. To the vast majority, however, there is a learning curve that requires experience under the heat and all of the factors that we've talked about before they know how to win. To experience your first big breakthrough, you must believe in yourself. You must believe that if you don't win today, then you will at some point in the not too distant future. You may draw some comfort while you are in this learning to win phase from the fact that a pool player's journey is a long one. It may take you years to learn how to win, but you'll then have decades to enjoy amassing victories.

Tournament play will provide you with great stories to tell of heart pounding victories and gut wrenching defeats. Post tournament story telling sessions are, for many pool players, one of pools greatest pleasures. I certainly wish each of you the best, but in the end all that matters is that you stepped up to the table and gave it your best shot.

 CAPELLE'S LAWS for POOL

Once you've paid your entry fee, you have nothing more to lose and everything to gain. So enjoy the ride for as long and as far as it takes you.

Our doubts are traitors, And make us lose the good we oft might win, By fearing to attempt.
— **Shakespeare**

I will not steep my speech in lies; the test of any man lies in action.
— **Pindar**

Enter to grow in wisdom.
— **Charles William Eliot**

Thou shalt not covet; but traditions approves All forms of competition.
— **Arthur Hugh Clough**

Matching Your Game to the Competition

I'm sure you love to win at pool and to feel the satisfaction that comes from beating a worthy opponent. And I'm also certain that it's not much fun for you to get your backside whipped regularly by more highly skilled opponents. These two observations should serve as your guide in helping you to choose the appropriate level of competition. The majority of the time (80 percent or so, to pick a percentage) you should be playing people within a range of 10-20 percent above or below your game. This will enable you to experience winning against significant competition.

Learning how to win under league pressure or in a $5 entry fee Eight-Ball tournament plays a big part in developing your game. Beating slightly better players can also serve as a stepping stone to higher and higher levels of play. The chart below gives you a general guideline for the quality of opponents that you should be playing on a regular basis. Each letter grade (A, B, C) is divided into three distinct levels. Most of your play should be in a range of 2/3 of a letter below your game (B+ plays B-) to 2/3 of a letter above (B plays up to A-). The exceptions to this rule come when you are A, C or below an A- or above, as noted in the chart.

Who You Should Play	
Your Game	**Range of Opposition**
A+	A+ to A-
A	A+ to B+
A-	A+ to B
B+	A to B-
B	A- to C+
B-	B+ to C
C+	B to C-
C	B- to C-
C-	C+ to C-

Now for the other 20 percent. You will occasionally be matched up against a vastly inferior opponent in league or tournament play. Beating this kind of player does little good for your development as a player. It should also provide little or no satisfaction to your ego.

Every so often you should purposefully match-up against people who play much better than you. The idea is to learn, by firsthand experience, how the game is really played. Winning is pretty much out of the question unless you receive a huge handicap. Don't waste time dwelling on your loss however lopsided the final score. Perhaps it would help to remember that world class Straight Pool players have lost by as much as 150-0 or more! Experience is a great teacher and that's what you're after when you compete against players who are three or more levels above your game.

CAPELLE'S LAWS for POOL

The majority of your competitive efforts should be with players a little worse to a little better than yourself.

You should begin your competitive career playing the game you like to play best. For 90 percent of all beginning pool players that game is Eight-Ball.

Understand that when you begin competing at pool that it can be highly addictive, and that may be a great thing.

There is nothing I love so much as a good fight.
> — **Franklin D. Roosevelt**

Experience is what you get when you don't get what you want.
> —**Dan Stanford**

While one person hesitates because he feels inferior, the other is busy making mistakes and becoming superior.
> — **Henry C. Link**

Getting a Jump on a New Season

I find it impossible not to play pool at least a few times a week, twelve months out of the year. However, I understand that for many readers pool is a seasonal sport. When the weather starts to warm, golf clubs, softball bats and fishing rods once again take precedence over your trusty pool cue. A five- or six-month absence from pool can do wonders for your enthusiasm for the game. The problem for seasonal players lies in rebuilding your game every year to where you can really enjoy playing again.

It seems like a shame to work your way into peak form by seasons end only to chuck it all aside for the next several months. Therefore, my first suggestion for thwarting the layoff blues is to never completely leave the game. An hour or two of practice once or twice a week could do wonders for your game. You'll retain much of your game, and you'll give yourself a big head start on your fellow competitors come next season.

Pool is largely an evening sport no matter what time of the year it's played, so you can still play a few games now and then in the summer when the sun sets on your other activities. A pool room also makes a wonderful oasis from exceptionally hot and humid days or from inclement weather. Yes, I'm making a concerted effort to turn each of you who are seasonal players into certified year around pool nuts.

Despite my pleas for continuous pool playing, however, many of you will continue to pack your cue away during the spring and summer months. If this describes your routine, then I advise you to at least consider going to Fall practice 2-3 weeks early. The pros in all seasonal sports follow this ritual. Fall practice will give you a big jump on your fellow competitors who show less dedication. You could build some early season momentum that might carry through until the season ends.

How To Get Your Game Back

⊙ On your first outing, play just for fun. Don't think about stroke mechanics. Just play and really enjoy your return to the game.

⊙ Early practice sessions should be used to work out the kinks. Create your own checklist of fundamentals and give yourself a complete tune-up.

⊙ Practice with a friend who is equally dedicated to the game. Take turns watching each other play and practice.

⊙ Don't be overly concerned with your results at first. Be patient and enjoy just being back at the table again.

CAPELLE'S LAWS for POOL

Practicing pool regularly during the off season can keep the rust off your game and help you get a fast start on the pool season.

The beginning is the most important part of the work.
— **Plato**

Absence diminishes mediocre passions and increases great ones, as the wind blows out candles and fans fire.
— **Francois, Duc de La Rochefoucauld**

Too much of a good thing can be wonderful.
— **Mae West**

Action may not always be happiness, but there is no happiness without action.
— **Benjamin Disraeli**

Bar Box Billiards

The very words "Bar Pool" bring to mind a unique world that's very much a part of today's pool scene and one that stands in stark contrast to pool played in billiard parlors. For starters, bar tables are much smaller, measuring 3 1/2' x 7' versus 4 1/2' x 9' for a regulation size table. The smaller playing field can be deceiving to those big table players who expect to have a field day on the bar box. You won't face the long green, and the corner pockets are usually much more forgiving. On the other hand, the side pockets are much smaller. The congestion factor makes running out extremely difficult at times as blockers seem to be stationed everywhere. And finally, you must master the specialty shots such as banks, combos, billiards and caroms if you wish to excel at bar pool.

Eight-Ball

Eight-Ball is by far the most popular game played on a bar table. It continues to be the favorite of casual players and is widely used in league play. Bar table Eight-Ball is a highly skillful game of cat and mouse when played by master technicians. The game calls for great patience. You must wait for the right time to attempt your run-out. This is the #1 principle for bar table Eight-Ball. It is also the very first piece of advice that you will hear from virtually anyone who knows anything at all about the art and science of winning Eight-Ball.

While you wait for your opportunity to run-out, you must move the balls (both yours and your opponents) like pieces on a chessboard. Needless to say, there are a million little tricks and traps that can build your advantage. You will learn to rejoice when you see your opponent quickly clear five ducks on his way to nowheresville. His early "lead" is really a mirage. Once he is done, you'll very likely have open season on your balls clear through to the Eight-Ball. Your ability to negotiate your way through a wide open pattern of six or seven balls along with the other tips we've discussed will enable you to beat 85 percent or more of the players you'll encounter. I guarantee it.

Etiquette

Most bar tables are coin-operated, which requires a steady diet of quarters. To get a game you must challenge the table. Most taverns have you secure a place in line by placing a quarter(s) on the rail. Some places use a chalkboard. It is considered proper etiquette to ask one of the contestants if challenges are accepted. However, this may not always be necessary, as the players will usually let you know if your challenge is welcome or not.

You would be smart to acknowledge your position out loud on the waiting list. This tactic can help you to avoid any disagreements about whose turn it is when it's your game. When there is a long wait, you should watch the table like a hawk when the game before yours is nearing completion. As the Eight-Ball drops, quickly swoop down on the table and confidently insert your quarter. Be prepared to explain your rights should a pool pirate attempt to steal your game. But also keep in mind that waiting an extra game may be a small price to pay for avoiding a nasty dispute.

Challenge Pool

Challenge pool is a real free for all. It offers some of the most intriguing match-ups and some highly entertaining people watching. Challenge tables are a haven for beginners, couples, singles on the make, ego trippers, showoffs, wannabes, hustlers and genuine enthusiasts.

Most taverns have more than one table open to challengers. This increases your options. Do you want to brag to your buddies about how long you held the table at Joe's Tavern last night? Is your goal to learn the game? If so, then look for the table with the toughest competition, even if losing costs you a beer. And, of course, you can choose to compete with those whose skill approximates your own. If playing for small stakes helps you to concentrate, don't be bashful about bringing up the subject. "What are you guys playing for?" will tell you if you are on a small stakes table.

Many establishments allow tables to be closed off to challengers. Your biggest tip-off is if Nine-Ball is being played. You should be respectful of the players' wishes to be left alone. After all, you may wish to have the same courtesy extended to you. When Nine-Ball is being played, there's a good chance that the players may be among the best in the bar. It might be both fun and educational to grab a stool and sweat the action.

Tips For Enjoying Bar Pool

⊙   Learn the local house rules, especially before placing a wager.

⊙   If you want to play serious pool, bring your own cue.

⊙   Don't be too surprised if the table rolls off.

⊙   Search carefully for a straight cue with a good tip if you are going to use a house cue.

⊙   Learn to shoot with a short stick.

⊙   Be assertive in asking people to move out of your way when you are shooting.

⊙   Offer to bank the eight-ball against much weaker competition. They'll appreciate your generosity.

⊙   Don't gamble with people who are intoxicated.

⊙   Develop a sixth sense for trouble.

CAPELLE'S LAWS for POOL

Big table pool and bar table pool are very much alike and yet also very different.

Small is beautiful.
— E. F. Schumacher

There is nothing which has yet been contrived by man by which so much happiness is produced as by a good tavern or inn.
— Samuel Johnson

Chapter 10
Preparing for Battle

"The die is cast."

— Julius Caesar

Bringing Your Game to a Peak

You may not give much thought to pre-tournament preparations prior to a weekly Eight-Ball tournament. Your approach should take a radical shift, however, when you are getting ready for a big 2–3 day Nine-Ball tournament or when you and your teammates are flying to Las Vegas for a national championship. Under these circumstances, you owe it to yourself to prepare as thoroughly as time allows.

To prepare for a big competition you should compete in smaller tournaments that can mirror the format of the big event as closely as possible. A money game for a few dollars is also good practice. You can tailor your match-up to the style used in the tournament. The idea is to sharpen both your game and your nerves to a fine edge.

Practice sessions will also help you to get in good stroke. Work with your instructor, if necessary, to fine-tune your game. Don't, however, consider making any radical last minute changes unless your game is in the pits and you are desperate for a tip that could jolt things back into place.

The majority of your last minute pre-tournament practice should be devoid of any thoughts about mechanics. Your goal is to develop complete trust in your stroke and to acquire a sense of rhythm to your game. You don't want to be fumbling around between different methods just before a big event.

Before embarking on your journey, make sure that your equipment is in order. Priority #1 is the condition of your tip. You'll want to bring along all of the little accessories that can mean so much to your game such as a tapper and shaft cleaner. Create a checklist of the items that you can't do without.

Establish your goals for the tournament. Start by telling yourself that you're going to have fun no matter what. This is a very obtainable objective, especially when compared with winning against several hundred or more determined competitors.

Pool games, matches and tournaments are the sum total of each and every shot you play. Your best chances of winning will come from accumulating as many successful shots as possible. Make it your goal to play each shot as well as possible. Other factors beyond your control, such as the rolls and the quality of the field, will have a big influence on the final results.

Arriving at a Tournament

 Arrive at the tournament site as early as possible so that you can spend time getting used to the tables and to the surroundings. Your knowledge of the tables can help you to refine your strategy. Perhaps the tables favor aggressive or defensive play. Regardless, you must learn to put a positive spin on the conditions no matter what they are like. Tell yourself that you are a master at adapting your game to the surroundings. This mindset will help you stay focused no matter how the table rolls or if the pockets reject well stroked shots.

It is beyond the scope of this book to delve too deeply into the whys and hows of the proper diet for shooting great pool. Suffice to say that certain foods, when eaten before a match, will sap your strength while others will give you the energy you need to stay completely focused on your game. There are many excellent books with diets that can be custom tailored for each individual. As part of your preparations, you'll also want to get plenty of rest just in case you wind up running a marathon in the loser's bracket.

Your Best Game

Tournament pool requires that you bring your best game to the table when it's time for your matches to begin. You must develop a routine that you use just prior to each match that enables you to call upon the absolute best that your game has to offer. This pre-match psyche-up session will ensure that you show up to play in body, mind and spirit. Hopefully, it will cut down on the number of post match laments such as "I just wasn't into it" or "I couldn't get up for the match." If you can't get up for a tournament, why bother to enter in the first place?

In the moments before a big match, you should be fully alive and feeling a sense of nervous anticipation. This will tell you that you are mentally stimulated and are psyched for battle. Be sure to knock some balls around on the table you will be playing on, if possible. Most big events schedule some time for this.

Give yourself enough time to get used to the table and to put the butterflies into formation. Also, consider evaluating the table using the checklist in the section on "Checking Out the Playing Conditions." Once the match is about to begin, you should feel quite confident because you have done everything in your power to maximize your chances for a top-flight game of pool.

Despite your best efforts, your game could be off. You could also be having trouble adapting to the table. In times like this, just remember that the pool gods reward patience and persistence. Therefore, part of your preparations should include a mindset that prepares you to slug it out to the bitter end. Pool is a funny game. You just never know when it all might start to click and you can do no wrong.

 CAPELLE'S LAWS for POOL

Your confidence will match your level of pre-tournament preparations.

Plan your work and work your plan.
— **Anonymous**

Organizing is what you do before you do something, so that when you do, it's not all mixed up.
— **A. A. Milne**

Most people don't plan to fail, they fail to plan.
— **John L. Beckley**

Dig the well before you are thirsty.
— **Chinese proverb**

It is a bad plan that admits no modification.
— **Publilius Syrus**

When Not to Play One-Pocket

When you are making final preparations in the days and hours before a big Nine-Ball tournament, you need to be thinking Nine-Ball and to be playing Nine-Ball. Nine-Ball has certain skill requirements that distinguish it from all other pool games. You must have you're A#1 rack smasher break in top gear. Your fear of the long green must be zilch, and your feel for the cue ball's rolling distance (speed control) must exceed that of a safecracker. These are all very specialized skills that don't necessarily fall into place on command. Instead, they must be nurtured together so that your game reaches its peak at the opening bell.

Your mind is a most wonderful piece of machinery. It can calculate 70 degree cut angles and program run-outs better than any computer. However, your mind is also extremely fragile. One minute you may feel down in the dumps. Seconds later you may soar to the heights of ecstasy as you come through in the clutch after your opponent hands you a reprieve.

Because of your minds transient nature, you must pamper it and constantly reinforce those thoughts and actions that enable you to play your best pool. Your mind needs all the help it can get. This, of course, includes the necessary pre-tournament preparations.

Pool is pool, but One-Pocket is not Nine-Ball. The whole set of terrific skills that go into One-Pocket cannot be denied. The game's growing popularity attests to the beauty and challenge of One-Pocket. The game, however, requires a ton of safety play, bank shots and short range position that run counter to the type of shots you'll be faced with in Nine-Ball. One-Pocket is a highly strategic game. Nine-Ball is a shoot-out in which you must be constantly pocketing one challenging shot after another even when your position is particularly sharp.

I'm sure you get the point; to play Nine-Ball really well you must play it very often and to the exclusion of all other games before an important event. I used One-Pocket as an example, but I could have inserted Eight-Ball or Straight Pool. Play only Eight-Ball before an Eight-Ball tournament and so on. Your goal is to hone your physical skills and to be thinking the game you will be competing at as well as possible.

The exceptions to the principles of preparation we've discussed above is that small segment of the pool playing population (about .0001 percent) that can switch from game to game at a moment's notice with no perceptible loss in skill. These players are mostly world champions who could run out using a broom handle.

CAPELLE'S LAWS for POOL

Playing One-Pocket right before an important Nine-Ball tournament is like taking a sleeping pill before a marathon race.

Beware of dissipating your powers; strive constantly to concentrate them.
— **Johann Wolfgang von Goethe**

The perplexity of life arises from there being too many interesting things in it for us to be interested properly in any of them.
— **G. K. Chesterton**

Scouting Reports Can Give You the Edge

You start each turn by playing what your opponent leaves behind. Since your game is unmistakably intertwined with theirs, it certainly helps to know about your opponents' game. The place to start is with a scouting report that details their strengths and weaknesses. This information can help you to plot a winning strategy. Keep in mind that the report is designed to help you win and not to create fear of a formidable foe. Respect for an especially skillful opponent is wise, but being fearful is not.

Your scouting reports can be as simple or detailed as you wish to make them. You can use them to build your confidence when the report indicates you are the favorite. Against a tough opponent your confidence can come from a particular weakness or two that you may be able to exploit. Your confidence can also spring from knowing what you are up against. Your opponents' solid play will not surprise or shock you into submission.

The more information you can acquire prior to the match, the better. With your game plan established, you won't have to waste any time or lose games unnecessarily while learning your opponents' game.

You can learn about your opponent by:

⊙ Watching them play in other matches and/or when they are warming up.

⊙ Having a knowledgeable friend scout their game.

⊙ Asking teammates or other players about their game.

⊙ Reviewing any previous matches against them.

⊙ Checking out their league or tournament records.

Once the match begins, you should continue to scope out your opponents' game. Is their game above or below the norm? Are they having trouble with any part of their game? You can also gain a valuable edge by critiquing their play even in the absence of any prior information. In Eight-Ball tournaments there is a good chance that your opponent is completely unknown. You must learn to "read" your opponents' game very quickly. This will enable you to make the necessary adjustments in your strategy. Suppose that your opponents' position or stroke shows that a five ball run-out on an open table is all but impossible. Now you can go ahead and maneuver the balls until a 100 percent cinch run-out is available. And you certainly need not bother with a heroic run-out attempt that springs from a fear that you might not get to shoot again.

Your scouting report can be as thorough as you feel is necessary. Your investigation should stop, however, short of the point where analysis of your opponents' game starts to take away from your play. The most critical pieces of information involve those skills that largely determine who gets to assume possession of the table.

A Top Flight Scouting Report

☑ **Break**—Does your opponent break and run-out very often? Do they lose control of the cue ball? Does this leave you with an awkward or difficult start to the rack? Does their break leave road map run-outs for their opponent?

☑ **Safeties**—Do they play extra tough safeties that require your kicking game to be on target? Do they leave tough, but open shots or return safeties? Do they play many safeties in the first place? (Note: less knowledgeable players don't bother much with safety play.)

☑ **Shot selection**—Do they play the percentages very carefully or are they offensive-minded shotmakers?

☑ **Kick shots**—Is your opponent skilled at making contact when hooked? If yes, this could require you to play airtight safeties. Can you get ball in hand very often with basic hook safeties?

☑ **Jump shots**—Does your opponent like to jump out of safeties? Do their jump attempts often lead to ball in hand?

☑ **Heart**—This is the big difference when there is no other deciding factor. Is your opponent a closer, or will they crack under pressure? Keep the heat on if they tend to weaken in the stretch.

Scouting your opponents' game can give you valuable information, confidence and the winning edge. If you are inclined to take the easy way out and not bother, just remember that your opponent may have a report on your game. Do you really want to spot him that advantage?

CAPELLE'S LAWS for POOL

Even though you've never played before, that doesn't mean that your opponent doesn't know your game.

A good scouting report can give you the winning edge.

When you are better than player B, and B knows it, then you have a big advantage. And when you know that B knows, then your advantage is overwhelming.

A man surprised is half beaten.
— **Thomas Fuller**

'Know thyself' is a good saying, but not in all situations. In many it is better to say 'know others.'
— **Menander**

Forewarned forearmed.
— **Cervantes**

All strategy depends on the competition.
— **Bruce D. Henderson**

Evaluating the Playing Conditions

Playing in familiar surroundings gives you confidence and a sense of comfort. Competitive pool, however, is a completely different animal. It requires you to duplicate your "A" game under a variety of conditions. As your knowledge of different playing conditions grows, so too will your ability to adapt your game to any and all circumstances. This skill is but another of the big factors in winning at competitive pool.

On occasion you will instantly fall in love with a new table and the surroundings. At other times, a part of you will rebel at what you consider to be unfair or unpleasant playing conditions. Since you are going to go ahead and participate in the competition, you should adopt a positive attitude towards the conditions. After all, the game can be frustrating enough without your getting upset about something that is beyond your control. In addition, stop to consider your opponent, who may also not find the table to his liking. You can gain an important edge by vowing to give it your best, while your opponent fumes about table rolls, poor lighting or tight pockets.

You may have to learn how the tables are playing by observing other matches. This is often the case in Eight-Ball tournaments on a bar table. At most big Nine-Ball events, you are usually given ample practice time before your matches begin. Use this time wisely by employing several, if not all, of the following techniques. Each will further your understanding of how the table plays.

Checking Out the Table

⊙ **Table speed**—Shoot several routine position shots and observe carefully the roll of the cue ball. Does it come to a rest on target, or is it stopping either short or past your position zone? Getting the feel of a table's speed should be your #1 priority.

⊙ **Pocket receptivity**—Pockets can be rated buckets (easy), medium difficult, and tight. Your first test is to place two object balls side by side at the pocket's opening. With average sized pockets there will be 1/4" to spare. Check out the depth of the opening. If the slate recedes well past the point, there's plenty of room to hang balls in the jaws. An improperly cut pocket that faces out excessively can also reject a reasonably well hit shot. Try shooting the cue ball down the rail. The main variables are how far the cue ball is positioned from the rail; how far from the pocket; how hard you shoot it; and how far up the rail you aim the cue ball. This test will tell you how much you can cheat the pocket and still make the shot into the corner.

⊙ **Table roll**—The object ball may curve just like a golfer's putt as it loses momentum on a softly stroked shot. Most tables have at least some measure of roll-off. You can test for this by shooting the cue ball slowly, both down and across the table. Closely observe its path as it slows down. The more a table rolls-off, the more you must avoid soft shots, especially from long range.

⊙ **The rails**—Bank shots, kick shots and a number of position plays are impacted by the condition of the rails. "Average" rails, if there is such a thing, play as *you* expect them to play. Bank shots and kick shots go where you expect them to without any adjustments on your part. Rails are said to play short when the cue ball or object ball rebounds at less than an "average" angle for that shot. The opposite is true when rails play longer than "average." Dead rails will cushion the cue ball's impact like a soft pillow. This requires you to use a more powerful stroke to arrive at your position zone. With live rails, the cue ball will rebound like a pinball. Be on the lookout for dead spots, which will severely retard the cue ball's rebound off the cushion.

⊙ **Straightness of the rails**—You need to know if an object ball that's frozen to the rail can make it past the side pocket without rebounding off the point. Freeze three balls against each other on the side rail. Shoot into the first ball from a fairly straight angle. Does the third ball travel past the side pocket and into the corner pocket? It takes just a few moments to test this from both sides of each side pocket.

- ⊙ **The cloth**—New cloth is typically very fast. It allows you to draw the cue ball monstrous distances with little effort. The cue ball tends to slide further down the tangent line before either draw spin or follow spin takes hold. The pockets also tend to play easier with new cloth. Old cloth can be super fast since the nap has been worn thin. Worn out cloth is unpleasant to look at and may cause big problems when racking the balls. A table with worn out cloth probably hasn't been leveled for ages, so roll-offs are to be expected.

- ⊙ **Break path**—After a table has been subjected to constant play, one or more well defined paths from the head string to the head ball get worn into the cloth. These markings will show you the preferred spots from which to consider playing your break shot.

- ⊙ **Cue ball**—There are a variety of cue balls in common usage. The biggest variation comes with the oversize cue ball, which is used only on some bar tables. It weighs more than a regulation sized ball, which makes drawing the cue ball quite a challenge. In addition, you must aim for a thinner hit on cut shots to compensate for its larger size.

- ⊙ **Object balls**—Balls that are cleaned and polished cannot be thrown as much as those with a layer of dust, sweat and pool chalk. Dirty balls have an annoying tendency of skidding unpredictably on soft shots. This is caused by excess friction between the cue ball and object ball at contact.

- ⊙ **Lighting**—Check to make sure that the lighting is spread evenly across the table. Also check for brightness. Good lighting is essential for long shots and for thin cut shots. Your shot selection could change significantly if the lighting is especially poor.

The environment also plays a big part in your success. Ask yourself if the place feels like a room in which you can play well? Does it require an adjustment in your thinking and your approach to the game? For example, you may have to be aware of matches on adjoining tables if the tables are spaced closely together. In some rooms or taverns, you may wish to avoid playing a position that results in a pillar or wall affecting your next shot. The noise level, the closeness of onlookers, and the temperature and humidity are also among the factors that you must learn to deal with effectively.

CAPELLE'S LAWS for POOL

No two tables play exactly alike, even in the same room. Better players have learned the importance of sizing up a table fast and adapting to the conditions.

Eighty percent of all surprises are unpleasant.
— William A. Marsteller

Plans are nothing. Planning is everything.
— Dwight D. Eisenhower

Chapter 11
Playing Under the Heat

"You can't think and hit at the same time."
—Yogi Berra

Pressure Proofing Your Game

Pressure adds a whole new dimension to the game. What you believe to be "your game" often disappears from sight. When pressure works for you, your concentration improves and your game may rise to a whole new level. You come through in the clutch. You may even experience dead stroke, the nirvana of pool.

The other side of the pressure equation is what, quite frankly, scares the hell out of all pool players: dogged shots, choking, the big apple. When pressure works against you, your mind gets focused on all of the wrong things. Out of nowhere your mind is screaming with thoughts about losing, the rolls, your opponent's good play, possible embarrassment and the score, just to name a few. Things may pop into your mind that have nothing to do whatsoever with pool. The sad result is much time in the chair contemplating your miserable state of affairs.

There is a very select group of players that are seemingly born to play their best pool under pressure. Their competitiveness and mental make-up enables them to naturally come through under the heat. Some are also blessed with superior hand-eye coordination and exceptional vision that allows them to rapidly develop into ball pocketing machines. Perhaps you are a natural born pressure player. If not, take heart, because you can still acquire the skill just like you would for any other facet of the game. You need to make the commitment to learning how to play like you practice when the winner's share is on the line.

Most players have a self-imposed limit to how much pressure that they wish to be under. When competing in a tournament or against a player that takes them out of their comfort zone, they will feel excessive pressure. This can cause them to crack. Some of the most well-known figures in the world of professional sports have succumbed to pressure, so don't feel too bad if you've dogged a few shots while under the heat.

Do You Like Pressure?

It is important for you to discover how far you really want to go with your pool game. Are you willing to suffer through dogged shots and blown matches to gain the experience you need to win? Can you stand to lose before you learn to win? Do you like to win more than you hate to lose? Be realistic when answering these questions, but don't sell yourself short. If competitive pool is not your bag, that's okay. Similarly, you may have set limits for your game because you lack the time or desire to push beyond. Keep in mind that the main purpose of this book is to help you enjoy the game of pool in whatever manner you feel is best suited to you and no one else.

The quiz below is designed to help you identify your true competitiveness. There are no right or wrong answers, just your answers. They may help you decide on your goals and whether or not you wish to scale the mountain as a competitive player.

Pressure Self Quiz

Do you now, or could you see yourself:

☑   Playing your best pool in front of a big crowd?

☑   Pocketing a long tough nine-ball on double-hill?

☑   Maintaining your game against a strong and intimidating player?

☑   Coming back strong after dogging a couple of routine shots?

☑   Winning your first Eight-Ball tournament?

☑   Running out to help your team win a league championship?

Do these pressure situations stir your competitive juices and make you want to master the mental game? Or do you wish to simply enjoy the game as a low-pressure means of relaxation? The choice is yours. The discussion that follows should be of value to those of you who have a strong desire to reach your full potential as a competitive player.

Playing Under Pressure

A large majority of professional athletes welcome a healthy case of the pre-game jitters. A mild case of nervousness lets them know they are up for the match. They are also a sign that they are ready to focus totally on their game. If you experience a bit of nervousness before an important match, don't let it shake your confidence. Instead, use it to help you get totally into the match from the word go.

Your warm-up routine should have you primed and ready for action. Still, once the balls are broken, things can change awfully fast. The first few shots and the first game can set a tone for the entire match. You will probably be a little tentative at the start. Don't let this be of too much concern. Just be sure to follow your routine, one shot at a time (more on this later). Have confidence in yourself and your game plan and stick to it.

Missing balls because of the pressure is a pool player's worst nightmare. Every player does their best to avoid the dreaded "C" word (rhymes with broke). Nevertheless, everybody misses balls because of pressure. There are certain times during a match when a miss is more likely to occur. We'll go through each of these high-pressure situations and offer some solutions.

Pressure Situations

EARLY IN THE MATCH—It takes a little time to let your stroke out and to shoot with complete abandon. Don't let an early miss throw you. Your opponent will also likely make a couple of mistakes due to early match nerves. The match has just started, so get refocused on playing your game.

YOU FALL A FEW GAMES BEHIND—There's a sinking feeling that comes when you see the match slipping away. At this point a pep-talk is in order. Tell yourself you're not a quitter. You have nothing to lose, so you might as well open up and fire away. You're the comeback kid. Your confident play and a change in momentum could serve to rattle your opponent.

YOU HAVE A BIG LEAD—You must avoid the tendency to let up and to celebrate your victory prematurely. The pool gods do not look kindly on those who don't fully appreciate a big lead. In your mind the match is over, but this feeling can change in a moment should your opponent start tearing into your once insurmountable lead. Again, a pep-talk is in order. Tell yourself that you'd rather have any lead than to be behind. Go back to playing the confident and assertive game that got you the lead in the first place. See yourself, in baseball lingo, as the ultimate "closer."

A CLOSE MATCH AT THE END—Pressure mounts during a match in direct proportion to how much of the contest remains to be played. The pressure can be suffocating at the end of a closely played match when both players can smell victory. Only one will prevail, and that's usually the one who can maintain their game when it matters most. The best advice I can give you is to enjoy yourself. Playing a tough match is what you've worked for. This is especially true when it comes down to the wire in the finals. If you win, great. And if you lose, you still had a great experience butting heads against a worthy opponent who is equally deserving of victory. After all, he had to beat a pretty darn good player (you) to win.

As a match wears on, you must be on guard for a drastic change in your pace of play. Under pressure you may have a tendency to play faster. This could be a misguided attempt to play right past the pressure. Unfortunately, the pressure will usually catch-up with you at the worst possible time near the end of a key game.

Another big mistake is to slow down to a snail's pace. The objective is to avoid making any mistakes, which is a big mistake all by itself. The solution for both the tortoise and the hare is to have a well-established shooting routine that you follow religiously on every shot. A routine gives you confidence. It helps you to maintain an ideal pace of play right up to the very end.

Your ability to maintain control over your emotions under end of tournament pressure, when world champions have been known to dog routine shots, is the acid test of your capacity to handle the heat. How well does your game hold up under pressure? That's the big challenge.

You must learn to trust yourself and your stroke. Sometimes you will handle the pressure like a pro, and at times maybe not so well. Focusing on each shot, enjoying the competition and staying in the moment, can work wonders. Experience also helps you in dealing with pressure.

I can write all about playing pressure pool, but it is really something that you must experience for yourself. I've choked on hangers and I've run-out when it matters most. So will you. And hopefully, you will learn not only about how to handle the heat but also about the sheer joy of participating in great matches, win or lose.

 CAPELLE'S LAWS for POOL

Your game almost never stays the same under pressure. You'll almost always play better or worse than your "average" game.

The pressure to win is inversely related to the frequency with which the event is held.

The only thing we have to fear is fear itself.
— **Franklin D. Roosevelt**

Courage is resistance to fear, mastery of fear, not absence of fear.
— **Mark Twain**

Fear defeats more people than any other one thing in the world.
— **Ralph Waldo Emerson**

> *We all choke, and the man who says he doesn't choke is lying like hell. We all leak oil.*
>
> — Lee Trevino
>
> *The greatest mistake you can make in life is to be continually fearing you will make one.*
>
> — Elbert Hubbard

You Gotta Have Heart

Many times the only difference between two closely matched competitors is who plays a little better or worse at the end of the match. And the ingredient that determines who comes through at crunch time is called heart. One of the biggest complements any pool player can be paid is "he's got the heart to take it off."

You can describe this essential characteristic of a top player as: courage, guts, nerve, tough, fearless, brave and resilient. These are just a few that come to mind. On the 1 to 10 scale, world champions rate a 9.8 or better with both their game and their heart. Anything short of this would certainly do them in under the heat of a major championship.

Heart is partly due to the inherent mental makeup of a player. Some players come by it naturally while others must work to develop heart. And then there are players that never acquire the quality called heart. Your degree of heart is related to your self-confidence and your belief in your ability to summon your best effort when it counts most.

Developing Heart

Heart can be built by improving your game and by a series of successful experiences while under pressure. With enough success under your belt, you'll come to believe in your ability to produce winning shots under fire.

Once you've come through in the clutch a few times, you'll really begin to understand the special feeling that comes when you've shown heart. You'll take additional pride in your game and you'll feel more like a genuine pool player. This process can feed on itself, and it can allow you to compete successfully at higher and higher levels of competition, assuming that your game is progressing in tandem.

Your heart content will be tested continuously in every match. For many players the first moment of truth comes when they miss a significant shot, possibly because of carelessness or nerves. At this point, one miss could lead to another. A player with heart, however, will shrug it off as an aberration and be ready to confidently approach their next turn. At moments like this you have a chance to add or subtract from your level of heart. Every time you react positively to a situation, you strengthen your heart for the next opponent.

Developing heart is essential for anyone wishing to advance very far in pool. In addition, it's just plain fun and very rewarding to show heart. When you do, you are able to mount serious comebacks, make pressure shots, beat supposedly better players and to run-out on double-hill. Your self-respect will grow. As a consequence, your opponents will no longer be able to feed off your defeatist demeanor.

An Example of Heart

There are a million examples that I could show of top players who have demonstrated heart, but the following should make the point. W.P.B.A. player Ewa Mataya Lawrence, a former World Champion, was mounting a strong bid to win her first pro title in some time. Her opponent in the finals was Allison Fisher, the dominant player on the women's tour. Needing but one game for victory, Ewa ran out beautifully to a relatively simple shot on the nine-ball—and missed. After Allison failed to pocket a ball on the break, Ewa methodically ran out a difficult layout to notch and emotional comeback win. Ewa had the perfect opportunity to fold or to show what heart is all about, and she showed it in spades.

CAPELLE'S LAWS for POOL

As long as you've got heart, you've got a chance.

A great game will take you only so far. You must also have a big dose of heart to complete the winning formula.

Self-trust is the first secret of success.
— **Ralph Waldo Emerson**

Great is the art of beginning, but greater is the art of ending.
— **Henry Wadsworth Longfellow**

What counts is not necessarily the size of the dog in the fight- it's the size of the fight in the dog.
— **Dwight D. Eisenhower**

> *Success seems to be largely a matter of the hanging on after others have let go.*
>
> **— William Feather**
>
> *Now this is not the end. It is not even the beginning of the end. But it is, perhaps, the end of the beginning.*
>
> **— Winston Churchill**
>
> *It is easier to begin well than to finish well.*
>
> **— Plautus**
>
> *Skill and confidence are an unconquered army.*
>
> **— George Herbert**

One Shot at a Time

Your results are the sum of each and every one of your shots. You cannot repeat shots you've already played anymore than you can sink the tournament winning Nine-Ball before you've even broken the rack. You can only play the shot you're faced with. You'll get your best results, therefore, by learning to focus fully on each shot, one at a time.

Every shot is important. It doesn't matter if it's in the first game or in the double-hill game. Yes, the shots seem a lot more important at the end of a match. But how many times have you replayed a losing match and said to yourself that if you hadn't missed the seven-ball in the fourth game, the match may have turned out differently. The score would have been tied at 2-2. Instead, you lost momentum and wound up trailing 1-3. You don't want to feel double-hill pressure on every shot, but you do need to treat each shot with the proper attention and respect.

A rock solid shooting routine you can repeat endlessly is the ticket to playing every shot to the best of your ability. You will have to think about your routine until it becomes a habit. Each segment of your routine must be followed without fail. Make it a priority to practice your routine until it becomes second nature. The following elements go into making up a complete routine. With enough practice and experience you will move smoothly from one segment to the next.

SHOT CYCLE

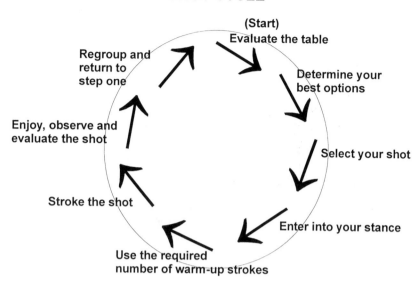

Shooting Routine

Your routine should flow at your most natural pace. Not too fast or slow, but with enough time to complete each element before moving on to the next. Just remember that any omission will very likely result in a poor shot. Take enough time, but not too much time. Also, beware of one of the most ruinous tendencies in pool, which is to change your mind when you are down in your stance. When you are uncertain about a shot, get up from your stance and reconsider your options. Make a firm decision and then pick-up again at step #4.

Playing in the Moment

Playing pool well requires an exquisite balancing of both your mind and body. During your routine you must take time for a bit of problem solving. You must then shift gears quickly into a purely physical mode like a well oiled machine.

Playing one shot at a time is another way of saying that you should live in the moment. Living in the moment is life enhancing advice that sages, gurus and wisemen have been advocating for thousands of years. It's not, despite its recent popularity, some trinket from the pop psychologists of the modern day self-help movement. Living in the moment is a way of life and a big key to your happiness in any endeavor. From a pool player's perspective, happiness is executing a series of successful shots under competitive conditions.

To play one shot at a time you must immerse yourself in to the moment. No thoughts of shots made or missed are welcome. The past is history. Daydreaming for even a moment about trophy presentations and the applause from your teammates or well-wishers also does you no good. The future will be upon you soon enough. All of your energy needs to be focused where it will do you the most good, which is on the shot you are about to play.

CAPELLE'S LAWS for POOL

You get your best results by concentrating 100% on the shot you are playing, so it makes no sense to think about anything but that shot.

You have no control over the past or the future so it's best to remain in the present moment when playing each and every shot.

Life is a succession of moments. To live each one is to succeed.

— **Corita Kent**

The passing moment is all we can be sure of; it is only common sense to extract its utmost value from it.

— **W. Somerset Maugham**

One should always think of what one is about; when one is learning, one should not think of play; and when one is at play, one should not think of one's learning.

— **Lord Chesterfield**

Attention—Yes! That's present! And present you see, makes past and future.

—**H. H. The Dalai Lama**

Dead Stroke

When a pool player falls into dead stroke, playing exceptional pool becomes about as difficult as eating cornflakes. Dead stroke is every pool player's dream come true. If you have experienced dead stroke, then you are fully aware of what I'm talking about. And if you haven't yet visited pool's holy land, then you have a monumental treat in store for you.

What is dead stroke? I'm going to list the first nineteen definitions that came to mind when writing this section. Perhaps one of them will ring a bell or jive with an experience you've encountered that could have been best described as dead stroke.

Dead Stroke Defined

Your unconscious	It's all so effortless
On top of your game	You're playing by feel alone
You can't miss	It's instinctual
You're in the flow	You're firing on all cylinders
You're on a roll	You're in the zone
You're on auto-pilot	The cue is part of you
You are freewheeling	You feel the magic
You're in the groove	Your game clicks
You're totally confident	You've completely let go
The game is easy	

When competing, one of the beauties of dead stroke is that it causes the pressure of playing big time pool to almost completely melt away. Some players become so enamored with dead stroke that they only enjoy the game when they are in dead stroke. Because of this fixation, they spend much of their careers looking for the secret to dead stroke, much like a treasure hunter's pursuit of buried gold. These players feel as if they are but one secret away from a lifetime pass to pool's Mecca. Dead stroke should be welcomed with open arms, but it only arrives intermittently as a result of your ongoing efforts to perfect your game.

When you are in dead stroke, you don't have to worry about stroke mechanics. You execute each shot by feel and instinct. Even your decision making becomes easier. This is a result of the extra mental energy that is freed up for strategic matters that would normally be spent on executing the shot.

What Causes Dead Stroke

We're going to discuss how you can establish a link between your game and dead stroke. Ideally, your goal would be to develop a magic switch that could put you in dead stroke. Realistically, your best shot at achieving dead stroke is to create those conditions that maximize its chances of appearing as often as possible.

Dead stroke can be defined, technically speaking, as the perfect combination of both your physical and mental games. Dead stroke occurs when both halves peak simultaneously. We'll now examine each component individually.

Dead stroke is largely a free-flowing expression of your absolute best stroking action. A consistently fine stroke should, even at its worst, be very functional. The more time you can spend in reasonably good stroke, the better will be your chances of it popping into the dead stroke groove. You're always close to, if not in, dead stroke. The zone near to perfection is where top players' games reside most of the time except for those moments when they truly feel the magic.

Your self-confidence also plays a big part in creating the ideal conditions for dead stroke. If you are a confident player by nature, then you are primed to really enjoy those times when your stroke matches your frame of mind. When this occurs, the two elements merge to create an even greater whole. A well-established shooting routine also works to put you in the proper mental state for dead stroke. A routine that is automatic relieves you of the anxiety that results when your game lacks a certain flow and rhythm.

The Formula: Great Stroke + Total Confidence = Dead Stroke

Dead stroke does not appear on command. To encourage dead stroke you must master the various elements of the game. Now you are set to enjoy those special moments when the stars line-up and all facets of your game unite in perfect harmony and you are transported to the land of dead stroke.

Dead stroke, as you might have guessed, is not an exact science. You can build a solid mental and physical game that will encourage its arrival, as we have just discussed. You could also stumble blindly upon it or spur its appearance by incorporating a tip or suggestion into your game. Anything might serve as the catalyst to the nirvana of pool. I certainly hope that one of the following tips may bring upon the spell, even if only for an hour or two.

How to Get in Dead Stroke Right Away (Maybe)

1. Forget completely about stroke mechanics. Try playing solely on instinct, feel and trust.

2. Take a lesson from your favorite instructor. Eliminating one glaring fault could send you instantly into dead stroke.

3. Practice stroking the cue ball only on the center axis. This will give you dead solid contact.

4. Play on a table on which you really feel comfortable.

5. Practice using an open bridge. This will smooth out your stroke and reveal any glaring deficiencies.

6. Play 10 percent faster. This will cure paralysis of analysis.

7. Practice some relatively simple straight-in shots. This will give you a better feel for your stroke.

8. While seated in your favorite easy chair, visualize yourself playing perfectly. Your subconscious doesn't know the difference between a real and an imagined experience. Your visualization could precede the actual event.

9. Find a stroke key that gives you something positive on which to focus your attention.

10. Check your tip to make sure it's in top condition.

Maximizing Dead Stroke

You will spend the majority of your pool playing days in something less than dead stroke. That should be perfectly acceptable, because you don't have to be in dead stroke all of the time to be an excellent pool player. Your approach to the game, for that matter, should not be centered on your being in dead stroke. Like the pros, you may feel like you are very much on your game, both physically and mentally, most of the time, but it wouldn't be what you could call dead stroke.

When dead stroke appears, you may hardly even notice it at first because you'll be immersed in the zone of complete concentration. Some sure signs that dead stroke has arrived are a slightly quicker pace; your stroke feels smooth and powerful; balls are splitting the pockets; the cue ball obeys your every command; you have no fear and you find yourself breaking most of the time. Your mind may lift from this dreamy fog for a moment to marvel at your feats of cue wizardry. But don't waste too much time congratulating yourself, for your energies are best spent enjoying dead stroke for as long as it lasts.

 CAPELLE'S LAWS for POOL

Although dead stroke seems to just appear out of nowhere, there is much that you can do to encourage its arrival.

Dead stroke comes from not trying after much trying.

> *I can live no longer by thinking.*
> — Shakespeare
>
> *You're not a man, you're a machine.*
> — George Bernard Shaw

> *Somehow, when we no longer feel in control, we become available to deeper aliveness.*
> — **Richard Moss**
>
> *As your faith is strengthened, you will find there is no longer the need to have a sense of control, that things will flow as they will, and that you will flow with them, to your great delight and benefit.*
> — **Emmanuel**
>
> *The highest point of life may be to live in a state of pure flow, a 'now-state' without past or future, in which prediction and control are not factors—a state of continual, instant-by-instant adaptation to the unknown.*
> — **Joseph Chilton Pearce**

Total Concentration

When you are totally focused on your game, then it's just you and the table. You are oblivious to noises and possible distractions from the crowd. People moving in the corner of your eye don't bother you. Three or four games may pass without you're even taking notice of the score. When your concentration is 100 percent, you may even fail to acknowledge the presence of a loved one in the first row despite making eye contact. Time seems to slow to almost a halt when pool is played under the spell of complete concentration.

We've talked about the wonderful but elusive nature of dead stroke. Playing pool with total concentration ranks second only to dead stroke. Fortunately, playing with complete concentration is a much more obtainable goal for the majority of your competitive play. You can concentrate fully while not being in dead stroke, but it almost never works in reverse. Total concentration can bring your competitive game to a whole new level of consistency and performance. When dead stroke appears along with 100% concentration, it will be like icing on the cake.

 You can't just turn on concentration like a switch. If you really try to concentrate, you may actually sabotage your efforts. A far better approach is to develop those attributes that can nearly guarantee your ability to concentrate on a regular basis. The game plan below gives you several suggestions for building your concentration. They all basically revolve around your interest in pool, your love for the game and your desire to compete.

A Short Course in Concentration

⊙ Play pool because you truly love the game and the challenge that it offers you.

⊙ Develop a consistent shooting routine that becomes completely automatic.

⊙ Become totally absorbed in the fine points of pool.

⊙ Become totally familiar with your style of play. Are you a socializer or are you better off staying completely to yourself?

⊙ Enjoy the process of playing each and every shot to the best of your ability.

⊙ Enjoy the feel of contact and become absorbed with watching the roll of the cue ball.

⊙ Get properly psyched up for every match. The event, your opponent and the opportunity to participate in a great match should have you sufficiently motivated. You don't want to play in a sleep walk or with the fire and brimstone of an NFL linebacker. Somewhere in-between is the happy medium.

Pressure can bring out the best or worst in your game. The same goes for your level of concentration. You may develop an acute case of rabbit ears. When this happens, every cough sounds like thunder. Ideally, you will be aware of nothing but the table and your extremely high desire to play pool as well as humanly possible. In other words, you will be concentrating 100% on your game to the exclusion of all else.

Total concentration, focus, the cocoon, the bubble, your own world, the zone, just you and the table—they all can be used to describe a state of mind in which playing pool is without a doubt one of the most pleasurable of activities known to mankind.

CAPELLE'S LAWS for POOL

When it's just you and the table, no matter what's at stake, then you have ascended to a place where you are at one with the game.

> *To do two things at once is to do neither.*
> — **Publilius Syrus**
>
> *Concentration is everything. On the day I'm performing, I don't hear anything anyone says to me.*
> — **Luciano Pavarotti**
>
> *Other people's interruptions of your work are relatively insignificant compared with the countless times you interrupt yourself.*
> — **Brendan Francis**
>
> *Attention to a subject depends upon our interest in it.*
> — **Tyron Edwards**
>
> *If your mind isn't clouded by unnecessary things, this is the best season of your life.*
> — **Wu-Men**

Playing with Confidence

When your confidence is high you expect good things from yourself and your game. Balls split the pockets and you can play shots you wouldn't ordinarily shoot. Your game has positive momentum and there is a purpose for everything that you do. Yes, there is no substitute for playing with confidence. Confidence, however, should not be confused with overconfidence, which can lead to poor decision making. Cockiness to a point that antagonizes others should also not be mistaken for confidence. True confidence is a belief that you hold deep inside yourself that you know how to play, plain and simple.

When you first pick up a cue, you can't be confident in your ability to pocket balls, much less run-out racks. At the beginning what you can be confident about is that you will eventually learn to play the game and reach whatever goals that you have set for your game. At the start you must have confidence in yourself and that you will learn to play the game. If you didn't believe in yourself, there's no way you would bother with taking up the game seriously in the first place.

Developing Confidence

 Building confidence goes hand in hand with developing your skills. Your success at various elements of the game breeds confidence… which leads to more success, which in turn increases your confidence still further. Once you get the cycle going, it can feed off itself. And again, it all starts with belief in yourself, not your pool game. This enables you to beat the paradox below that troubles so many players.

You can't play well without confidence.
You can't have confidence unless you play well.

But how, you ask, can you be confident about making a tough new shot or beating somebody you've never beaten before? You must learn to see yourself doing successfully that wish you hope to accomplish. Visualization can help, because your subconscious doesn't know the difference between a real and an imagined experience. Relax in your favorite easy chair, take some deep breaths, close your eyes and take few moments to allow the thoughts and cares of the day to vacate your mind. Then visualize yourself accomplishing your objective in as rich detail as possible. This exercise will help to sow the seeds for achieving your goal.

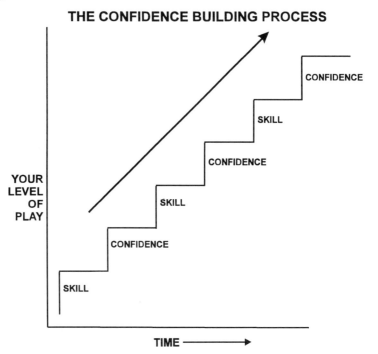

THE CONFIDENCE BUILDING PROCESS

Your successes may seem rather small and insignificant, but each one is nevertheless an important link in the chain of building a solid game. You may have made a long straight in shot only once or twice in ten tries. That success, however, is the foundation from which you can up that percentage to 30 percent, to 50 percent, to 75 percent or even more. Each success, however infrequent or accidental it may seem, can and must serve as the springboard for growth.

Your Level of Confidence

The confidence spectrum ranges from total doubt to total belief. Your mind may rest on any part of the spectrum at any time, primarily as a result of your response to one or more of the confidence factors.

Confidence Factors

- How you are playing
- What game you are playing
- Who you are playing
- The shot you are playing
- The significance of the competition
- The table (conditions)

Your skill at the various elements of the game combines with the confidence factors above to determine your level of confidence at any particular moment.

You could have confidently run-out to win a match in a single game Eight-Ball tournament. A couple of minutes later you can't make a ball because you're up against the pre-tourney favorite. Nothing that much is different except your opponent and your level of confidence.

As your game develops, you will discover more factors that go into making you an experienced and confident player than you would have ever imagined when you first started playing. And you can't downplay the significance of any element that goes into making you the 100 percent confident player that you wish to become. As you develop your skills and experience competitive success, your confidence will grow accordingly.

As long as your goal is to improve, you've got to keep feeding yourself valid reasons why you should be feeling even more confidence. Valid reasons are tangible evidence of advances in your skills and success in competition. They are not gimmicks that may only serve to pump you up over the short-run.

You must stay focused on the process of building your game piece by piece. You must also retain the belief that you are a better player today than ever before, and that you'll be even better tomorrow. To reach higher and higher levels of play, you need to build your confidence along with your skills. As your confidence grows, you should also remain open to a sudden surge in confidence. This jump could result from a significant victory or a major discovery that raises your level of skill.

Changes in Your Confidence Level

Your game will occasionally reach a series of plateaus once you've been playing for awhile and the rapid development phase of the growth cycle is over. It's possible you may start to doubt whether you will get any better. You may even wonder what happened to the belief that you could continue to learn the game, a belief which enabled you to get this far in the first place. You may also be wondering what it takes to raise your game and your confidence to the next level.

 It's hard for your overall level of confidence in your game to stay perfectly flat for any length of time. Most of the time your confidence will be growing or receding, even if ever so slightly. Your best antidote against losing your hard won belief in your game is to keep trying to advance your level of play, even if only by the smallest of increments. Building and maintaining your confidence should be viewed as an ongoing process. The process will enable you to retain positive momentum and to minimize the impact of any apparent leveling off of your game.

Bringing Your Game to the Table

In the process of developing your game you may acquire a new skill at the practice table. Perhaps you can now make a certain shot nineteen times out of twenty in practice. This should give you every right to feel confident about that shot. Now you need to carry that same belief over to the tournament table or to whatever competition will test your ability to make that shot in a pressure situation.

You can be told a thousand times that you should play the shot and the table and not your opponent. Still it's not the easiest thing for most people to put this theory into practice when trying to perform some newly developed shot or skill under pressure.

The fact that you've learned to make a shot in practice is one thing. To make that same shot under pressure is another matter. So don't be too upset if your newly developed skills in practice don't initially carry over to a pressure situation. With enough experience, practice, and belief in yourself, you will come closer and closer to achieving under pressure that which you can do so successfully in practice. And when you do, your confidence will ascend to the next level.

The next time you are in a pressure situation and you are facing a shot that you know you can make 95 percent of the time, but you feel some doubt at this moment, stop and ask yourself why you feel this way. Ask yourself if it really makes any sense to question your ability to make a shot that you are perfectly capable of making. You may even find that you will laugh at yourself for entertaining such a ridiculous thought. Then refocus on the task at hand, give it your best stroke and let the cards fall where they may. Even though you're not 100 percent certain the shot will fall, you've at least given it your 100 percent best effort.

 CAPELLE'S LAWS for POOL

Confidence building is not a straight-line growth process.

Significant victories and major discoveries can fuel a sudden and lasting surge in confidence.

A certain shot under pressure is not the same shot you made in practice even though it is.

You've got to believe that you can do it when you haven't yet until you know you can do it because you have.

There is a direct link between confidence and skill.

It's nearly impossible for your level of confidence to remain perfectly flat for any length of time.

You've got to have the confidence that you will play well until you do play well.

Pool, by its very nature, will continuously test your level of confidence in yourself and your game.

Confidence replaces fear with fun.

Confident thinking produces positive results most of the time, but not always.

Regardless of the situation, your level of confidence ultimately rests entirely in your hands.

You can if you think you can, at least most of the time.

Confidence doesn't guarantee results, it only guarantees the best that your game has to offer.

Even the very most confident and skillful of players will still make mistakes, so don't let errors throw you.

Every thing that you add to your arsenal of skills is one more thing that can enable your confidence to grow.

If you don't believe in your game, who will?

The years of searching in the dark for a truth that one feels but cannot express, the intense desire and the alterations of confidence and misgiving until one breaks through to clarity and understanding, are known only to him who has experienced them himself.

— **Albert Einstein**

As soon as you trust yourself, you will know how to live.

— **Johann Wolfgang von Goethe**

Be not afraid of life. Believe that life is worth living, and your belief will help create the fact.

— **William James**

No pessimist ever discovered the secrets of the stars, or sailed to an uncharted land, or opened a new heaven to the human spirit.

— **Hellen Keller**

Confidence is that feeling by which the mind embarks in great and honorable courses with a sure hope and trust in itself.

— **Cicero**

Self-confidence is the first requisite to great undertakings.

— **Samuel Johnson**

Man is what he believes.

— **Anton Chekhov**

Confidence, like art, never comes from having all the answers; it comes from being open to all the questions.

— **Earl Gary Stevens**

Anger

No one escapes the less than pleasant aspects of a game of pool. Within the course of a match or two, you can expect to suffer blown shots, bad rolls and your opponent's ridiculously lucky good fortune. What can go a long ways in separating you from other players is your response to adversity. Do you calmly analyze each situation, put it in its proper perspective and move on? Or do you blow your stack and then have to struggle to restore your concentration?

Early in the development stage, anger may indicate that you have an intense desire to learn to play very well and that you expect a lot from yourself. There have been many champion athletes who began their sport with a fiery temper. Without a strong desire, it's difficult to succeed in pool or any other endeavor, for that matter. Ultimately you must learn to control your anger when playing because pool is a sport that lends itself best to those with an even disposition.

Anger stems largely from playing below what you feel you are capable of. Careless mistakes cause anger, which then clouds your thinking and creates excess tension. When this happens, both your mental and physical games suffer.

When you mess up a shot, excessive anger can lead to subsequent misses and blown opportunities. Obviously this is not in your best interests if your goal is to maximize your talents and to play winning pool. Simply put, staying mad is a luxury that you can't afford in pool. If you let one bad shot or lousy break upset you to the point where your very next shot is adversely affected, then your anger is out of control, at least from the perspective of a champion pool player.

Anger is largely behavioral. We all react in our own way to the same events. Anger is also, however, a habit or conditioned response to certain situations. Your response can be altered with some work on your part. The next time you play pool, take careful note of those times when you feel like blowing your top. Take a few moments to regain your composure. You needn't totally dismiss your annoyance with yourself because of a silly mistake. Instead of losing your cool, however, try to analyze your mistake as objectively as possible.

Chances are your anger is really only a result of poor concentration or some flaw in your stroke. Whatever the reason, it is most likely something that is totally within your power to correct prior to your next shot. And if not, then you have discovered a weakness that needs to be attended to in an upcoming practice session. The main thing is to let anger alert you to areas that can stand some improvement right now, or in the very immediate future.

As we said a moment ago, everybody has a different length fuse. You may be one of those people who has to blow off steam occasionally regardless of your desire to remain cool, calm and collected. If you must show your displeasure, hopefully you can at least learn to quickly regroup so that you can play the next shot to the best of your ability.

Keep in mind that excess displays of temper are a sign of weakness to some of your opponents. Many of them will take delight in pushing your buttons to the point where you're so angry that you can't play, but not so angry that you'll resort to physical measures.

Your Level of Anger

It may be helpful for you to look back on your experiences to discover if there is a pattern of excessive anger that is harmful to your game. Pay particularly close attention to those times when you really "lost it". Your answers to the following questions should alert you to the possibility that your game is suffering from bouts of anger.

- ☑ Have you ever broken a cue?
- ☑ Have you ever broken a very expensive cue?
- ☑ Do you occasionally throw the rack down hard on the ground?
- ☑ Do you occasionally toss balls around the table?
- ☑ Have you ever snapped at a friend of loved one who had nothing to do with your game?
- ☑ Do you sometimes let one bad shot ruin your game that day?
- ☑ Have you ever quit in the middle of a match because of anger?
- ☑ Do you curse out loud regularly?

If you discovered that you have a tendency to get excessively angry, then perhaps it's time to go a little easier on yourself. Allow yourself the luxury of an isolated mistake here or there. That way you can avoid the much bigger mistake of letting your anger turn one bad shot into a string of misses.

CAPELLE'S LAWS for POOL

Channel your energy into your game, not your temper.

A hot temper does not lead to a hot game of pool.

When your anger causes one additional mistake, it is excessive.

Why play pool if it upsets you so?

Your overriding rule of thumb should be to do what's best for your game at the moment you're playing.

Excessive anger is simply a weakness in your game.

Anger is never without a reason, but seldom with a good one.
— Benjamin Franklin

When anger rises, think of the consequences.
— Confucius

We boil at different degrees.
— Ralph Waldo Emerson

A man is about as big as the things that make him angry.
— Winston Churchill

Anger is really disappointed hope.
— Erica Jong

Those who God wishes to destroy, he first makes mad.
— Euripides

The angry man always thinks he can do more than he can.
— Albertano of Brescia

Anger is a sort madness.
— Horace

Chapter 12
Winning Techniques

"A man who has committed one mistake and doesn't correct it is committing another mistake."

— Confucius

Winning Without Your "A" Game

It's not possible for you to bring your "A" game to every match. Even professional athletes of the highest caliber experience fairly substantial fluctuations in their play from day to day. A golfer may shoot 75 one day and a 65 the next. A basketball player may can 11 of 12 free throws one day and 6 of 11 the next day. Nobody has their "A" game working all of the time. And you know, of course, that the tournament officials are not going to reschedule your matches until you feel the magic has returned.

It is imperative, therefore, that you learn to compete successfully when your "A" game is on vacation. You must, in other words, learn how to grind it out and to win ugly. Winning in this manner may not be pretty, but you can derive a great deal of satisfaction from your competitiveness and "never say die" attitude.

First you must accept that your "A" game is temporarily on hold. Now you can go about your business of playing pool without getting too upset about the mistakes that are bound to take place. As long as you keep grinding it out, a whole host of good things could happen, any or all of which could translate into victory. You could become the beneficiary of several good rolls in close succession. Your opponent could also suffer through a spell of poor play. Unusually tough conditions could also be affecting both you and your opponents games.

While you are out of stroke, you may adopt a more conservative strategy. Continue to go for the run-outs that you can complete on your off days and play some smart safeties when you are in doubt about a particular shot.

You should remain optimistic about the possibility of your "A" game kicking into gear at any time. If you can hang tough until a turnaround in your play, you will give yourself a much better chance of winning.

 CAPELLE'S LAWS for POOL

Playing badly well is a difficult but invaluable art form.

There are many ways to win pool games. You don't have to depend on dead stroke or poor play from your opponent to win.

We conquer by continuing.
— George Matheson

> *To persevere, trusting in what hopes he has, is courage in a man.*
> *The coward despairs.*
>
> **— Euripides**
>
> *I have nothing to offer but blood, toil, tears and sweat.*
>
> **— Winston Churchill**
>
> *I am not the smartest or most talented person in the world, but I*
> *succeeded because I keep going, and going, and going.*
>
> **— Sylvester Stallone**

Using Feedback to Elevate Your Game

Your mind is exposed to a dizzying array of information during the course of a match. When you are concentrating 100% on your game, you will handle this onslaught of data rather easily and effortlessly. Useless or negative information will be automatically filtered out. Valuable information, such as how the table is playing, will be assimilated and kept for future reference.

Ideally, your mind will be functioning on automatic pilot and you won't have to consciously activate your filtering mechanism. However, there will be moments when your concentration is less than 100%. Negative input could hurt your game, such as crowd noise or a roll-off. At times like these you must quickly and objectively analyze the data. Then you must determine its value to your game. Blatantly negative and useless information must be filtered out immediately before it can affect your play.

You must understand your game well enough so that you can cure common errors during a match. Some otherwise negative feedback can be turned into a positive that can help you to quickly solve a problem. For example, you may have a tendency to miss to the right of the pocket when you twist your wrist. A couple of misses to the right could provide you with information that can be used to correct your stroke on the spot.

Positive feedback that comes from playing excellent position will confirm that you are in tune with the table. This could bolster your confidence and allow you to extend your game. You may now tackle tougher position plays than you might normally go for.

This process of adapting and fine tuning your game goes on continuously throughout a match. The information you receive is of the same value to you as the readings on the instrument panel that allow a pilot to stay on course.

CAPELLE'S LAWS for POOL

Every shot you play can provide you with valuable information to help you improve your game.

A man who has committed a mistake and doesn't correct it is committing another mistake.

— Confucius

The great virtue of man lies in his ability to correct his mistakes and to continuously make a new man of himself."

— Wang Yang-Ming

How to Use Your Sitting Time Wisely

I've had the pleasure of watching some of the greatest Straight Pool players in history play in tournament games to 150 points. On many occasions one player would be sentenced to his chair while the other rattled off a run of over 100 balls. At the 1974 U. S. Open in Chicago, Ritchie Florence tore through a run of about 105 balls before missing. Hall of Famer Joe Balsis, apparently unfazed by his long wait, proceeded to run 138 balls to win the game.

Nine-Ball and Eight-Ball are a breeze compared to Straight Pool when it comes to how long you must wait between turns. And yet, many players feel as if the chair is like a penalty box that you're confined to for poor play. It is often viewed as a place to suffer and whine about everything that's going wrong. It's also a place where your anger can grow by the second as you watch your opponent run out a game that could have been yours. These ways of looking at your time between turns obviously don't do you much good.

Smart pool players, on the other hand, know that they will spend a good part of every match in the chair no matter how well they play. They also know that this waiting time can be used to rest, relax and to gain valuable information.

While seated you may be harboring a not so secret wish that your opponent misses as quickly as possible so you can get back to the table. Praying for a miss, however, is not in your best interests. Neither is stressing out over your opponents' good play. And I'm certainly not suggesting that you shark your opponent into a mistake. Instead, I propose that you adopt the following techniques. They will give you the most positive mindset for your next turn at the table.

How to Wait for Your Next Turn

⊙ Watch the roll of the balls and evaluate how the table is playing. Perhaps you will learn something about the table speed or the pockets.

⊙ Analyze the layout. How you would play it compared to your opponent's pattern. This homework will also have you ready to deal with the layout if your opponent misses.

⊙ Learn about the game from your opponent. That's one of the big reasons why you play good players.

⊙ Appreciate the good pool that your opponent is playing. It could serve as a model for your game, and it could help to bring out your best pool.

⊙ Discover their strengths and weaknesses and plot your strategy accordingly.

⊙ Build your confidence by evaluating their play. Tell yourself after a questionable shot or a miss that "I can beat this guy."

⊙ Relax, drink some water and take a few deep breaths.

⊙ Give yourself a pep talk if needed.

CAPELLE'S LAWS for POOL

The time you spend waiting for yout turn should be spent wisely to help you win the game.

He that can have patience can have what he will.
— **Benjamin Franklin**

Everything comes to he who hustles while he waits.
— **Thomas Edison**

Never be afraid to sit awhile and think.
— **Lorraine Hansberry**

Genius is eternal patience.
— **Michelangelo**

Timeouts Can Change the Momentum

A classic example of the power of a time out occurred during the first meeting between Eddie Felson and Minnesota Fats in the movie "The Hustler." After getting whipped soundly for hours, Minnesota Fats retreated to the restroom to revive himself. A few minutes later he emerged all spiffed up and ready to play. From that moment on Fats dominated the match.

Time outs, half-times and breaks between innings of a ballgame all provide athletes with a welcome break from the action. These interruptions in play, however brief, give the athletes a moment to rest, reflect and regroup for the remainder of the contest. A pool match typically has no scheduled breaks other than your time in the chair. This continuous action can be mentally exhausting. In the absence of a formalized series of timeouts, you must create your own.

Have you ever noticed how quickly an NBA coach will call a time out when it appears that the other team is on a run? You can use the same tactic to break your opponent's momentum. Just don't go turning an acceptable tactic into an obvious form of gamesmanship.

 Little things like taking a break at the proper time can help you win pool games. A trip to the restroom to freshen up can do wonders for your game. Washing the chalk off your hands can restore the smooth feel of the shaft in your bridge hand. Leaving the table for five minutes to get a breath of fresh air or for a beverage may be all that it takes to give you a whole new perspective on the match.

 CAPELLE'S LAWS for POOL

Momentum plays a big part in any pool game. A short break at the right time can slow you opponent down and/or revive your game.

The time is always right to do what is right.
— **Martin Luther King, Jr.**

In all things rest is sweet.
— **Pindar**

Time cools, time clarifies; no mood can be maintained quite unaltered through the course of hours.
— **Thomas Mann**

Chapter 13
How to Think Like a Player

"A man is what he thinks about all day long."
—**Ralph Waldo Emerson**

The Mind of a Pool Player

There are three phases of your pool playing experience, each of which is handled in a different manner. When you are learning the game, you need to remain open to new information that can help you improve. You need to evaluate each new input. A firm decision must then be made as to whether or not to incorporate it into your game.

Under friendly or low pressure game conditions you should continue to experiment as you work to sharpen your game. In this second phase, you are learning, practicing and competing in more or less equal parts.

Phase three is not the time to be experimenting with your game. Instead, it is the time to make the most of what you've got. Under the heat of tough competition you should be executing what you already know to the best of your ability.

The learning process that takes place in phases one and two sets the stage for thinking like a pool player when you are in serious competition. During these phases you learn all you can about the game. At the same time, you need to develop filters that can quickly weed out those thoughts that add nothing constructive to your game.

Evaluating Input

There are two broad categories of information: **1)** that which can help you play better, and **2)** everything else. It would certainly be foolish to allow anything from the second category to enter your mind while you're in the heat of battle. And yet it happens to pool players constantly. Developing the proper filters and a thick hide will help ensure that your thinking will be confined to the first category the majority of the time.

Although you want to be thinking positively as much as possible, negative thoughts are bound to appear. Dealing with negative and potentially harmful thoughts quickly and effectively will keep their influence to a minimum. Quickly casting aside negative input will also enable you to concentrate more of your energy on playing great pool.

Let's assume that you are getting ready to play an important tournament match against Joe Player. A few feet away you overhear a spectator remark to a friend that "that guy (you) hasn't got a chance against Joe." How would you handle this potentially devastating remark? Under the worst case scenario you would allow the spectator's comments to take up permanent residence in your mind. You may be motivated to show the spectator wrong. More likely, however, you would begin to doubt your ability to beat Joe, especially if the remark confirmed what you already knew about how well Joe plays. Your chances of winning may have just dropped about 50 percent or more.

A better response is to consider the comment, evaluate it, and then discard it. You don't need useless and potentially destructive information. You might say to yourself that Joe's a good player, but that you have confidence in your game. Joe may have an edge, but the match is still up for grabs. As long as you play your game, you've got a decent shot at winning. This line of thinking is definitely better than caving in because of the spectator's remark. Still, you had to stop and expend some time and energy to process and eliminate this potentially negative input.

When your pool player's mind becomes like hardened steel, you probably would not have even heard the comment in the first place. And if you had, in a flash it would have bounced right off. You would have quickly recognized it as useless information.

The Value of Experience

Experience can be a great teacher. It can help to train your mind to think in the best way possible about your game as often as possible. When you have already experienced a negative input, then you should know how to handle it. This thought process is similar to the way a comedian handles a heckler. They know a zinger for every comment because they've heard them all before. The comedian can deal with the unwanted remark and go right back into their routine without skipping a beat.

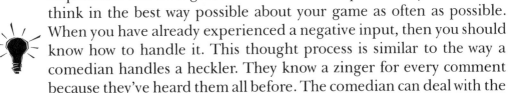

With enough experience you will spot worthless information in a split second. And just as quickly, you will discard it and go on about your business. You may even get to the point where you can quickly categorize and eliminate negative input you have never previously encountered. When your opponent hits you with a new and unusual shark, you may respond with "That's a good one. I've never heard that one before." And just as quickly you will go back to playing your game with your concentration 100 percent intact.

While Shooting

Once you're down in your stance and are getting ready to shoot, a whole host of thoughts may make themselves felt. They run the spectrum from you can't miss, to you're sure you'll miss.

Possible Beliefs While You're in Your Stance

1. I'm in dead stroke and I can't miss. I don't need to worry about whether or not I'll make the shot.

2. I'm grinding just a little, but my stroke feels fine and I'm sure I'll make the ball.

3. I'm not 100 percent certain that I'll make it, but I'm going to give it the very best effort I can.

4. I'm not too sure that I'll make the shot.

5. I feel like I'm going to miss.

You can feel very comfortable firing away when you believe either number one or two. Belief number three is the absolute minimum for playing any shot. Whenever your mind is focused on either four or five, you need to back off the shot and start your routine all over again. It is possible that you won't be able to escape beliefs four or five, even after resuming your routine from the start. If not, then you have some serious work to do on your physical and/or mental game.

Doubts about your game set the stage for a battle within yourself. Now it's you vs. you as your positive and negative thoughts compete for your attention. Part of you certainly wants to play your best. But at the same time, another part doubts your ability to do so. Are you continuing to wage a civil war within your mind? If so, wouldn't it be wise to let the positive side win out so that peace of mind can be restored? When peace offers you the possibility of playing pool better than you ever have before, it kind of makes you wonder why there even has to be a battle in the first place.

 CAPELLE'S LAWS for POOL

As you gain experience, your mind develops to the point where you can quickly filter out unnecessary or unwanted data.

When you're playing pool you're not in the garbage business, so don't let it into your mind.

It all comes back to you, not the negative outside forces, but to your reaction or lack of reaction to them.

> *There is nothing either good or bad, but thinking makes it so.*
> —Shakespeare

A man is what he thinks about all day long.
— **Ralph Waldo Emerson**

It is not enough to have a good mind. The main thing is to use it well.
— **René Descartes**

An open mind is all very well in its way, but it ought not be so open that there is no keeping anything in or out of it.
—**Alfred North Whitehead**

There are two sides to every question.
— **Protagoras**

Putting Opponents in the Proper Perspective

Imagine you are playing in a very special pool tournament. When it's your turn, you exit your private waiting room and enter into a room with a pool table and a referee. That's it. You never meet your opponent and never get to watch him play. Your opponent follows the exact same routine. Back and forth you go until the referee announces a winner.

You would think this is the way tournament pool should be played the way some players complain and moan about their opponents. Those players with poor concentration or a weak mental game who are easily thrown off their game by their opponent's reputation, personality or silky smooth stroke, would probably welcome this approach to competitive pool.

Common sense tells us that pool will never be played this way, not in a million years. Your opponent is part of the game. It's unrealistic to think, however, that you can completely eliminate the possible negative effects of your opponent. You must, however, reduce their influence to the point where you lose only 2–5 percent of your effectiveness under a worst case scenario.

When you let opponents, for whatever the reason, cause you to miss shots, lose games and even matches that you could have just as easily won, then your whole line of thought about the very nature of opponents is in need of a serious overhaul. Take a moment to consider what pool would really be like without someone to do battle against. You should give thanks that there are fellow pool nuts with which you can match your skills. You may even learn to value your opponents highly because they help to bring out the best in your game and because they teach you things you didn't already know about the game.

The Impact of Your Opponent

At its best, pool is a fierce head-to-head competition without tackling, blocked shots, or 120 mile-an-hour serves to return. Even though you do not physically interact with your opponents, you are subjected to their personalities and to what they leave you on the table. People and personalities can enter heavily into the win-loss equation. The degree to which your opponent tips the scales depends largely on your thinking about opponents, or perhaps your ability to not think about them much at all.

Ideally, you can reach a stage very quickly in match where you are concentrating fully on your game. You are using your time in the chair between turns wisely to scope out their game. You have, at this stage, come to terms with the unique pool person that you are playing and you have donned your suit of bulletproof armor. Intimidation is out. Playing your game is in. Getting to this stage can be accomplished rather quickly when you've acquired enough experience and knowledge about the divergent personalities that you'll encounter.

Opponents come in all shapes and sizes. Some are loudmouths while others are sphinxes. You'll play nice guys and jerks, racehorses and turtles. Some are comedians while others play the role of the silent assassin. Each personality brings to the contest their unique blend of characteristics. Sometimes you'll mesh with your opponents and the game will take 100 percent center stage. At other times your personalities may grate like chalk on a blackboard. It just may be poor chemistry. The bottom line remains the same: no matter who you play, you must make it your business to play your game to the best of your ability. No excuses allowed.

One of the most intriguing moments of a big-time boxing match occurs when the two fighters come face-to-face for instructions from the referee. The TV camera zooms in tight for a shot at the look in each boxer's eyes. Before the bout has even begun, the battle for intimidation is raging. Pool players experience a similar but much more subtle battle with their opponents for emotional dominance.

You may begin thinking about your opponent well before the coin toss or lag for break. Several thoughts may run through your mind about past match-ups (if any), your opponent's awesome stroke and reputation or how their game appeared when they were warming up.

You may have a detailed scouting report that instills confidence or maybe a dose of fear.

Your opponent brings both their game and their personality to the table. With enough experience, you can quickly categorize your opponents' personality. Now you will not be overly surprised or upset by their behavior. For example, a little voice may tell you that you're playing a jokester who pretends not to take the game too seriously. That's okay for them, but you're not going to fall for that act. You're there to play your best game. Besides, you may have had some of your best successes against jokesters. Jokesters tend to become unglued when you don't play along with their "pool doesn't really matter" routine.

How to View Your Opponent

Some players like to adopt a certain attitude towards all opponents. They may, for example, develop a healthy dislike for every opponent regardless of how wonderful their adversary may be in real life. Complete indifference towards your opponent falls in the middle of the spectrum. At the other end is a genuine feeling of warmth and compassion for a fellow warrior. It may help you to keep your opponents in the proper perspective by recognizing that they most likely love the game as much as you do and that they also deserve to win on occasion.

The following lists give you some food for thought on opponents. They fall into two categories: The high road and the low road. Which path do you chose and why? Could you gain from a change in attitude towards your opponents?

What is an Opponent?

The High Road

⊙ A fellow traveler on the journey called pool.

⊙ Someone to test your skills against.

⊙ One who can help you to bring out your best game.

⊙ A person who deserves your respect.

⊙ Someone to learn from.

⊙ A unique individual who you can accept as is.

The Low Road

⊙ Somebody to hate while you're playing.

⊙ Someone to walk all over.

⊙ Someone to torment.

⊙ Someone to resent or fear because they play so well.

⊙ Someone to shark and openly root against.

⊙ An adversary who must be beaten by whatever means are at your disposal.

 Your decisions in pool related matters should be based on what can help you to play your best game. This is not the same as advising you to win at all costs by purposefully sharking your opponent into submission. You may not care much for your opponent. Nevertheless, you should consider adopting an attitude that fosters mutual respect for a fellow traveler. After all, their journey in pool is not so different from yours.

 CAPELLE'S LAWS for POOL

Don't be surprised at the quality of your opponent's play.

When your opponent's ways are way out of line, you are foolish to continue playing without putting them to a halt.

You can discover more about a person in an hour of play than in a year of conversation.
— **Plato**

There is no little enemy.
— **Benjamin Franklin**

Dignity does not consist in possessing honors but in deserving
— **Aristotle**

He that wrestles with us strengthens our nerves and sharpens our skill. Our antagonist is our helper.
—**Edmund Burke**

Sports do not build character. They reveal it.
— **Heywood Hale Broun**

The man who is swimming against the stream knows the strength of it.
— **Woodrow Wilson**

Shark Proofing Your Game

We all have quirks in our personality. Pool has a way of magnifying them in the heat of competition. As a result, some of your behavior may be less than perfect, so you can't expect your opponent's actions to be flawless. Both you and your opponent must give each other some latitude to express valid human emotions. An attitude of acceptance and amusement at your opponent's off-beat behavior will bring you the peace of mind necessary to focus on your game.

Pool players come fully equipped with a variety of playing styles and personalities. Some player's mannerisms, by their very nature, could seem like a shark. Their motivations for some of their antics are certainly open to interpretation. What you think is a shark, however, may be a harmless gesture in the eyes of your opponent.

You could monitor your opponent's behavior like a pool room vigilante. If you do, you'll waste mental energy that could be better spent focusing on your game. The last thing you want is for your opponent's somewhat questionable behavior to chip away at your concentration. Instead, simply observe your opponent with a sense of amusement. Understand that their act is most likely an attempt to make up for something that is missing in their game. Quickly and surely filter out their supposed sharks before they have any chance of gaining access to the sanctuary of your mind.

A pool player's conduct can be rated on a spectrum from the most perfectly behaved gentleman clear through to the most blatant and morally corrupt of shark artists. As we run through the spectrum, take a few moments to see where you and some of your opponents fit-in.

The Spectrum of Behavior

⊙ **The perfect gentleman**—You can attempt to exhibit absolutely perfect behavior which may be devoid of all personality, but nobody really expects you to. Perfect behavior is both unrealistic and unnecessary. It also takes some of the humor and fun out of the game.

⊙ **Exhibit your unique personality**—When you do this, you are behaving pretty much as you normally do. This assumes, of course, that you do not purposefully engage in tactics that are designed to throw your opponent off their game. You are operating within the boundaries of good taste and good sportsmanship. You are also being you.

- ◉ **Gamesmanship**—These are relatively harmless tactics (but not totally) that test your opponent's mental strength. One example is to place the chalk at the opposite end of the table. Another would be to compliment your opponent on their unusual but effective stroke. Gamesmanship is a sometimes controversial approach that's going to continue whether you use it or not. You've got to learn to recognize these ploys for what they are and not let them get to you.

- ◉ **Sharking**—There is a fine line where gamesmanship turns into sharking. Sharking is a deliberate and not so subtle attempt to throw you off your game. When your opponent engages in low level sharking, he has crossed over the line from gamesmanship to questionable tactics. A muffled cough as you are about to shoot is just one example. You must decide whether to police his actions or put them out of your mind. If you put up with low level sharking and it disrupts your game, you are almost as much to blame as your opponent when you miss. Another option is to engage in a battle of sharks, but this really turns a great game into something far less.

- ◉ **Blatant sharking**—Jingling change, talking loudly or walking in front of your line as you are about to shoot are all examples of blatant and unacceptable sharking. There has to be a limit to either you or your opponent's behavior and this is it. You must put a stop to blatant sharking quickly and firmly. In tournament play you have every right to enlist the aid of an official or referee. Under extreme cases, offenders will be disqualified. Blatant sharking is really cheating, which you shouldn't let your opponent get away with under any circumstance.

In the final analysis, you must decide where to draw the line on your and your opponent's behavior. Are you going to engage in gamesmanship and sharking? And how much are you willing to let your opponent get away with? Remember back to your childhood when you and/or the other students would test a new teacher to see what they would take? Well, your opponent knows what he's doing when he engages in excessive sharking. He is testing you to see how much you'll take. He expects to be reprimanded for his shady tactics. In fact, he will be surprised if you let him continue to get away with murdering your chances for a fair contest.

 Experience and a healthy dose of common sense, along with a willingness to assert yourself, will be your best allies when it comes to ensuring that your play and not your opponent's underhanded tactics decide who wins the match.

The Best Sharking I've Ever Been Subjected To

I remember beating a pretty good player named Johnny Katella out of several hundred dollars. Unfazed by the loss, he demanded a rematch. The next night he came fully equipped for battle with his shark team. His first move was to position "a little honey" named Dee Dee on a barstool not four feet from the table. Dee Dee was dressed to kill (my chances) in a short tight polka-dot mini dress. Next to Dee Dee he positioned Keith McCready (of "The Color of Money" fame) to do the color commentary. We posted up $600 each and the "fun" began.

Johnny unleashed a barrage of combos and billiards that had me on the ropes at seven down in an eight-ahead set. I fought back to even, and then came the big shark and my big mistake. Johnny had missed, leaving me a cut shot into the side with the cue ball on the end rail. The shot was not a hanger, but rather the type you can easily miss if your mind's not right. Johnny had left his cigarette on the rail. I asked him to move it, which he did, all of one foot further down the rail. I played the role of Mister Cool and went ahead and dogged the shot, lost the momentum and of course, the money.

If I had taken the advice that I gave you a moment ago and had policed his sharking, quite possibly the match would have turned out differently. Sometimes experience can be a painful teacher. On a positive note, I learned from that tough, streetwise player because he came out on the short end in several subsequent meetings.

 CAPELLE'S LAWS for POOL

If your opponent sharks you, that indicates they don't think their game alone is good enough to beat you.

Every player sharks at least a little, whether they know it or not.

Nobody expects you to behave like a saint, but you should be at least within the ball park of good behavior.

Let me listen to me and not to them.
— **Gertrude Stein**

He who passively excepts evil is as much involved in it as he who helps to perpetuate it.
— **Martin Luther King, Jr.**

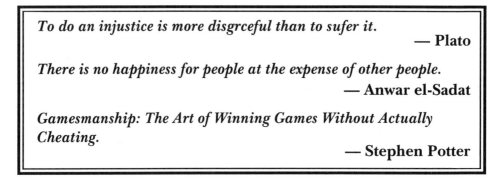

> *To do an injustice is more disgrceful than to sufer it.*
> — **Plato**
>
> *There is no happiness for people at the expense of other people.*
> — **Anwar el-Sadat**
>
> *Gamesmanship: The Art of Winning Games Without Actually Cheating.*
> — **Stephen Potter**

The Value of Experience

Less experienced players are often befuddled at how the beautiful game they play on league nights or against the pool room regulars can disappear under the heat of big time competition. Has your game ever unraveled when you traveled to a new room to play in an important event? Did this nightmare leave you shaking your head in disgust? Well, don't feel too bad. You just got a taste of what it's like to play competitive pool against stiffer competition in unfamiliar surroundings.

Your ability to cope with the additional elements that are a part of a big event will determine if your "A" game accompanies you to the competition. The list below gives you some factors that could negatively impact your game.

- New equipment
- Big name opponents
- Big prize money
- Prestigious title
- Crowds
- Noise
- Nerves

Your game could be affected by a table that's not compatible with your game. Your mental game could also suffer from intimidation at the hands of a big name player or from having a big crowd watch you play for the first time. And, of course, when your mental game suffers, it takes your physical game down with it.

If your goal is to play your best pool against higher and higher levels of competition, you must learn how to deal successfully with the elements on this list. That's why we are taking the time to go over things like how to handle pressure, crowds and unfamiliar equipment.

I can't offer you a magic solution that will enable you to bypass the lessons that come from experience. I can promise you, however, that your attitude towards learning and your desire to compete successfully will accelerate the process. And while you're learning and making some mistakes, please understand that there may be nothing much inherently wrong with your game. It simply takes most players time to bring their top game from their home room to the bright lights of big time competition.

 The more experience and confidence you acquire, the quicker you will be able to fill-in the gaps when conditions are unlike your previous experiences. Ultimately, you could enter that select group of the super quick adapters. Now you're prepared for just about anything. Super tight pockets and boisterous crowds will be handled with ease. At this point, there's not much left that can catch you by surprise.

CAPELLE'S LAWS for POOL

There is so much more to pool than shooting straight, playing shape and blasting a rack into pieces.

Try like hell to keep the snowball from starting it's descent. That's your best defense against your game completely unraveling.

It is not the same to talk of bulls as to be in the bullring.
— **Spanish proverb**

Experience has two things to teach: the first is that we must correct a great deal; the second that we must not correct too much.
— **Eugene Delacroix**

I am not discouraged, because every wrong attempt discarded is another step forward.
— **Thomas Edison**

Fool me once, shame on you, fool me twice, shame on me.
— **Proverb**

The things we know best are the things we haven't been taught.
— **Vauvenargues**

Never Give Up

Pool is a game of intimidation. When you feel that you are a lessor player than your opponent, then your game is primed for a fall. Your opponent's reputation or your losses in any previous encounters may have you feeling nervous and unsure before a match has even begun. Already your confidence is starting to slip. Intimidation can also set in during a match. This can result from your opponent's excellent play and/or you being off your game. Stir into the pot a few bad rolls and you have the ingredients for a disaster.

The capper arrives in that moment when you mentally concede the match to your opponent. Your belief in your ability to win has all but disappeared. Your confidence is shot. You are now just going through the motions. You've given up, even though the match is not over. I was astonished once to hear a friend tell me he hoped his opponent, who was a lessor player, would run out so he wouldn't have to miss again. This collapse occurred in a game of Straight Pool by a player who has run over 100 balls on numerous occasions. Imagine that.

 Pool players have a not too flattering way of describing when a player has mentally given up. When a player mentally caves in, he is said to have "brokendown." This has a much more distasteful ring to it than simply losing. You can lose gracefully and with honor. When you breakdown, you have literally deserted yourself. You have thrown in the towel.

I hope that this negatively charged subject matter has stirred something within you, especially if you've been plagued by a case of the give-ups. Hopefully a fire will now burn within you that says you'll never roll over and play dead again for anyone, no matter what. You may not win when trailing badly, but at least you'll win your opponent's respect for hanging-in-there until the bitter end. You'll win your own self-respect as well.

Breaking Down is a Bad Habit

 There are several good reasons why you should never allow a breakdown, even if you are playing a superior player who is on their game. Giving up can develop into an extremely bad habit. Every time you breakdown it makes it that much easier to concede defeat on subsequent outings. Pretty soon you'll start slumping in your chair at the slightest sign of adversity. Worse yet, you may turn into a chronic whiner.

People are highly intelligent animals with a well-developed sense of the human condition. Your opponent, therefore, need not own a Ph.D. in psychology to be able to sense when you are down and possibly out. Under these circumstances, a skillful player's confidence will grow and they will circle in for the kill. Obviously, you don't want a breakdown to add more fuel to your opponent's game.

Word tends to travel in the pool world about your skill in handling the mental game. Opponents in future matches will love to hear that you can easily be brokendown. Phrases like "He can't handle the heat" or "He'll fold if you fire at him" are used to describe players who give up easily. They're not too complimentary, are they? The grapevine is just another reason not to ever give up because you don't want to spot future opponents any kind of mental edge.

Great Comebacks

Perhaps one of the worst reasons for quitting prematurely is that you negate any chances for a heroic comeback. Just ask pro player, Roger Griffiths. In a big pro event he faced a 1-12 deficit in a race to 13. Roger rattled off eleven straight wins before losing the double hill (12-12) game. Even though he lost, he won over the fans and he no doubt gained a lot of confidence that should help him in future matches. He also sent out a warning to his fellow pros that no lead is safe when playing Roger. Talk about heart!

In the now classic and immortal words of former New York Yankee great, Yogi Berra, "It ain't over till it is over." There is no clock that can prevent a comeback from occurring at anytime in pool. As long as your opponent needs a single game or point, you've got a chance. You may not be the favorite. The rolls could be going completely against you and, to make matters worse, you may be playing like a dog. So what. Until it's over, you've got a chance. A couple of rolls could come your way. You could fall into stroke, and the momentum could shift to your side. You could end up dominating play all the way to the finish line. You can always give yourself the opportunity for a great comeback as long as you steadfastly refuse to breakdown, no matter what.

CAPELLE'S LAWS for POOL

When you breakdown, you've given up before it's over. This makes a comeback all but impossible.

Every match is a battle for intimidation. Each player knows when his role has been clearly established.

> *You can measure a man by the opposition it takes to discourage him.*
> — **Robert C. Savage**
>
> *Adversity causes some men to break; others to break records.*
> — **William A. Ward**
>
> *All men do not know how much strength is in poise, that he goes the farthest who goes far enough.*
> — **James Russell Lowell**
>
> *The fearful unbelief is unbelieve in yourself.*
> — **Thomas Carlyle**

Effective Crowd Management

Pool is an intimate game played in very close surroundings. There's just no escaping the fact that people, noise and a variety of distractions all can enter prominently into the pool playing equation. Once you venture from the home rec room into league and tournament action, you will encounter several pairs of eyes focused in on your game.

Tuesday night league play can easily draw 15–20 spectators. These include the contestants, well-wishers and other locals who choose to watch. You need to become as comfortable as possible with people watching you play for the sake of your enjoyment of competitive pool and for the quality of your game. After all, you may one day (if you haven't already) find yourself in the finals of a big event with a hundred or more spectators watching and evaluating your every move.

Whether you are playing on league night, in the finals of a weekly Eight-Ball tournament or for a few dollars, your game could attract a crowd, however small. Crowds move, talk, cough and generate a wide variety of possible game ruining distractions. A crowd can be friendly or hostile. A crowd will develop a relationship with you if you let them. Crowds can pump you up and motivate you to give your best performance. At their best, a crowd can be like a big gathering of your best friends who have showed up to applaud your great shots and to root you on to victory. At their worst, a crowd may seem like a formidable opponent on top of the one you're already playing.

Management Skills

Only a certain element seems to feed off the energy of an unfriendly crowd. Most "normal" people like to be liked. Effective crowd management skills can, therefore, be a big plus for your game. Any efforts to build rapport should be based on a genuine desire to connect with the crowd. People can spot a phony. If crowd relations is not your thing, you're probably best off remaining totally in the bubble of complete concentration.

Because pool takes so much concentration, you'll need to spend most of your time focusing on the match. Opportunities will arise for meaningful interaction following a spectacular shot or game winning shot or between racks. A skilled crowd manager uses these moments to acknowledge the cheers, make eye contact and to give off friendly and positive body language. All of these actions communicate to the crowd that you fully appreciate their support.

Your Role as a Player

The arena of competitive pool is truly a stage and the players are actors with roles to play. Philippine star Efren Reyes plays the role of the consummate gentleman. He even goes so far as to smile on those rare occasions when he plays a shot poorly. Earl Strickland, a winner of numerous major Nine-Ball titles, seems to relish playing the role of Dr. Jekyl and Mr. Hyde. His outspoken and volatile temperament seems to bring out the best and worst from the crowd.

Perhaps you should take a moment to analyze your style and your relationship with a crowd. Do you play the good guy or the villain? Are you one of those rare birds actually like to have the crowd root openly for your opponent. Do you enjoy adopting an "I'll show them" attitude. These type of players, amazingly enough, sometimes succeed at winning over the crowd by the time they've won the match. Some people take to a "winner" regardless of their behavior.

Dealing with Friends and Foes

A good percentage of your tournament and league matches will be contested in front of the locals. While it's great to have their support, you also need to focus on your game. Crowd management can become a delicate matter. You can run the risk of alienating your buddies when you choose to concentrate your energies on pool and not on social interactions. Good crowd relations can be both a blessing and a concentration draining responsibility. For this reason, some players actually prefer to play away from home where there are far less distractions.

On some occasions the crowd is clearly not on your side. If you are playing away from home and didn't bring a rooting section with you, this is clearly understandable. It is also possible you did something to turn the crowd against you. The negative vibes could be because they don't know what a great person you really are, or because you are the type of person who keeps to yourself. In any event, you must be able to go about playing your game without letting their preferences get you down.

Crowd Noise

As a competitive pool player you must learn to deal with crowd noise. Applause or cheers can erupt at any time. These could come as a result of heroics on a nearby table. Crowd noise may even cost you a shot once in a while, especially if it sharks you in mid-stroke. You can choose to play through crowd noise. If your concentration is really strong, you may not hear a thing. Another solution is to develop a sixth sense that tells you when to shoot and when to wait until the fireworks are over.

Most recreational pool is played in relatively noisy surroundings. Laughter, music and the sounds of twenty tables being played on all at once provides a constant level of noise that can actually block out distractions. Once you arrive at the finals of a big tournament, the noise level can change drastically. The more important the event, the quieter it gets. Under these conditions, the jingle of a few coins may sound like a stereo going at full blast to a player whose concentration is slipping. It takes experience to get used to playing in front of a crowd when the quiet is broken intermittently by a variety of sounds.

Pool crowds come in all sizes and shapes. There are beer drinkers as well as the coat and tie set. Some crowds are very responsive while others appear to be half asleep. Crowds can be extremely knowledgeable on the fine points of pool. They also may not know the difference between a long-rail bank and a slop shot. And, of course, a crowd can be any mixture of the above and more.

Crowds add a certain vibrancy and richness to any pool game. As a player, you can chose to love 'em or hate 'em. You can join with them in their cheers and suffer when they suffer when you are a spectator. But one thing is for sure: you don't ever want the crowds to go away because they are as much a part of pool as the table, cues and balls.

CAPELLE'S LAWS for POOL

The acceptable noise level is inversely proportionate to the importance of the match.

Your hearing gets much better or much worse when you are under extreme pressure.

But the great man is he who in the midst of the crowd keeps with perfect sweetness the independence of solitude.
— **Ralph Waldo Emerson**

To know the art of impressing the imagination of crowds is to know at the same time the art of governing them.
— **Gustave Le Bon**

Man in a crowd is quite a different creature than man acting alone.
— **William Jennings Bryan**

Every crowd has a silver lining.
— **P. T. Barnum**

Chapter 14
All About Winning and Losing

"The credit belongs to the man who is actually in the arena; whose face is marred by dust and sweat and blood; who strives valiantly; who errs and comes short again and again; who knows the great enthusiasms, the great devotions, and spends himself in a worthy cause; who at the best, knows in the end the triumph of high achievement; and who, at the worst, if he fails, at least fails while daring greatly, so that his place shall never be with those cold and timid souls who know neither."
— **Theodore Roosevelt**

Goals and Expectations Should Fit the Competition

Good reasons for playing competitive pool include the opportunity to play your best game under pressure and to experience both winning and losing. Competitive pool is also played for the sheer enjoyment of the sport and for the chance to learn about the game.

The emphasis usually shifts back and forth between winning and learning and is unusually dependent on the quality of the opposition. You can win most of the time against weaker players, but you won't learn very much. On the other hand, learning may take precedence over winning when you are playing a decidedly superior opponent.

Your goals for any competition should be directly related to the strength of the field. Your objectives could also change from match to match. If you draw the top seed, your goals could be to learn and to score a moral victory by playing a solid game and by keeping the score reasonably close. Your objective is to win if you play someone around your speed or below. The table below suggests some reasonable and obtainable goals when factoring in the ability of your opponent. The table assumes that you are playing a long enough match so that luck is not a large factor in the outcome.

Competitive Goals

YOUR OPPONENT IS:	THE ODDS SAY YOU CAN EXPECT TO:	YOUR GOAL IS TO:
Much better	Lose	Learn and a moral victory
Better	Lose, but you could win	Learn and/or Win
Equal	Have a competitive match	Win and Learn
Worse	Win, but you could lose	Win
Much worse	Win	Win

You should enter into every contest with the goals of playing your best pool and of enjoying yourself. You may also harbor a notion about the expected result. You always want to win, but if you are a developing pool player that may not be realistic against certain opponents. Anger that arises from losing to a considerably better player could keep you from learning much about the game.

I can't begin to tell you how many times I've witnessed an extremely raw beginner quit playing a good player on a 50 cent challenge table just because they were losing. Their need for victory completely overshadowed their desire to learn some very valuable lessons from an accomplished player.

 Certain rather uncomfortable and disturbing thoughts can flood your mind in the moments following a loss. Losing can leave a bad taste in the mouth of some people while others get over a defeat very quickly. Those who continue to do a slow burn have a true hatred of losing. This attitude towards losing ironically keeps them from the learning that can help them to win in the future. When you maintain a realistic set of expectations for each encounter, you will encourage growth, reduce anger and frustration and have much more fun.

When your thinking is right, you can emerge as a winner every time no matter what the outcome. When you win, you will feel good because you won and possibly also because you played well. And when you lose, you will eventually feel good as long as you learned something that can help you play better in the future.

 CAPELLE'S LAWS for POOL

The outcome of any match rests mostly on the play of the better player. When they are on, they will usually always win.

When you're not so worried about the outcome of a match, then it has a much better chance of turning out the way you want it to.

Oft expectation fails, and most oft there
*   Where most it promises.*
> **— Shakespeare**

The significance of a man is not in what he attains but rather in what he longs to attain.
> **— Kahlil Gibran**

Blessed is he who expects nothing, for he shall never be disappointed.
> **— Alexander Pope**

When you aim for perfection, you discover it's a moving target.
> **— George Eisner**

Keep high aspirations, moderate expectations and small needs.
> **— H. Stein**

How Winning Can Improve Your Game

Imagine yourself in the finals of an important Nine-Ball tournament. The score's tied at eight in a race to nine (double-hill) and you've just pocketed a couple of balls on the break. Methodically and confidently you work your way through the rack until only the nine-ball stands between you and victory. The crowd starts buzzing and your mind begins to race in anticipation of the big shot. For a moment you stop to think about what winning would mean: first prize money, a trophy, cheers from your supporters and the satisfaction of winning a big event.

The nine-ball is far from a hanger, but it's the kind of shot that you've made thousands of times in practice or under much less pressure. The nine is a shot you know you really can and should make 85–90 percent of the time. You could, however, easily miss it under the heat of battle. Before your nerves overreact to the situation, you remember to take a couple of deep breaths and refocus your mind on the task at hand. You follow your shooting routine flawlessly and fire the nine into the center of the pocket. You've just won your first big tournament.

Now that the match is over, what comes next? After shaking your opponent's hand, it's time to accept the congratulations of your friends, family and others who are enthusiastic about your victory. You've worked hard to accomplish your biggest win yet, so now is the time to enjoy yourself by engaging in activities that give you pleasure at a moment like this.

Maximizing a Victory

Once the excitement has died down, it's time to reflect on what you've accomplished. You've jumped a big hurdle by beating a tough player to win the most important event of your career. Now's the time to gain maximum value from this experience. Start by letting your confidence and your belief in your ability grow to a whole new level. Winning breeds winning, so you should let it. Your increased confidence helps ensure that there will be an encore to your winning performance.

It is okay to tell yourself that you must be a pretty darn good player since you beat Joe Player to win first prize. This conversation is just between you and yourself. Its sole purpose is to pump yourself up for future encounters. Your goal is to build the kind of quiet confidence and self-assurance that's a part of all strong players. It is really not necessary or even appropriate to go around bragging to everyone about how great you are. For some strange reason, Muhammad Ali was the only athlete who could ever get away with proclaiming that "I'm the greatest" without turning people off.

 Your victory came as a result of your doing something better than usual. Take some time to latch onto what you were doing right. In our example, you were able to follow your shooting routine under extreme pressure. Whatever facets of your game that worked at an even higher level must become a permanent part of your game. Perhaps some new safeties or an increased emphasis on speed control will be the keys to a future victory.

Most matches, especially the close ones, have a key turning point or two. These are the critical moments where things turn for or against you. Turning points hinge on things like a good roll or an opponent's missed shot. They can also stem from a clutch shot or a brilliant position play. Turning points often occur because of the mental toughness of the winner. You would be wise to evaluate your matches to discover what shots and tactics were instrumental in your victory.

 Another technique for learning from your victory is to replay run-outs in your mind while relaxing at home. This gives you the chance to review your patterns and position play and to replay some of your particularly strong shots. This exercise can build your confidence as you see yourself playing your best. You may even recall the feel of your stroke and the sound of the balls hitting the back of the pocket.

Even the best played matches are rarely error free, so take time to evaluate your mistakes. Look for areas of your game that could use some improvement. You've just won the biggest event of your career and yet there is still room for improvement. This should excite you about your chances for more victories after you shore-up any deficiencies.

As a practical matter, you should make a few notes about your opponent's game for future encounters. Catalogue their most obvious strengths and weaknesses. If you both play locally or are members of a league or regional tour, this information could really come in handy.

 Pressure situations have a way of galvanizing your stroke. Try practicing soon after an important match, especially if you were in very good stroke. You'll be amazed at your ball pocketing prowess when you're free to fire away at will without worrying about the outcome of a match.

A big win can motivate you to set new goals and to rethink your stature as a player. Tougher competition could be in order. You might consider traveling out of town to play in big tournaments where the competition is particularly fierce.

My final suggestion after a big win is to relax and just let it all sink in. Look back on your journey in pool from the first day that you picked up a cue. Recall your practice sessions, lessons, studies, conversations and competitions that have brought you to where you are today—in the winner's circle. Remember how hard you have worked to achieve success. A victory can do wonders for your career. Take some time in your favorite easy chair or while watching the sunset to reflect on where you've been, how your game has grown, and where you're headed next.

 CAPELLE'S LAWS for POOL

How you feel about losing goes a long way towards determining your chances of winning.

Winning can lead to more of the same if you believe and let it happen.

I came, I saw, I conquered.

— Julius Caesar

A winner must first know what losing's like.

— Malcolm Forbes

The world is won by those who let it go!
But when you try and try,
The world is then beyond the winning.

— Lao-tzu

Winners Learn from Losing

After losing go shake hands with your opponent and congratulate him on his play. After all, he must have done something right to beat a good player like yourself. Once this formality is over, your pool personality kicks in. The recovery time after a loss varies for each individual. Perhaps you are the type who can return to your normal sweet self moments after even the toughest of losses. I once saw a friend ask Johnny Archer for his autograph not one minute after he had just lost a heartbreaker 12-13. Johnny was very friendly, and he signed his name without hesitation. Amazing!

It's possible that you'll need time to shake off the sting of losing. Sometimes it can help to inject some humor into your post-game state of mind. One of the beauties of pool is the absurdly ridiculous ways in which the hands of fortune dole out victories and defeats. Crazy rolls and one-in-a-million shots are all part of the game. Laughter, therefore, can be a valuable alternative to tears. It also helps if you can keep the game in its true perspective. Your self-knowledge can also help in making sure that your post-match blues do not adversely affect those closest to you.

Your reaction to a loss also depends on the nature of the contest. Among the toughest losses to swallow are those where you had it won in your mind, but not on the scoreboard. Blowing a big lead is painful, but completely understandable once you analyze why it happens. Switching from an aggressive style to one in which you are trying to protect your lead can backfire. A shift in momentum and/or the rolls could also let your opponent back in the match.

Sometimes a contest will remain close from start to finish as you trade games with your opponent. On other occasions you may be on the receiving end of a blowout. No matter how or why you lost, once you've recovered from defeat, it's time to think objectively about the match. This will allow you to gain something positive from what is an oftentimes painful experience. The following tips should help the process.

Learning from Losses

⊙ Realize that losing a pool game is not the end of the world. By actually believing this and not just theorizing about the concept, you will make winning easier next time.

⊙ Analyze the match. What were the key shots? How did you let it get away from you? What could you do differently? What area(s) of your game need work?

⊙ Replay your run-outs and your run-out failures. Give yourself credit for your good play. Discover where your run-outs failed and why.

⊙ Appraise the overall quality of your performance as objectively as possible. Also consider your opponent's play and the rolls. It could be that you played well, but it wasn't your turn to win. Your opponent might have played very well and/or have been very lucky.

Hopefully you will discover the gift that comes with each losing effort. The lessons that you learn from a loss could be among the most valuable you will learn because they can help you to win in the future.

Avoiding the Ill Effects of a Loss

You must guard against allowing the ill effects of a loss to linger. A defeat could eat away at your confidence and windup costing you matches in the future. Harboring doubts about your game could trigger a slump or, worse yet, a complete demise of your game. I'm harping on these unpleasant possibilities because you must realize the potential impact of a loss. It is crucial for you to put each loss in its proper perspective, learn what you can and move forward with your game.

After a loss, choose to exercise your powers of choice. Make a commitment that from now on you will view all losses in the most constructive way possible. Learn what you can, forgive yourself for your mistakes, and prepare your mind for a winning effort next time.

 One of the most counterproductive ways that pool players use to deal with losing is to make excuses. They love to tell you how they would have won if they had: gotten a couple of rolls; weren't sharked; weren't stuffed from lunch; weren't this and weren't that; and so on and so on. The list of excuses goes on, limited only by the imagination of the player who has just lost.

By making excuses, a player is trying to say they won, but with an asterisk. Likewise, their opponent really lost once you factor in the excuses. It's almost as if each excuse is worth a game or two on the wire. The trouble is, they are not. The loser lost and the winner won, period.

Excuse making may make you feel better, but it prevents growth. When you make excuses, you'll walk away from a loss thinking that you really won, sort of. What this does is keep you from being fully accountable for your game. It also prevents you from learning the valuable lessons that can make you a winner next time.

  ### CAPELLE'S LAWS for POOL

Lopsided losses or a stinging defeat at the hands of a much weaker player are wake-up calls that your game needs work.

After some losses, it is unfortunately not over when it's over.

Look for the gift in every defeat. It will come as a lesson that will help to prepare you to win next time.

When you've lost, it does not really matter whether you have a perfectly valid excuse unless the excuse somehow makes you feel better.

> *He that is good for making excuses, is seldom good for anything.*
> — **Benjamin Franklin**
>
> *The greatest test of courage on earth is to bear defeat without losing heart.*
> — **Robert G. Ingersoll**
>
> *If I lose, I'll walk away and never feel bad because...I did all I could, there was nothing more to do.*
> — **Joe Frazier**
>
> *Men's best successes come after their disappointments!*
> — **Henry Ward Beecher**
>
> *We have forty million reasons for failure, but not a single excuse.*
> — **Rudyard Kipling**

Putting Your Matches in the Proper Perspective

When you play pool competitively, two of your main goals (most of the time) are to play well and to win. It's least preferable, of course, to play poorly and lose. If you are like most people, you would rather play poorly and win than to play well and lose. The rationale is that you have at least achieved one objective, which is a win. You can always redeem yourself as long as you remain in the hunt. Although it's always nice to play well, you hate to be rewarded for your efforts with a loss.

After every match you will walk away with a feeling that's based on how you played and the outcome. The ideal perspective makes you feel your best about your pool playing experience or that, at worst, can help you learn something that will increase your enjoyment in the future. We will cover the most typical results and some recommended ways of viewing each outcome.

Thoughts About Winning

You won when you:

⊙ **Played well.** You should feel good about your game and about winning. Let your confidence grow and allow success to lead to more success.

⊙ **Played average.** You should feel good about your ability to hang tough and to win without your best game. Feel proud of your mental strength but do what's required to sharpen up your game.

◉ **Played poorly.** You should feel a sense of relief to escape with a win when you know you didn't do much to deserve it. Take advantage of your good fortune by finding a way to rebound to a higher level of play.

Thoughts About Losing

You lose when you:

◉ **Played great.** You should feel very satisfied, even though you lost, because you played your best pool. What more could you do? Take heart and applaud yourself and your opponent for a great match. If you keep playing like this, you'll win your share.

◉ **Played well but your opponent didn't.** This is usually attributable to an avalanche of bad rolls. It hurts the worst because you feel cheated. Realize that there is nothing wrong with your game. You were just unlucky. The pool gods now owe you one.

◉ **Played an average game.** You can live with this if your opponent played a fine game. In any other case, losing like this bugs you because you know you could have done better. Ask yourself what minor change or two (mental or physical) could get your game to a higher level.

◉ **Played poorly.** You should not be too upset at the loss as you are about your poor play. You know in your heart that you really didn't deserve to win anyway. Look for lessons that can turn your game around.

Your perspective on winning and losing can be influenced by the margin of victory or defeat. Getting on a roll and totally dominating your opponent is a great high. As your lead grows and your confidence swells, your game may shift into overdrive. You can do no wrong. In one respect, this is pool at its best because of the quality of your play.

Being on the receiving end of a rout is certainly no fun. On the bright side, your opponent could be treating you to an exhibition of great pool. Oftentimes you can learn more from watching pool when you are involved in a match because you tend to pay complete attention to your opponent's play.

Most of your matches will fall between the extremes we discussed above. In a competitive match, both you and your opponent have a fairly equal chance for winning. The victor usually is the one who gets an extra roll or two or who plays a little better. Winning a competitive match is quite satisfying. When you lose a match like this, you can usually pinpoint two or three mistakes that made the difference. This can be frustrating because you "should have" or "could have" won "if only" this or that had not occurred. You can also draw some encouragement from a competitive loss. A 6-9 loss could easily be reversed next time by eliminating the kind of mistakes that caused you to lose.

CAPELLE'S LAWS for POOL

You should look at wins and losses in a way that helps you improve your game and that provides the maximum of joy or that minimizes the pain.

You can be a winner without winning.

He made too many wrong mistakes.
— **Yogi Berra**

Every man's got to figure to get beat some time.
— **Joe Louis**

Victory is in the quality of competition, not the final score.
— **Mike Marshall**

In a game, just losing is almost as satisfying as just winning... in life the loser's score is always zero.
— **W. H. Auden**

The Magic Formula for Winning Tournaments

You needn't be the best player to win a tournament. As long as you play reasonably close to the best players, you have a chance. Against a particularly rugged field your goal may be to gain valuable experience and to finish in the money. However, you must also prepare mentally for the possibility that the magic formula for winning could propel you to the top.

A host of factors can contribute to winning any tournament. The better you play, the less you will have to rely on many things going your way. If you are in a little over your head, you'll need more components of the formula to fall into place. Some of the factors have to do with the quality of your game. Other elements have to do with luck, good fortune, destiny or to simply having everything work in your favor.

The Magic Formula for Winning

- ⊙ You play very well, possibly your best.

- ⊙ You beat all of the players that you are supposed to beat.

- ⊙ You pull-off an upset or two.

- ⊙ You benefit from a good draw.

- ⊙ Players that you have little chance of beating are upset by players that you can compete with, even though you are the underdog.

- ⊙ You get more than your share of good rolls.

- ⊙ You "steal" a match or two with a subpar effort.

- ⊙ Your opponents suffer through some horrendous rolls.

- ⊙ You take advantage of your good breaks and your opponent's poor play.

- ⊙ The tournament's format encourages upsets. This can come from handicapping and/or short races.

- ⊙ You never give up.

 When you get on a roll and are playing well, many, if not all, of these factors could align themselves in your favor. You can encourage the arrival of the formula by believing in it. Now you are ready for those special moments when the pool gods smile down upon you. In one fell swoop they will make amends for every bad roll that you've been subjected to over the last ten, twenty or more tournaments. With the pool gods and destiny on your side, you will roll into victory lane. Just remember that the best player doesn't always win. That's why they hold the tournament.

 CAPELLE'S LAWS for POOL

There are many ways to win a tournament. You do not always have to be the best player or to be on top of your game to emerge on top.

Everything comes gradually and at its appointed hour.
— **Ovid**

Destiny grants us our wishes, but in its own way, in order to give us something beyond our wishes.
— **Johann Wolfgang von Goethe**

The secret to success in life is for a man to be ready for his opportunity when it comes.
— **Benjamin Disraeli**

The Rolls: The Luck Factor in Pool

Ah, the rolls—pool's jargon for the luck factor which plays such a big part in the game. The rolls give you hope one minute and drive you nuts moments later. The rolls turn sure victories into gut wrenching losses. They hand you games that you have no expectation of winning. The rolls are totally unjust and eminently fair. The rolls are pool's greatest blessing and it's damnedest curse, depending on your current point of view.

There's no denying the importance of the rolls. But then again, luck plays an important part in most sports, so why should pool be any different? If it weren't for luck, the same players would almost always win and lessor players would soon lose hope and quit.

Without the luck factor, pool would be only a little more exciting than a snail race. In addition, the game would lose much of it's humor. Indeed, one of pool's biggest attractions is the rolls. People just love to applaud, curse, rejoice and laugh uncontrollably at the oftentimes absurd things that take place when 2¼" balls roll with reckless abandon on a smooth, hard, flat surface covered with cloth.

The Randomness of the Rolls

It is sometimes difficult to explain the actions and motivations of the pool gods, who are the invisible but all powerful keepers of the rolls. The pool gods will make sure that you get your fair share of the rolls providing you play the game for a sufficiently long period of time. But if you expect justice and equality over the course of, say, a race to nine, forget it. You're in for a big disappointment. Rolls are not divvied out one at a time to you, then your opponent. On the contrary, you may be showered with good fortune one set and be stuck with nothing but bad luck the next.

Recently I was all smiles as I took a 6-4 lead in a race to seven. So guess what happens next? My opponent, who was getting spotted the eight-ball and the breaks (in a game of Nine-Ball), snaps in the eight. Now it's 6-5. He breaks again, makes a ball and has a dead billiard on the nine-ball. Score tied, 6-6. He then sinks the eight on the break to win the set. I'd conservatively placed the odds of this trifecta at about 125-1. S—- happens. I can't begin to tell you in the course of thirty years of pool how often I've fallen prey to a scenario like this. And I'm sure that you've got your horror stories. But I still love the rolls, both good and bad, for they help make the game what it is.

After you've played pool long enough, you learn that it's useless to fight the rolls. They'll come when they come, both the good ones and the bad. The rolls cannot be controlled. Once you accept this, your mind is free to concentrate on that which is within your control—your game. You will no longer spend any of your valuable mental energy fussing and fuming in self pity over the bad breaks and the great injustices of the game. You will be able to concentrate on your game, secure in the knowledge that the best player usually wins, but not always.

Testing Your Mental Strength

While you proceed through your matches, the bad rolls will appear at random. This will test your mental strength. You can choose to make of them exactly what you wish. You can allow bad rolls to eat away at your frame of mind. A far wiser choice, however, is to develop a carefully crafted point of view towards bad luck. A calm and detached view of the rolls will help you to maximize your chances of victory. The latter approach takes some discipline, but your game will be well rewarded. Below is the whiner's and winner's guide to the rolls. The attitudes and thoughts that you choose to follow will largely determine your success as a pool player.

Guide to the Rolls

For Winners

- Over the long run I'll get my share of good rolls.

- I can only control my game, so why waste valuable energy worrying about something that is out of my control.

- I can make up for a few rolls going against me by keeping my mistakes to a minimum.

- I've got to stay patient and remain prepared to capitalize on any good rolls that come my way.

- The game is not meant to be fair. Sometimes I'll lose because of the rolls, and not from poor play. So be it.

- During a match one player will get more than 50% of the rolls almost every time. I accept this as fact. This frees me to concentrate on my game.

- I can't really second guess the rolls. Pool is a game of what was, not what if.

For Whinners

⊙ I think I've been permanently cursed with bad luck.

⊙ Every time I miss, I sell out.

⊙ I can't understand how my opponents can be so lucky.

⊙ This game is so unfair.

⊙ The rolls are going against me again. I've got no chance.

⊙ I could have won the match if I'd gotten the rolls.

⊙ I never get a shot when my opponent misses.

⊙ The eternal favorite: "I can't get a roll."

The Rolls Versus Reality

The rolls have a way of distorting reality. Even seasoned pros who should know better, buy into the notion that the rolls largely determine the outcome of their tournaments. The facts say otherwise. The winner in a field of 100 top players is almost always one of the top ten players in the world. Despite the role that luck plays in any pool game, the cream still rises to the top when the pros play. The reason is that great players exert such control over the table that they minimize the luck factor.

 If you are like most players, then you have a tendency to take good rolls for granted. When you win, it's because you played well, period! And when you lose, it's often a result of getting too many bad rolls. When you add up these two misperceptions, it appears, on balance, as if you are getting more than your share of bad rolls. The rolls are evenly distributed over the long run even though it doesn't seem that way.

Pool is so much fun when you are getting the rolls that allow you to run rack after rack. While you're in this delightful state, you really do believe that those runs come strictly as a result of your brilliant play. And you can hardly stand it when your opponent catches a break or two. This rather lopsided view comes from your bias towards your own cause.

You may magnify the importance that luck plays in the outcome of your matches. There is a tendency to focus on the lucky shot your opponent made to win a key game rather than on your mistake that gave him the opportunity to get lucky in the first place.

 A destructive delusion can creep up after you receive a few bad rolls. You start believing that all you're going to get are more bad rolls. This erroneous kind of thinking can develop into a self-fulfilling prophecy. This in turn can cause you to lose your cool and your concentration.

You may see yourself as an extremely lucky player. This can help your attitude and your game as long as you don't windup depending on your good rolls to win. Your reputation as a lucky player can cause your opponents to exaggerate your good rolls even more than they normally would. Your good breaks will start to really upset them. They will feel sure that you've been blessed at their expense by the pool gods of good fortune.

Some players become so focused on the rolls that they extend their definition way beyond the accepted limits. Bad rolls come to define mistakes like scratching and missed position that result from poor play, not bad luck. By enlarging the definition of a bad roll, you have replaced responsibility for your game with a litany of excuses. Crying the blues about your bad rolls could ease the pain of bad play. Complaining also causes you to miss out on the real reasons why you lost. The next time you hook yourself, consider what you need to do to improve your cue ball control rather than angrily cursing your bad luck.

Taking a Chance

On occasion you will need to throw caution to the wind and take a chance on a shot that's part luck, part skill. One example is playing 3-rail shape to a small position zone when there is a 30–40% chance you could get hooked or scratch. The shot must be played because there is no viable alternative. The result is either a great shot combined with a good roll or a decent shot that fails partly because of bad luck. This is the kind of shot that can make you or break you. It's also the type of shot that adds real spice to the game.

Minimizing the Impact of the Rolls

A statistical study on the various probabilities of the rolls would reveal their impact on the game. For instance, it would be valuable to know how often you can expect to get one, two, three or more good or bad rolls more than your opponent in a race to seven. I'm fairly certain that the odds of your getting completely out-rolled to the point where you have no chance to win with even your best game are quite slim. In other words, in most matches you can counteract your opponent's slight rolls advantage with superior play.

When the rolls are going against you, you simply must limit your mistakes and take full advantage of every opportunity. When either you or your opponent has been blessed with an overabundance of good rolls, it just means that fate has entered in to chose the winner on this occasion. That doesn't mean that you should ever give up when you're on the short end of the rolls. It just means that you are up against a statistical aberration.

"Lucky" Shots

Each pool game has its own unique characteristics. On some shots luck is a big factor while on others the result can be attributed almost entirely to skill. Let's consider some key shots in a game of Nine-Ball. The break shot is the ultimate blend of skill and luck. A player with a powerful and well controlled break is still subject to the fickle hands of fate. Stop and think for a moment of how often that you've witnessed a player smash open a rack, park the cue ball in the middle of the table and get shafted. Typical bad rolls include: not making a ball, having no shot or getting kissed into a scratch. If golf was pool, they'd position hazards near the middle of the fairway. Yes, the luck factor in pool is brutal. Rolls also enter in heavily on nearly every kick shot no matter how skillful the player. Counterbalancing luck is the skill factor that determines the results of nearly all safeties and position plays.

In Eight-Ball, the break is far less subject to the whims of fate. If you make a ball, chances are nearly 100 percent that you'll have a shot at something. The luck factor shows up primarily in the layout of the balls. You could face a road map to the eight while your opponent is stuck with an obstacle course. And naturally these positions could be reversed. Position and safety play in Eight-Ball are primarily a test of skill. Sometimes you will need a bit of luck when you are breaking clusters apart.

 CAPELLE'S LAWS for POOL

The better you play, the less you need to depend on rolls.

The worse you play, the more you need good rolls to win.

Your number of mistakes is the most accurate indicator of the quality of your game.

If you expect bad rolls, that's what you'll get.

A 100 percent total mismatch occurs when the lessor player gets every roll and loses even though his opponent plays his worst match of the year.

Keeping your mistakes to a minimum is under your control. The rolls are not, so why waste energy worrying about them?

Breaks balance out. The sun doesn't shine on the same old dog's rear every day.

— **Darrell Royal**

Diligence is the mother of good fortune.

— **Cervantes**

Laugh, and the world laughs with you;
Weep, and you weep alone.

— **Ella Wheeler Wilcox**

The only sure thing about luck is that it will change.

— **Bret Harte**

Thorough preparation makes its own luck.

— **Joe Poyer**

I am a great believer in luck, and I find the harder I work the more I have of it.

— **Stephen Leacock**

Chapter 15
Playing for the Cash

"When I am getting to reason with a man, I spend one-third of my time thinking about myself and what I am going to say, and two-thirds thinking about him and what he is going to say."
— **Abraham Lincoln**

Wagering Sensibly on Pool

Perfectly respectable people from all walks of life gamble regularly on the lotto, football, basketball, bingo and their weekly golf game, to name just a few examples. Sports heroes, show business people and other household names have admitted a fondness for games of chance. I'm not here to argue the pros and cons of gambling but to suggest that a realistic view of the subject is in order. Quite simply, a very large percentage of our population enjoys placing a harmless wager. Most people who travel to Las Vegas, for example, don't go with the expectation of winning. They look at gambling as part of the entertainment package.

Even though gambling modest amounts has widespread acceptance, wagering on pool is still frowned upon in many circles. This blatant case of hypocrisy has its roots in pool's supposedly shady past. Pool has fought an image problem for a long time because of the big money gambling and hustling of a small segment of the pool playing population. The undesirable aspects of pool were most likely magnified all out of proportion.

The gambling element still exists today, but it is overshadowed by pool's new image as a wholesome activity that's played in very pleasant surroundings. Therefore, it makes no sense to punish the vast majority of participants who enjoy gambling reasonable sums because of the "sins" of the past. It is also unrealistic for the game to be held to lofty standards that completely discount the wishes of the majority of its participants.

What is Gambling?

Let's take a moment to consider Webster's definitions of gambling as they relate to pool.

1. To play games of chance for money, etc.

2. To take a risk for some advantage.

You could argue that playing pool is a game of skill and not chance. Therefore, under the first definition, playing pool for money is not really gambling. The second definition of gambling is very far ranging. Playing pool for money or even bragging rights could be construed as gambling. Under this catchall definition, you could also include your entry into a weekly Eight-Ball tournament or the fees for league play. In short, just about every game of pool represents some form of gambling by its participants.

The most commonplace gambling in the traditional sense (one-on-one money games) are the low stakes games between friends and pool room regulars. These contests are a primary source of fun and recreation for millions of amateur players, all of whom share a deep love for the sport. It is simply preposterous to suggest that these pool aficionados are engaged in evil and destructive deeds.

Most of the participants in friendly matches spend a good part of the time trading each other's money back and forth. These players love the constant haggling over handicaps which, in the long run, ensures that very little money actually exchanges hands. In sum, if you put gambling into the context of a friendly game, league play or tournament competition, it should be viewed as a harmless diversion rather than the ugly beast that some would make it out to be.

Problems from Gambling

The problems that come from gambling at pool are not unlike those that befall addicts who overindulge in any activity of their choosing. Most pool players wouldn't think for a second of betting their rent money on a pool game or anything else, for that matter. There is, however, that small core of gamblers who will bet their very last dollar on a Nine-Ball game or the flip of a coin. These people are not pool players who gamble. Instead, they are gamblers who also happen to play pool. Huge difference. Unfortunately, it is this small, but colorful, segment of the pool playing population that has given the sport its black eye.

Fortunately, the day has finally arrived when all of the positive developments that have upgraded the game's image are now starting to receive the lion's share of media attention, and rightfully so. The hardcore gambling element, to be realistic, will never entirely disappear. Besides, it adds a certain spice to the game. In today's enlightened times, however, hard-core gamblers no longer represent pool in the mainstream as that is an era that has come and gone.

 When gambling at pool, the real question becomes where to draw the line. When does a harmless pastime turn into a destructive vice? When does a respectable wager turn into the kind of gambling that hurts you and those within your world? And when are your activities more closely aligned with a hustler or a sucker than with a sportsman? Common sense should provide you with the answers. If you think there's a chance that you are anywhere close to engaging in harmful activities, then it's time to reappraise your approach to the game. The questions that follow can help you to evaluate your practices.

Is Your Gambling Excessive?

☑ Do you regularly wager large sums that could cost you money that's needed for rent and bills?

☑ Does your gambling upset your family life?

☑ Have you ever borrowed money to keep playing a losing game?

☑ Have you thought about quitting your day job to play pool?

☑ Do you enjoy taking advantage of human weaknesses?

☑ Do you sneak into tournaments that you clearly don't belong in?

☑ Do you enjoy telling stories of how you beat someone out of four times more money than they have ever lost before?

What did the quiz reveal? Do you think you might have a problem when it comes to your gambling or to your pool room ethics? Perhaps an objective opinion from someone who knows you well could be of value in diagnosing any destructive behavior. If you find that gambling at pool is a problem, do what's necessary to curb your abusive tendencies.

Everybody Gambles on Something

There are purists who may argue that because of the potential for excessive gambling, why tempt fate by engaging in it at all? If pool is such a great sport, then why don't people just play for pride? The answer lies partly with the very nature of our capitalistic culture, which emphasizes money. The game is the main thing, but most players also enjoy the added excitement of wagering a few dollars. They enjoy the pleasure of needling their buddies even more than they dislike the discomfort that arises when they must reach into their wallet.

In sum, life is really a big gamble no matter what you do. Taking a new job, moving to a new city, investing your money, choosing a mate, and buying a home are all "gambles" that have much more riding on them than a recreational game of pool for a few dollars. When it comes to pool and gambling, we simply must bow to the wishes of its participants. Any problems that arise usually stem from those who would lose their money at cards, the track, or betting on football. With these people, the problem is not pool, but rather their addiction to gambling.

 CAPELLE'S LAWS for POOL

The bottom line is that life itself is a big gamble. In comparison, wagering a small amount on a pool game is really just a harmless diversion.

CAPELLE'S LAWS for POOL

When you put up your money on the hope of receiving back even more at the end of the competition, then you are gambling on your game.

Losing small sums to significantly better players is one of the best and least expensive ways of learning to play pool.

There's nothing wrong with wagering small sums on a pool game. Never has been and never will be.

Playing for nominal stakes can improve your game by raising your desire for competition.

There will always be those people who take whatever they are doing, pool included, and carry it to an unhealthy extreme.

The sport of pool has nothing to be defensive about when it comes to gambling, anymore than do those who wager at golf, football, and basketball as well as those who vacation in Las Vegas.

My pride fell with my fortunes.
— **Shakespeare**

Whoever plays deep must necessarily lose his money or his character.
— **Lord Chesterfield**

Money is always there but the pockets change. It is not in the same pockets after a change, and that is all there is to say about money.
— **Gertrude Stein**

The gambling known as business looks with austere disfavor upon the business known as gambling.
— **Ambrose Bierce**

Money...brings out the best and worst in people.
— **Herb Goldberg and Robert T. Lewis**

A man has one hundred dollars and you leave him with two dollars, that's subtraction.
— **Mae West**

The Art of Handicapping Pool

Handicaps are used regularly in tournaments, money games and some leagues to even out the competition. Handicapping gives players of all levels of skill an opportunity to taste victory. Handicapping also encourages more people to participate in competitive pool.

Tournament Handicaps

Tournament handicaps are largely left up to the description of the tournament director. Your record in a tournament, your ranking within a region and your reputation as a player are some of the factors that enter into the equation. The director will assign you a rating which determines how you will match up against other contestants.

Rating players is not an exact science. Ratings can often become the subject of debate between the director and a player who questions his logic. Tournament directors make mistakes. A director, after all, must keep tabs on the ability of perhaps 20-40 or more people. It's asking a lot for them to know every player's true level of skill within a tolerance of 3-4 percent. Because of this, these overworked and under-paid servants of the game deserve a break. Besides, some of the players who complain the most are really the same types that will regularly seek an unfair edge in any competition.

If you have a question about your rating, present your case as courteously as possible. Understand, however, that the director is trying to be as fair as possible. He must look out for the interests of the entire field, not just yours. If he completely underrates you because of your whining, then he'll catch hell from the other players.

The real scourge of any tournament are those players who lie about their game or who are experts at concealing their true speed. These hustlers will play just well enough to win. Sometimes they will even settle for second or third place just to avoid suspicion. Any experienced tournament director knows that the surest way to kill off a tournament is to allow a small group of hustlers to take turns winning every week. A director in charge of a "B" or "C" level tournament must make every effort to keep "A"s from sneaking into the field.

Making a Money Game

Securing a fair game is a challenging proposition when you play head-to-head for money. Negotiating a fair game plays a huge part in giving you at least a reasonable chance of winning. You will need to hone your skills at the give and take that goes into making a game. Some players feel that the negotiating process is a bothersome chore. On the other hand, there are certain types who relish playing the role of the pool room lawyer. These players, because of their attitude towards the negotiating process, are much more likely to emerge with the game they are after.

The reason to enter negotiations with another player is to arrive at a satisfying game of pool. So don't give in prematurely to your opponent's demands, especially if you feel the game is tilted in their favor. A bad game will affect your play. You will start out thinking you have little chance of winning. When a game doesn't appeal to you, suspend negotiations. Within a few minutes, your opponent might make an important concession. If they refuse, just remember you don't have to play. Sometimes it's better to walk away than to give into the urge to play a bad game. Also, keep in mind that some players prefer bad action to no action. If you are one of them, you only have yourself to blame when it comes time to pull out your billfold.

The game making process may start with you and your opponent some distance apart. As each component is entered into the equation, you gradually come closer and closer until an agreement is reached. Once the game is made, it is time for action. The following list gives you some of the most important points on which to base your negotiations:

Factors in Negotiating a Pool Game

- Your game.
- Your opponent's game.
- How you've been playing lately.
- How your opponent's been playing lately.
- Your previous encounters (if any). Who won and by how much. Were there any unusual circumstances?
- How you each have fared against common opponents.
- Unusual strengths or weaknesses in either player's game.
- The amount of the wager.
- The format.
- Which table you'll play on.
- How long you'll play.
- Will there be an adjustment clause?

This list may intimidate a newcomer. With enough experience, however, you can learn to zip right through most of these items rather quickly. Most negotiations ultimately will center around one or two key issues.

The whole idea behind the pregame conversation is to arrive at a "fair game," not to become fair game for your opponent. To some players a fair game gives each player an equal shot at winning. A hustler, on the other hand, will only play when the game is 80/20 in his favor (or better).

Some contests are really more like playing lessons. There is an unspoken agreement that Player "A" will get the money and Player "B" will receive an education. This type of "gambling" is really just another form of instruction.

Adjusting the Spot

The weight you are either giving or receiving is not cast in stone. In fact, many negotiations include an adjustment clause. Player "A" could, for example, agree to play Player "B" on the provision that the spot be changed if "A" loses. Player "B" might also insist on an adjustment if he loses the first set.

Weight is adjusted depending on the outcome of play. The final score may or may not be a valid indicator of the fairness of the match-up. Your ability to precisely reconstruct how you won or lost is crucial to your success in the renegotiating of a spot. The primary variables are the rolls and how each person performed.

You could feel justified in keeping the game the same if you won a close set 9-7 largely because you got better rolls than your opponent. If your opponent thumped you 9-2 and the rolls had little to do with the outcome, then you should, in most cases, request a sizable adjustment in the spot. You should always be on the look out for those players who always manage to win by a narrow margin. They could be manipulating the score to avoid giving up too much weight in a subsequent match.

When two players' games are far apart, the weaker player can fall victim to another hustler's trick. The hustler will start out giving up a small spot. Each time the hustler wins (usually be a small margin), he ups the spot slightly. The closeness of the final score and the increased spot keep the victim thinking that he's got a chance. This tactic continues until the hustler proclaims that "I can't give you that much weight." This usually happens when his chances of winning have dropped to about 75-80 percent.

If you sense that your opponent is substantially better than you, then immediately request a huge increase in the spot. If they refuse, cut your losses and quit playing. As a matter of fact, you might be wise to quit if they do offer you the world because they have obviously been concealing a vastly superior game.

When you play with friends or pool room regulars, you can expect to make adjustments constantly. The net result is that you windup passing each other's money back and forth. If you discover you are consistently losing, you should consider your motivations for playing a bad game on a regular basis. Perhaps you enjoy your friends' company and the competition. You may not mind losing small amounts that you can easily afford. It could be that you simply need to work on your negotiating skills.

Nine-Ball Spots

Nine-Ball is pool's most popular money game. Part of the reason is the mind-boggling array of possible handicaps. Most handicapping starts with the designation of an additional ball that the weaker player receives as a spot. He can now win by sinking either the nine or the spot ball. Most players consider the last-two to be the smallest spot. The player getting spotted wins when he pockets the ball before the nine when the nine is the only other object ball on the table. The benefit of the spot is that you need not bother playing shape on the nine-ball or worry about having to sink it.

Next in magnitude is the call eight-ball. The call eight can be pocketed at any time providing that the lowest numbered ball is contacted first and the player calls the pocket. This spot brings into play combos, billiards and the break as potential winning shots on the extra money ball. Calling the money ball eliminates slop shots. It also cuts out five of the six pockets on break shots.

The wild eight, also known as the eight, comes after the call eight. A player receiving this spot wins the game any time he pockets the eight on a legal shot. This opens the doors to all six pockets on both the break shot and slop shots. The call eight and wild eight are sometimes mixed together. For example, a player could receive the call eight on the break and the wild eight during the rest of the rack.

The same rules and definitions which we discussed above apply when designating other numbered balls as money balls. The next biggest spot after the wild eight is the call seven ball. This is turn is followed by the wild seven ball. The seven is a bigger spot because you don't need to run out to the eight ball.

Even though the seven comes first, some players would rather receive the wild eight than the call seven. They prefer the right to slop shots at the cost of having to run one more ball on games which are won by run-outs.

Large Spots

When there is a large gap in the level of play, then a multiple ball spot is in order. One of the most commonly used is the last three. This spot requires that you run-out through the third to last ball on the table. Weaker players may also request the last four, last five or even more.

Another popular multiple ball spot is the seven-ball and eight-ball. This spot is also referred to as the seven-out or the seven and eight. Both balls can be wild or both must be called. A variation of this spot is to make one ball wild while the other must be called. The six-out is a huge spot that is typically given when an "A" player plays a "C" player. Sometimes a stronger play will even go so far as to give up alternate money balls such as the five and the seven.

The break can play a big part in Nine-Ball. This is especially true when two excellent players match up, or when wild balls are in play. The break is often a huge negotiating chip. If a "C" player makes a game with an "A" player, he will routinely ask for the breaks. His goal is to eliminate his opponent's break and runs so that he has a chance to shoot in every game. The combination of the breaks and a couple of wild balls is a substantial spot.

Games on the Wire

Another commonly used handicap is called giving up games on the wire. One player is given a head start in a race to X number of games. Let's say you are playing a race to nine and you are giving up two games. Your opponent would mark two games on his side and effectively start the set with a 2-0 lead. Selecting a spot to give or receive is largely a matter of personal preference. For example, you might prefer to get two games on the wire and forego any additional money balls. Meanwhile, another player would rather go to the same number of games but get the wild seven, for example.

I'm sure you can tell, at this point, that the possible combination of money balls is truly astounding. When you mix in the break and spot games into the equation, the possibilities then become as limitless as your imagination.

The discussion above is merely an introduction to the wild and wacky world of handicapping Nine-Ball. In sum, your ability to arrive at an equitable game depends on your experience, negotiating skills, creativity and desire for action, all sprinkled with a liberal dosage of common sense.

 CAPELLE'S LAWS for POOL

When all is said and done, the person giving the spot wins more often than not.

Constantly adjusting the spot is a means of making sure there is no big winner or loser. This is done among friends who gamble all of the time.

If you are a terrible negotiator, then stick to tournaments or leagues.

Approximately 50 percent of all pool games are over before the balls have been broken.

It is truly amazing how the game that your opponent plays and the one that he talked about in pre-match conversation barely resemble each other.

Pool players are prone to extreme cases of false modesty during negotiations. After the game they metamorphose into boastful egomaniacs.

When I am getting to reason with a man, I spend one-third of my time thinking about myself and what I am going to say, and two-thirds thinking about him and what he is going to say.

— **Abraham Lincoln**

Liars when they speak the truth are not believed.

— **Aristotle**

The fox barks not when he would steal the lamb.

— **Shakespeare**

Let us never fear to negotiate. But let us never negotiate out of fear.

— **John F. Kennedy**

An experienced, industrious, ambitious, and often quite picturesque liar.

— **Mark Twain**

All I wanted was compliance with my wishes after reasonable discussion.

— **Winston Churchill**

I think crime pays. The hours are good, you travel a lot.

— **Woody Allen**

Some Perspectives on Giving Weight

A handicap should create a fair game for both participants. In spite of this lofty goal, certain match-ups are difficult, if not impossible, to handicap fairly. For example, it's tough to make a fair game when one player is significantly better than the other. Game making is also a problem when one player is marginally better than the other.

Most players fall into the "C" category, which denotes an average player. Average players don't have the benefit of an established handicap, unlike golf, for use in making a money game. Another problem stems from the minimum spot that one player normally gives to another. The last-two was mentioned in a previous section as the smallest practical spot in Nine-Ball. When two "C" players match-up, one is usually a consistent favorite over the other. If the better player spots his opponent the last-two, now he is the underdog. The reason is that the player giving the spot cannot consistently run-out. He'll end up handing over enough games to create a margin of defeat.

The player receiving the last-two will win many games he would have lost were he also required to run-out through the nine-ball. The spot, however small it appears, turns into a big advantage when two average players match-up. One solution is to keep adjusting the game back and forth from even to the last-two. Another solution is to calculate odds on the money, such as 5 to 4, in favor of the weaker player.

When two excellent ("A") players match-up, the last-two or the call eight does not amount to much of an advantage. Both players will make the nine almost every time if they have run through the eight. Most games between "A" players are decided in the early or middle portion of the rack. Because of an "A" player's run-out power, an "A" can spot an "A-" the seven-ball easier than a "C+" can give a "C" the last-two.

Some of the easiest games to handicap evenly are when an average player matches-up against an above-average player in the "B" category. The two players' games are far enough apart so that they can fine tune the spot precisely. For example, the game could be adjusted between the wild seven or the call seven. At the same time, both players' games are close enough to where each player should get enough chances to play their game. Intimidation and lack of playing time are not big factors. All of this adds up to a reasonably fair game. The outcome depends on how each person plays rather than on the spot. When an excellent ("A") player gives up weight to someone at the "B" level or below, that spot can really become rather meaningless. This fact leads to the following:

A spot can look very tempting on paper. When a match-up between two players of vastly different levels of skill takes place, however, other unseen factors enter into the game-making equation.

Key Factors in Games Between an A vs. B or A vs. C

"A" Players Advantages	"B" or "C" Players Disadvantages
Dominates table time	Lack of playing time
Feels confidence	Feel intimidated
Gets into great stroke	Falls out of stroke in chair
Enjoys playing	Feels frustrated

Notice that none of these key factors has anything to do with skills such as position play, safeties or kick shots. The "A" player's big advantage comes from several items that are rarely given proper weighting or consideration by the "B" or "C" player when the game is being made. A short time after the match has begun you'll hear the player getting the spot complain that "I just can't play my game against this guy. He never let's me shoot!" Remember that the more weight that you need, the more weight you really need to make up for the fact that your game will probably get as cold as ice.

When Two Good Players Match-Up

A single ball spot may not amount to much when two very good players (B+ or better) match-up. Now let's take this concept a couple of steps further. Let's assume an "A" player can give a "B+" the six ball and win. The "A" player is better, but the "B+" is certainly not completely out of his league. To some it's a mystery how a perfectly capable player can lose with this kind of spot. The answer partly lies in balancing the benefits of getting a spot with the disadvantage of losing valuable playing time.

Now suppose that the "A" and "B+" players have played for awhile, and they have split games 50/50. Every time the "A" player wins, he pockets eight balls. When the "B+" player wins, he sinks five balls on average. We're assuming one ball falls on the average break and that the balls each player sinks on losing racks cancel each other out. Simple math reveals that the "A" player is pocketing about 60 percent more balls after the break than the "B+" player. (This advantage could be even larger if the "B+" player is occasionally sinking the six-ball out of rotation.)

After they've played for awhile, it's clear that the "A" player is building a huge time of possession advantage. The big question concerns the advantage the "B+" player has in not having to run-out to the nine vs. the advantage the "A" player receives from getting into great stroke, because of his additional playing time. So what's better: to have an easier win or to get in stroke? The answer lies primarily in the mental make up of the "A" player. Good players love to play. They don't mind "practicing" on the 7, 8 and 9 while their opponent gets out of stroke in the chair. Good players know when giving up weight, that how you play is more important than the spot, as long as the weight is within reason.

Psychological Factors

There are psychological factors that coincide with both giving and getting weight. Players that are accustomed to giving up weight have a work ethic that keeps them from slacking off at any time. They know that the weight forces them to concentrate fully on every shot. They also believe that winning doesn't always come easy, and that part of the fun is in trying to play your best game at all times.

The mindset for the player receiving weight is often quite the opposite. They, at times, have a tendency to ease up because they think that the spot can win the game for them. A game that can't be lost (at least in the mind of the player) is commonly referred to as "the nuts." People who get spotted often falsely believe that they have the nuts. "How can I lose, I've got the nuts!" is a popular refrain.

A player with a large spot may even feel guilty for receiving such big weight. Well, just remember our law that says that big spots usually beget even bigger spots. To sum it all up, whether you are giving or getting weight, you still have got to play the game, shot by shot, to the best of your ability at all times, no matter what.

 CAPELLE'S LAWS for POOL

Getting enough table time to get in stroke is often more important to your chances for winning than getting a big spot.

The more weight you think you need, the more weight you really need.

The nuts is not always the nuts.

> *Nothing is so good as it seems beforehand.*
> — **George Eliot**
>
> *Life is a very sad piece of buffoonery, because we have...the need to fool ourselves continuously by the spontaneous creation of a reality which, from time to time, reveals itself to be vain and illusory.*
> — **Luigi Pirandello**
>
> *People who have no weaknesses are terrible; there is no way of taking advantage of them.*
> — **Anatole France**
>
> *It is natural for man to indulge in the illusions of hope.*
> — **Patrick Henry**

Backing Pool Games for Fun... and Profit?

A stakehorse, or backer, is someone who finances a money game in exchange for a split of the winnings, if any. Stakehorses are a vital part of the aspiring pool players' economy, especially when you consider the almost total lack of corporate support in comparison to other sports. In the absence of a big money tour, players not in the top ten need to supplement their incomes with endorsements, lessons, clinics and, for some, an occasional money game.

Some pros and semi-pros must use stakehorses or give up playing serious pool. Indeed, without stakehorses, the minor leagues for developing talent as well as the sponsorship for many excellent pros would cease to exist. In addition to top level play, there are also backers who stake amateur players mostly as a form of entertainment.

 People become stakehorses for many reasons that, strangely enough, have little to do with money. Stakehorses like action. They enjoy rubbing shoulders with top players, and they relish being an important member of the pool scene. Because stakehorses lack the skills of the players, they substitute for this by living vicariously through the players' games.

Backing pool players provides a stakehorse with a gut wrenching form of entertainment. They experience the highs and lows of winning and losing just like the players do. In fact, they may get an even bigger charge out of the action because it's their money on the line.

Stakehorse Economics

The economics of stakehorsing are definitely not in the backers' favor. The typical split of any winnings is 50/50. The backer absorbs 100 percent of the losses. To break even over the long run, the stakehorse has to win twice as much as they lose. In other words, the stakehorse needs to back games in which he and his player have a 67 percent chance of winning just to break even. There are a few top notch game makers that manage to beat this figure. How do they do it? By consistently making games with people who have less than a 33 percent chance of winning.

Let's assume that all backers are equally skilled at making games. This means that they all win 50 percent of the time. Using a 50/50 split again, the backer over the long run will average a 25 percent loss on every dollar wagered. This is a little worse than keno in Las Vegas. Unless you and/or your player are among the elite at making games, you will, in the long run, lose money as a stakehorse.

As we said previously, people don't necessarily get into the stakehorse business to make a profit. The typical backer is a successful businessman who can easily absorb the few dollars (relatively speaking) that he may lose backing pool players. They love to bet what a pair of courtside tickets to an NBA game might run. In exchange, they can watch great pool. From a distance of 5'-10' from the table, a backer can closely observe every twitch in their player's eyebrow and every wretched twist of their player's wrist.

Stakehorsing is definitely not for everyone. You'll need to have fun money that you can easily afford to lose. A cast iron stomach is a must because those lousy rolls and dogged shots will drive you three times as crazy as when you're playing. Just think about the tirades you have seen thrown by managers and coaches in a variety of professional sports. This is the price you pay for becoming emotionally involved in something that becomes out of your control once the game starts. The pleasure you get from winning must far outweigh the pain that comes from losing. You'll certainly get your answer after your first, and possibly last, heartbreaking defeat while backing a player who "had the nuts."

Recruiting a Player

Now that we've covered some of the pros and cons and you've decided to give it a shot, the next step is to recruit a player. I suggest you start off slow and easy. Don't broadcast your intentions until you've done your homework. Visit the action spots within your area. Watch some games and ask very discreetly about the top players in town. Strike up conversations with your leading candidates. Find out what they like to play, how good they think they are, their ethics and how much they like to play for.

You should verify your research with objective and reliable sources. Try to get at least two "he's honest" replies that are delivered with conviction. If you get even one "does business," that's far worse than TRW saying forget it on a credit check.

Once you've decided to back a player, start small. Let them prove their ability to make a good game and to win before you up the ante. Ideally, this will turn into a long-term relationship, so there's no point in blowing a big wad and killing the deal before it even gets off the ground.

Players Treatment of Their Backer

Now let's assume that you are an aspiring pool player who is in search of a backer. You must be an excellent player who makes good games and who knows how to win. You must also establish a reputation for honesty. That means that you never resort to losing on purpose. This is referred to as "dumping" or "doing business." It is also the single worst crime that any pool player can commit. If you give in to the lure of easy money and dump your backer, it will come back to haunt you a thousand-fold.

Be patient while you work your way up the ladder. Establish a winning record against your level of competition. Backers appreciate a winner who knows his true speed. Backers also appreciate a player who respects their money. To be a pool player, you must also be part salesman. Confidently present your games to a stakehorse, but avoid over-hyping your chances for winning. If you oversell a game and lose, you'll lose credibility and possibly your backer as well. Always view your relationship as a long-term deal that can last as long as you hold up your end of the bargain.

A good stakehorse believes in you and your game. They will offer encouragement when needed, but they will not get on your case when you are playing below average. An excellent stakehorse will also take care of the little things while you are playing so that you can concentrate on your game. Some of their duties may include crowd control, fending off sharkers, handling the money, playing your music and getting you a glass of water.

As a player, you probably know considerably more about the fine points of the game than your stakehorse. Therefore, one of your duties is to educate your backer, especially if they are new to financing pool games. Help your stakehorse so you can both profit. And by all means, don't take advantage of their newness to the sport by risking their money on bad games.

Firing a Player

Pool players are often great talkers. Some could, as the saying goes, sell ice to an Eskimo. This kind of player can be particularly annoying when it comes time to quit a losing game or, worse yet, when its time to fire a player. If you are going to back pool players, you must learn to stand firm when it's time to cut your losses or let your player go. Some of the most common reasons for firing a player include:

- Consistently makes bad games.
- Oversells games and then losses.
- Plays just to be in action when they are short of money.
- Advises you poorly on money management.
- Lacks heart. Gives up too easily.
- Does "business" on you. (The #1 no-no. Instant and perma-nent dis-missal.)

CAPELLE'S LAWS for POOL

If you truly insist on making money as a stakehorse, you must be prepared to bat .750.

Never back a player that you wouldn't allow in your home while you're away.

There are two times in a man's life when he should not speculate: when he can't afford it and when he can.
— **Mark Twain**

It is not the return on my investment I am concerned about; it is the return of my investment.
— **Will Rogers**

Finance is the art of passing currency from hand to hand until it finally disappears.
— **Robert W. Sarnoff**

> *The greatest waste of money is to keep it.*
>
> **— Jackie Gleason**
>
> *The darkest hour in any man's life is when he sits down to plan how to get money without earning it.*
>
> **— Horace Greeley**
>
> *The safest way to double your money is to fold it over and put it in your pocket.*
>
> **— Frank McKinney**
>
> *A fool and his money are soon parted.*
>
> **— Anonymous**

How Tempo Affects Time of Possession

Big spots can affect your time at the table, which can affect your ability to get in stroke. On top of this there is another big factor which also can severly impact your game: the pace of you and your opponent's play. If you play like a jackrabbit, you'll spend much time watching your opponent. This is even more true if your opponent plays at the speed of a tortoise. A steady and methodical pace of play can drive a quick shooting player crazy as they fidget in their chair.

 To play your best pool, you must stay within your normal tempo, whether it is slow, moderately paced or fast. One of the big challenges of pool is to maintain your tempo and your best game while waiting for a few moments to several minutes for your next turn. This, of course, is far easier said than done.

Slow Players

Slow or moderately paced players have the least trouble adjusting to players with a similar pace. Their patience at the table carries over to their time spent in the chair. They also have an advantage over a racehorse as long as they don't fall into the trap, consciously or otherwise, of mimicking their opponent's pace.

A slower player must avoid feelings of intimidation because their opponent only takes half as long to run a rack. Faster play is not better pool. Faster play is simply faster. That's it. A slower player must remind himself that his style is right for him. A slower player should draw comfort from knowing that a methodical approach can help to eliminate the mistakes that fast play often encourages.

Fast Players

Fast players tend to perform best when they are competing against a fellow speed demon. Waiting time is at a minimum. Each player is able to flow with their ideal pace and style of play. Fast players can go nuts watching a plodder at work. They start to think things like "what is he thinking about," "hasn't he ever played before" or "I can't get in stroke against this guy."

If you are a fast player, you need some method for relaxing in your chair while at the same time retaining the particular psyche or flow of adrenaline that makes your game tick. The advantages of a fast pace are that you can get on a roll where you're playing completely on instinct. This can intimidate a slower paced opponent who lacks experience.

An Example of Time of Possession

Let's look at an example of how different tempos can affect the time of possession. This analysis should be especially pertinent to football fans because of the announcer's habit of reinforcing the importance of retaining possession of the ball. In pool it's the cue ball. The longer you can stay at the table, the more chances you have of winning games and of putting your opponent's offense in the deep-freeze.

We'll assume that your opponent plays twice as fast as you, and that the number of shots you each play is directly related to the score. You are currently twelve games into a race to eleven.

Time of Possession

Score	You	Your Opponent
6-6	67%	33%
4-8	50%	50%
8-4	80%	20%

Notice with the score tied 6–6 that you've retained possession of the table 67 percent of the time. This could work to your advantage in the later stages of the match. Your opponent has not been able to get on a roll and may start to be feeling a bit frustrated at the pace of play. At 4–8, your disadvantage in the score is obviously a big handicap. On the bright side, your game may not have turned stone cold simply because your fast shooting opponent has only an equal share of the total table time. As you can see, a fast player has to win nearly every game to achieve an advantage in time of possession.

The big advantage that comes with your lead of 8–4 is further magnified by your 4–1 margin in time of possession. In this case, you have a sizable lead in the score, and your opponent could be turning into a nervous wreck.

 You are now aware of the plusses and pitfalls that come with each style of play. Your awareness of your and your opponent's ideal pace of play should be put in its proper perspective so that you can go about your normal game. If your opponent plays quickly, don't purposefully slow down or this could throw your game off. And don't increase your tempo against a fast player because this could lead to unnecessary mistakes. Fast players should avoid being taken out of your tempo by a slow player. Your challenge is to maintain your ideal tempo even though you'll probably spend the majority of your time seated. Your mentality is kind of like a sprinter as you must always be ready to run at top speed when the gun goes off.

 CAPELLE'S LAWS for POOL

Your tempo affects your time of possession, which can affect your ability to play your best game.

Slow or moderately paced players have an advantage in that their pace of play helps them to play their normal game more often.

I am the owner of the sphere.
— **Ralph Waldo Emerson**

Wisely and slow; they stumble that run fast.
— **Shakespeare**

The style is the man himself.
— **Georges Louis Leclerc de Buffon**

When I rest I rust.
— **German proverb**

Slow and steady wins the race.
— **Aesop**

Haste maketh waste.
— **John Heywood**

Chapter 16
League Pool

"Grief takes care of itself, but to get full value of a joy you must have somebody to divide it with."

—**Mark Twain**

An Introduction to League Pool

Take the rugged individualism of pool and stir it with the highly social nature of pool players and you've got the winning recipe for league pool. When you join a team, you get the camaraderie that comes only from team sports while still enjoying the thrill of head-to-head competition. This explains why league pool has experienced a surge in popularity over the last dozen or so years.

As a member of a team, you can count on an evening of fun and possibly serious competition. Team play gives you a sense of belonging to a group that is united in a common cause. Leagues also offer the chance for players of all levels to experience pressure pool. Newcomers may be getting used to playing in front of spectators for the first time while experienced players can fill the heat that comes from fighting for a league title or from attempting to qualify for a national championship. Pressure also comes from wanting to do well for your teammates. This is similar to the pressure that the pros feel in competing for the Mosconi Cup.

League play also offers a valuable learning experience for each player. During the course of a season you may test your game against perhaps a dozen to thirty or more players. You and your teammates can also be a big help in raising the level of each other's games.

There are a wide variety of formats in use, too numerous to include in this book. You'll find, however, that most leagues fall within the parameters that follow. Teams are usually comprised of four or five regular players and one or two substitutes. Eight-Ball is the mainstay of league pool, but Nine-Ball is gaining in popularity. There are also a handful of Straight Pool leagues.

A season will typically last from ten to thirty weeks. Matches are held weekly and they alternate between your home room or tavern and your opponent's home ground. A match usually lasts between two to three hours. There are men's leagues, women's leagues and coed teams. Many of the leagues offer the chance to compete for national championships, but there are a number of homegrown leagues that also offer participants a very satisfying experience.

 CAPELLE'S LAWS for POOL

When a team is truly together, league pool combines the best of an individual sport with the virtues of team play to create something very special.

> *Who is happiest of men? He who values the merits of others, and in their pleasures takes joy even as though it were his own.*
>
> — **Johann Wolfgang von Goethe**
>
> *All men seek the society of those who think and act somewhat like themselves.*
>
> — **William Cobbett**

Putting Together a Winning Team

Once you decided to play league pool, the next step is to join a team. Many players go about this in a haphazard manner and then have to suffer through a season with a team that's not right for them. I advise that you take some common sense measures to make sure you windup with the right group. Your selection process must be even more exacting as your skill level rises and as your desire for serious competition increases. Obviously you won't have much fun with a group of beer drinkers who use league night as an excuse to get out of the house if you are hellbent on winning a league championship.

If you are a relatively inexperienced player or if you play in leagues to socialize, then you can look to your pool playing friends as potential teammates. As your game improves and winning takes on added importance, then the process of finding the right team becomes increasingly complex. If you are particularly sensitive to playing with only those who share your commitment to the game and you like to organize things, you could be best off founding your own team.

Let's assume for a moment that you've decided to recruit a team of reasonably serious players. What would you look for? What screening criteria could help you ensure that you'll have an enjoyable season? The following items should be useful in your search for the perfect team.

Elements of a Winning Team

Good attitudes: Team chemistry is crucial. Although you can't necessarily love everybody, it's important for teammates to feel positive towards each other and to be tolerant of each person's unique characteristics.

Common goals: At the start of the season, all teammates should agree on what they would like to accomplish.

Player's level of skill: All players should be relatively close so that the low man doesn't feel like he is holding the team back. Handicap leagues go a long ways toward eliminating this concern.

Reliability: One of the biggest headaches for any captain is players who cancel out, especially at the last moment. Team members must make a firm commitment to show up every week and to inform the captain when they can't play as early as possible.

Substitutes: They must meet the team's standards and be available when called upon. A good sub usually lacks the time or desire to play every week but relishes their role as a pinch hitter.

Recruiting a solid unit takes time. If you wait until the last minute, as many captains do, then you may have to take what you can get. I advise that you start the process as early as possible and nail down commitments from those who you can count on to show up when the season begins and that meet your criteria.

When you choose your team wisely, you won't have to suffer through the agony of when and how to can a bad apple. If you windup with a spoilsport, you could choose to suffer until the end of the season and then not invite the person back for next season. Either way it's an unpleasant situation.

It's possible for you or anyone to make an error in judgment when putting together a team. One sure way to reduce the stress that comes from "firing" a teammate is by creating an understanding at the start of the season of what is expected from everybody. Having done so, you then have every right to give a player the boot if they consistently break the team's rules and code of behavior.

 CAPELLE'S LAWS for POOL

The success and fun that a team experiences is directly related to the quality of the captains recruiting efforts.

Man must be disciplined, for he is by nature raw and wild.

—Immanuel Kant

I really believe my greatest service is in the many unwise steps I prevent.

— William Lyon MacKenzie King

> *He knows should rule, and he who does not know should obey.*
>
> — **Italian Proverb**
>
> *In case of dissension, never dare to judge till you've heard the other side.*
>
> — **Euripides**

Choosing the Right League

Picking the right league can be just as important as being with a team that you enjoy playing on. If your team is interested in socializing and you don't care much whether you win or lose, then any league will do fine. On the other hand, if your team is full of serious competitors, then you owe it to yourselves to find a league that's around your level of skill. It's certainly okay if you finish on top at season's end. After all, somebody's got to win. It won't be too satisfying, however, if you win by such a ridiculously wide margin that your only competition is for who's No. 1 on your team. You could also finish in the lower half if you are in over your head. This might not be a complete waste of time, however, if you are intent on learning from playing better players.

Some leagues handicap players as a means of evening out the competition. Assuming that the system is fairly accurate, you can avoid the mismatches, which we discussed above.

Your league season will consist of several matches away from home. It may not matter to you what the other rooms or taverns are like. On the other hand, you may wish to avoid leagues where your away matches are played in a series of dives that you would never otherwise consider frequenting. Likewise, you should not consider a league where every team has more than its share of head cases.

If your team is entering into a league for the first time, you may be unaware of any problems with rooms, taverns or opposing teams. As the season progresses, you will have a chance to assess the league to see if you wish to play in it again next season. You can also get a reading on the appropriateness of the competition. If a league doesn't meet your expectations, hunt for one that you can switch to next season. When you decide to move to a new league, it's also a good time to review your roster and to weed out any spoilsports.

CAPELLE'S LAWS for POOL

You'll get much more satisfaction from playing in a league where you must fight hard to win.

> *Look for your choices, pick the best one, then go with it.*
> — Pat Riley
>
> *When you have to make a choice and don't make it, that is in itself a choice.*
> — William James

Choosing Your Team's Home Room

Since 50 percent of your matches will be played at home, its important for you to select a room or tavern that you enjoy spending time in. Very often this will be your home room since you have already chosen it on the basis of your exacting criteria. Your home base may also be centrally located if your teammates must travel from different parts of town. When you play away from home, you will more than likely wear shirts that bear the name of your home room. Your home base should therefore be a place with which you are proud to be associated.

An owner who takes an active role in sponsoring the team is also a big plus. A number of owners really get behind their teams and treat them like they are a major league franchise. A particularly generous owner/sponsor will buy team shirts, pay for team beverages and often spring for travel and/or entry expenses to big events.

A supportive owner will occasionally attend matches and act as a cheerleader. He will also do the little things that make the team feel welcome. In addition, he will post team records and schedules and may even construct a trophy case to proudly display mementos of the team's success. Season ending barbecues and diners are another method that owners use to show their appreciation and support for their team(s).

CAPELLE'S LAWS for POOL

A big part of your teams success rests not only on how you play but where you play your home matches.

> *To be able to fill leisure intelligently is the last product of civilization.*
> — **Bertrand Russell**
>
> *Like all blessings, leisure is a bad thing unless it is used well.*
> — **James A. Garfield**

Setting the Teams Goals

Having fun should be a primary goal of any team. This goal is easily achieved by those teams who look at league night as a time to get together with friends, shoot some pool, have a beverage or two and have an enjoyable evening regardless of the outcome of the match. This rather simple approach to league night only requires that team members show up on-time with a good attitude. Fun oriented teams are usually the kind that win the seasons award for good sportsmanship.

 Teams that our serious about winning and playing their best should establish some concrete goals at the start of the season. These could include several from the following list:

Team Goals

⊙   Improve on last seasons finish in the standings.

⊙   Contend for first place.

⊙   Win the league title.

⊙   Best an arch rival.

⊙   Qualify for the nationals.

⊙   Help each other improve your game.

⊙   Learn to play is a team.

⊙   Have fun and maintain a positive attitude.

⊙   Play in the nationals at Las Vegas and do extremely well if not win it all.

The team members should all agree on their goals. The captain should write down the team goals, make copies, and distribute them to each player. As the season progresses, your goals could change in light of your progress and your record. You might find first place an obtainable objective at midseason even though you were just looking to improve on last year's fourth place finish at the start of league play.

Even though league pool is a team sport, each individual is still largely responsible for his performance. As a result, it is very useful for each team member to establish personal goals.

Individual Goals

⊙ Learning to play under pressure and with people watching.

⊙ Learning to cope with the increasing tension that comes with contending for league titles and national championships.

⊙ Improving your game. This could include choosing one or more areas that need work.

⊙ Raising your winning percentage by a certain amount over last year's percentage.

⊙ Having the best record in the league.

⊙ Winning or placing highly in a season ending league tournament.

⊙ Qualifying for the nationals and doing well in Las Vegas.

It is easy to keep track of your progress towards your goals as the season progresses since all leagues and team captains keep accurate records of the team and of each player's performance. The results each week are usually posted on a bulletin board in your home room or tavern. In addition, some leagues also send out newsletters filled with the details of who is doing what.

 Although individual goals are a strong motivator for any serious player, all team members should keep in mind that league pool is a team sport, first and foremost. I mention this because I've seen teams where competition among teammates led to sharking and bitterness. This can be especially prevalent when two or more players are competing for perhaps a single spot in a post season tournament or when they are each vying for league MVP. On a highly unified team this shouldn't be a problem. If rivalries erupt, it's the captain's job to strongly remind each player that the team comes first.

 CAPELLE'S LAWS for POOL

Team goals must always take precedence over individual goals. Only when team goals are completely realized should individual goals come to the forefront.

The team should agree upon a set of goals before the season starts and only change them when they've been exceeded or when it's absolutely clear they won't be met.

> *If you don't know where you're going, you'll end up somewhere else.*
> — **Yogi Berra**
>
> *The secret of success is constancy to purpose.*
> — **Benjamin Franklin**
>
> *The most absurd and reckless aspirations have sometimes led to extraordinary success.*
> — **Vauvenargues**

Achieving Team Unity

In the landmark bestseller, "The 7 Habits of Highly Effective People", Stephen Covey advises when undertaking any activity that you "begin with the end in mind". Now visualize how you would like to feel at the end of your next league season. Would you like to say something like "I really enjoyed the season, I played with a great bunch of guys" or "I couldn't wait for the season the end"? The choice is obvious. You can realize the goal of an enjoyable time by working to build team unity.

 Every team is comprised of people with distinct personalities as well as their own reality about how to play pool and how a pool player should conduct himself. A group of opinionated individuals must put aside some of their notions about the game so that the team can come together and develop into a unit. It takes time to learn about each other and to get used to playing as a team. The process can be made a whole lot easier if the team is put together wisely.

Before the season starts it's important for a leader to emerge and to set the tone. This can be accomplished in a practice or team meeting. At this all-important session every player should share their thoughts about the upcoming season. From this meeting of the minds an understanding should be reached regarding team rules, goals and of what's expected from all players.

It takes time for a new group of players to mold into a unit. There is also an adjustment period when a new player joins a team with a few seasons under its belt. While there is no exact timetable, you can figure on at least four to six weeks, possibly longer, before a team really begins to jell. Ideally the break-in phase will be over before the season reaches the halfway point. During the second half of the season you can really make a serious run at your goals (first place or whatever) and hone your game's still further for postseason play, if any. Personality conflicts, petty rivalries or any number of things could keep a group of individuals from becoming a unit. It is important, therefore, for the captain or team leader to monitor the situation and to make sure that all members are living up to their end of the agreement that was struck before the season began.

 Team unity can be fostered by doing the little things that, when added together, can make a big difference. You can start by picking a cool name that reflects your team's personality and goals. Your name will, of course, be fashioned into fancy type or a logo that will be prominently displayed on your team shirt. Since your appearance can affect the other team, it's important to show your togetherness by wearing your team shirt to every match.

A positive sign of each player's commitment is their willingness to show up on time each week. Every player should go out of their way to help make the captain's largely thankless job as easy as possible. Once the matches are underway, each team member should not hesitate in helping each other with things like watching their cue or fetching a glass of water while a teammate is in action.

Physical togetherness is but another technique commonly used by successful teams to build unity and to create positive energy. Before the start of play your team may want to get together in a circle, and repeat a mantra to get pumped up and to reinstill your solidarity. As the season progresses, your team may develop a whole set of rituals that add meaning to the experience. After each player wins a match, you could slap hands, bump fists or give a high-five. Some teams will ring a bell after each victory. Keep in mind that one of the big benefits of league play is that you get to share your successes with others who truly care about you and your game.

 You need to develop a means of maintaining unity when a player loses a game or when the team is behind. You can start by not treating a player as if he had a social disease when he loses a game. Someone on the team should always make an attempt to console a loser. Give the player a pat on the back and offer some words of encouragement that will keep them from brooding about the loss and that will get them mentally prepared for the next game. It's important that poor play and the anger and hostility that can accompany it does not get out of hand and disrupt the morale of the team.

Whatever rituals you and your teammates develop, it's important that you all participate in them. Unfortunately not all players go for much in the way of physical contact. If this is the case with anyone on your team, you may have to face the fact that this could be a hard nosed loner type who is best off playing solo.

 League pool is an individual sport played in a team setting. While you are at the table, it helps if your teammates enthusiastically support your efforts, rather than having them observe your play like a hostile jury. Your team can develop a series of codes or signals that will remind each player that they are not at the table alone. These gestures could be as subtle and simple as the raising of an eyebrow or movement of the hand that could tell a player not to rush their shots. These communications are designed, in part, to help build team spirit. They are not illegal as long as they remain nonverbal and are not blatantly obvious.

 CAPELLE'S LAWS for POOL

When your team plays together as a unit, $1 + 1 + 1 + 1 + 1 = 10$

You'll enjoy league pool even more if you visualize how you'd like to look back on the season when it's over and then work to make that vision a reality.

We must all hang together, or assuredly we shall all hang separately.
— **Benjamin Franklin**

The energy of our differences can produce a precious gift we could never have experienced alone.
— **Thomas Crum**

Superstition is foolish, childish, primitive and irrational—but how much does it cost you to knock on wood?
— **Judith Viorst**

What gives a team richness, texture, and, ultimately, resourcefulness is the uniqueness of its members and an artful linking of their diverse gifts.
— **Allan Cox**

A long pull, and a strong pull, and a pull all together.
— **Charles Dickens**

Every Teammate Has a Role to Play

In most team sports the various members each have a specific position to play such as running back, forward or outfielder. League pool players, at first glance, would seem to all play the same position. When you look a little deeper, however, you will discover that each player may assume a role at the table as well as in a variety of team activities.

The one member whose role is well defined is the captain. The captain is in charge of running the team, attending to a host of details such as bookkeeping, setting the lineup and arranging for sponsors. Captains are people persons who love to take charge of the things that most players dislike doing. The captain is also the logical choice for team leadership, although he may delegate this responsibility to a more charismatic teammate.

On every team there is one player who is regarded as their top gun. This player's main job is to consistently win the majority of their matches week after week. By doing so, the other players feel a little less pressure. They know their top player will hold up the team. In baseball, this player is known as a stopper. Top players are serious competitors who are really into their game. Because of this, they may not necessarily be the best of cheerleaders. And even though they play the best, they may not always be the best teacher on the team.

In a group of approximately 5 to 8 team members there is the core or nucleus that makes up the bulk of the squad. These are the "average" players on the team. Although they also feel some pressure, it is not like that experienced by the top gun or the low man. One week, one or two might be up, while the others are down. Their performance each week is often viewed as the sum of the group.

There's usually one player on every team who occupies the bottom rung. The player with the worst record is under some pressure because he may feel that he is holding the team back. On a team that's truly united the pressure the low man feels is usually self-imposed. After all, most players recognize that somebody's got to fill the role.

The majority of players will have no problem tolerating the play of the low man as long as he maintains a positive attitude and is willing to help the team in other ways. The low man must be willing to sit out a week here or there when the team feels they can benefit from inserting a substitute. This is typically called for when playing a particularly tough team or against an arch rival.

For a team to function as a unit, it is important that there be some maximum differential in skill between the best and worst players. This assumes, of course, that we are not talking about a league with a handicap system. When this differential is exceeded, chances are that the top player belongs on a stronger team or tougher league or that the weakest player belongs on a weaker team or easier league.

 Every team that is serious about improving their record and the games of each player can benefit from the advice of their in-house instructor. This player is recognized as the best at analyzing each player's game and at delivering constructive criticism effectively. The team guru can spot recurring flaws in each player's technique and can offer advice and analysis on shot selection after a match is complete.

In some leagues, players can solicit advice from a teammate on how to play a shot while a game is in progress. This rule can make the services of a guru especially valuable. As mentioned earlier, the guru may not necessarily be the top player. On some especially knowledge-able teams, two or more players may share in the teaching and analysis.

 Every team member should have a very positive and supportive attitude at all times towards his teammates. Nevertheless, there is typically one member who really stands out as a cheerleader. This unflappable optimist can see the silver lining in every defeat. He will unfailingly make a conscious effort to root teammates on to victory and to help pick them up when they are down.

 CAPELLE'S LAWS for POOL

The team leader, usually the captain, sets the tone but every member has an important role to play on a successful team.

A leader is a dealer in hope.
— **Napoleon Bonaparte**

I hold the world but as the world, gratiano;
A stage where every man must play a part,
And mine a sad one.
— **Shakespeare**

You're either part of the solution or part of the problem.
— **Eldridge Cleaver**

> *I've got to follow them — I am their leader.*
> — **Alexandre Ledru-Rollin**

Giving Your Best Effort on League Night

You and your teammates can make your preparations for league night as brief or extensive as you wish. The time you spend getting ready for each opponent will be a reflection of: your desire to win, your available time, the quality of the upcoming opponent, and the need to get familiar with the table, to name just a few.

Any team that's at all serious about winning and building team unity should plan on showing up at least thirty minutes prior to the start of the first match. This will help reduce the captain's stress level. Arriving early gives all team members a chance to play a practice game or two. During this period, team members may wish to share information on how the tables are playing. This is especially important when you're playing away from home.

A detailed knowledge of your opponents games and styles of play can significantly raise your winning percentage in Eight-Ball. With an accurate scouting report, each player knows exactly what to expect and how to adjust their game accordingly. A knowledge of your opponent's games will also raise your level of confidence. You can acquire intelligence on your opponents by watching them practice, by casually asking around, from previous league encounters and from tournaments in your area where you may have seen them play. You will get a read on Who's Who on a team by their position in the lineup and their handicap ratings, if handicaps are being used. If your team plans on staying in the same league for many seasons, you may wish to develop a scouting report for each player on every team. This report can also help your cause if you play a team more than once during a season, which is almost always the case.

Your preparations may extend beyond league night if your team is committed to an all-out effort. A practice session can help everyone to work on weak points which were evident in the previous week's matches. Your team may even consider bringing in an instructor for a team lesson.

The very best teams that are gunning for a national championship will use the regular season as a means of honing their games and for building team unity. With this approach, the regular season loses none of its importance because it is a means to realizing an even bigger goal.

Every week there should be some factor that motivates your team and keeps you from coming in flat. Although it may seem easier to get up for a match when your team is fighting for first place or some other valued objective, there is always a reason to give it your best shot even if it's just pride. Below are a number of reasons for giving a match your very best, any one of which may apply on any given week.

Motivating Factors

⊙ Get the season off to a fast start.

⊙ End a losing streak.

⊙ Atone for last weeks poor play.

⊙ Keep a hot streak going.

⊙ Increase your lead.

⊙ Challenge for the next spot in the standings.

⊙ Avoid or get out of the cellar.

⊙ Beat an arch rival.

⊙ Score an upset against a much stronger team.

⊙ Pad your place in the standings against a much weaker team.

⊙ Finish strong no matter where you stand so you can end the season with a positive note.

⊙ Qualify for a postseason event.

⊙ Move into the top half of the league.

 Prior to the start of play the captain must finalize his starting lineup. During this period team members should discuss any unusual conditions that may affect the captain's decision-making. A player may confide that he's not feeling well or may be a little off his game. Another may advise the captain that he seems to have the number of a member on the opposite team. These and other pearls of information could help shift the balance in your team's favor.

While setting the lineup, the captain may also wish to factor where his players like to be positioned. Some players love to go first while others relish the role of the closer. Each of these positions carries with it a little extra pressure. The last shooter may really feel the heat if his match breaks a tie. Most players seem to prefer the middle matches which are less stressful.

The captain may also decide to create certain match-ups that optimize the team's chances for success given the quality of their opponent. There are five basic expected outcomes from any match-up: heavy favorite, favorite, equal, underdog, heavy underdog. A captain could sacrifice the worst player against the opponent's best player in order to improve the other four match-ups. He may also wish to employ this strategy if the opponent's top player happens to be the leagues best player by far. Another strategy, when your team is quite a bit better than your opponent, is to have your #1 play their #1, your #2 play their #2 and so on down the lineup. This will make your team the favorite in every match. As you may have guessed, the possible combinations and maneuvers are limitless.

Once play begins, that's no time for your team members to scatter across the room, at least not if your team is united in a quest for victory. While one player is shooting, another could be actively rooting him on. This could include employing the codes and signals that remind the player to hang tough, slow down or to call the eight.

The team's guru and perhaps another player or two should be watching the match and analyzing their teammates play. We'll get more into this in a moment. In many leagues you'll play three or four members of the opposing team. Therefore it is a good idea for every team member to scout the games of players they'll be facing later in the evening. Some leagues also require extensive record keeping during a match so there must always be a person available for this duty. Should the player in action need a favor, no teammate should be above helping him out. One person who may be excused is the next player, who may be better off warming up on another table for his upcoming match. A number of rooms or taverns will host two or more team matches on a given evening. A smart team may also wish to dispatch a scout to check out the opposition for a future match.

Your team may do very well without attending to the details mentioned above, but think how much better you'd be if you did all of the things that the very best teams do. All too often, however, I've seen teams disassemble while a match is still in progress as each player runs out the door when they are done shooting. At the end, one player is pitted against his opponent and their cheering section. No team with the true spirit of league pool would ever let this happen.

One of the big benefits from league pool is that you and your teammates can help each other's games improve. While every player is shooting, someone should be observing the game closely and analyzing his play. The following suggestions will help you to make the most out of the learning process.

Tips for Improving

- ⊙ All players should be open to constructive criticism.
- ⊙ Have blank pool table diagrams available so you can go over shot selection after the game is over.
- ⊙ Often there is one player who the team recognizes as their expert.
- ⊙ Correct any flaws in the player's mechanics.
- ⊙ No two players play exactly alike. It helps to know each player's style of play.
- ⊙ Reinforce the things a player did correctly.
- ⊙ Mistakes come from poor execution or picking the wrong shot.
- ⊙ Post game consultations can take many forms: the guru advises the player; two players discuss a third players game; the player actively solicits advice.
- ⊙ Bad play and losses must be taken in stride. Nobody wants to lose or play poorly, but it happens.

 CAPELLE'S LAWS for POOL

No matter where you stand in your league, there is always a reason why you should give it your best effort even if it's just so you can hold your head up and say you tried your best on every turn at the table.

Your success can be ensured by doing all of the little things that winners do and that the also rans never think of doing.

League pool is not just about winning but about helping each other grow as pool players.

All that we do is done with an eye to something else.
— Aristotle

We all our are imbued with the love of praise.
— Cicero

I like people to come back and tell me what I did wrong. That's the kindest thing you can do.
— Lillian Gish

> *Reprove privately, praise publicly.*
>
> — **Arnold Glasow**
>
> *The breakfast of champions is not cereal, it's the opposition.*
>
> — **Nick Seitz**

The Nationals at Las Vegas

Every year approximately 20,000 amateur pool enthusiasts travel to Las Vegas for a series of tournaments hosted by the three major associations. Each event lasts about ten days during which numerous tournaments are held for both teams and singles.

The already huge convention facilities at the Riviera Hotel and Casino were enlarged and can now house over 200 pool tables. When the tournament rooms are filled with activity, there's an incredible buzz in the air. With each victory, you'll hear a chorus of cheers from the winning team and possibly from spectators who have traveled to Las Vegas in support of their hometown heroes.

Trick shot exhibitions and instructional sessions by some of America's leading teachers do much to enhance the proceedings. There are a number of vendors on hand that create a carnival like atmosphere. At the booths players can find cues, T-shirts, instructional materials and a wide variety of pool accessories. Players who need on the spot repairs will find the services of cue repairmen readily available.

Another measure of the pool addiction of the participants are the seemingly unending series of mini-tournaments. These take place daily once the regular competition has ended or on any tables that aren't needed for the main tournaments. All of the tournaments are run very smoothly by experienced teams of professionals. This is no small feat when you consider the logistics of managing thousands of pool players.

The tournaments proper are the culmination of the prior twelve-months series of league seasons. Each association has its own requirements for qualifying to play at Las Vegas for a national championship. At stake is some substantial prize money as well as the prestige of doing well in the big time of amateur pool. Winning teams will return home to victory celebrations and their photo will be featured in the national publication of their association.

With hundreds of teams competing, finishing in the top 32 (or even 100 for that matter) is a major accomplishment. As a result, the sponsors generously award prize money to a substantial portion of the starting field in each event. As you might expect, the possibility of winning a national championship and a big check creates a pressure packed atmosphere. The closer a team moves towards the top, the more the pressure mounts. I've seen players turn into statues as their brains locked up while trying to decide what shot to play next. One league director told me of a time when a player broke down in tears near the conclusion of a match. These reactions are completely understandable when you consider that nearly every player nearing the finals is in a position so totally unlike the first week of league play.

Despite the pressures, I would advise any player to join a league and, if eligible, to make the trip to Las Vegas. The pleasure of the whole experience – the tournament room, thousands of players in their team shirts, the carnival like atmosphere and so much more makes it a completely memorable adventure. Remember that as an amateur player your goal should be to have as much fun as possible despite the seriousness of your quest for fame and fortune.

CAPELLE'S LAWS for POOL

League players in the national tournaments should approach them with the attitude that they have everything to gain, not everything to lose.

League players at Las Vegas have everything to gain, but they often play as if they have everything to lose.

Fame is the perfume of heroic deeds.
— Socrates

We must look for the opportunity in every difficulty instead of being paralyzed at the thought of the difficulty in every opportunity.
— Walter E. Cole

The successful man is one who had the chance and took it.
— Roger Babson

Chapter 17
Playing Pool with Class

"Always do right. This will gratify some people, and astonish the rest."

— **Mark Twain**

Playing Pool with Class

Pool players are really very well behaved, especially when compared to athletes in the major professional sports. Just consider for a moment the organized mayhem of the NFL and NHL, bean-balls thrown at 90 plus mph and the flying elbows and trash talk that characterizes the NBA. Yes, pool players, despite their bad rap, are relatively docile and mild-mannered sorts when compared to the multimillionaire athletes in the glamour sports.

The close quarters of a pool room and the highly social nature of pool leads to a level of conduct that is quite admirable. Because of this, pool need not suffer due to the two percent that will always try to spoil things for the majority no matter what the sport. Indeed, the vast majority of pool is played today with a degree of conduct, etiquette and sportsmanship that would make it the envy of many sports with supposedly superior images.

Pool is held by many to a very high standard of behavior. As a result, the industry is doing its best to compensate for and overcome the past. The nature of a game that requires intense concentration also fosters good behavior. You won't see constant yelling, screaming, and booing from a crowd at a pool tournament. The emergence of women players in a big way has also provided a calming influence for a sport that was once dominated by males.

Your Approach to Pool

Every pool player must decide for themselves the level of class and sportsmanship they bring to the game. The following questions will give you some food for thought.

☑   Do you care about how you behave?

☑   How do you feel when your opponent behaves poorly?

☑   Should there be a double standard regarding your behavior and that of your opponent?

☑   Do you enjoy playing the role of the villain?

I certainly hope that you choose to join the majority who approach pool with dignity and class. Besides being the right thing, the high road enhances the image of the sport. When you exercise good sportsmanship, you will feel better about winning and you'll make your opponent feel better when they win.

Sportsmanship in Action

When you compete at pool, you have three distinct opportunities to show good sportsmanship: at the pre-match greeting; during the match and after the match is completed.

Pre-match greeting—This is the easiest time for anyone to show good conduct because nothing bad has happened yet to test your sportsmanship. At this time, both you and your opponent will get an early read on the type of person you are each up against. You'll quickly find out if your opponent is a nice guy, a serious competitor, or a jerk.

During the match—Once the match begins, good sportsmanship demands that you adhere to the game's etiquette. You should treat your opponent with respect. You don't have to act like he's your best friend, but you should be mindful of the tradition of the game. Some of the rules to follow include:

Pool Etiquette

⊙   No excessive gamesmanship or sharking.

⊙   Give your opponents a decent rack.

⊙   Don't hoard the chalk.

⊙   Stay seated when it's not your turn.

⊙   Be ready to play when it's your turn.

⊙   Pay attention to the game.

⊙   Retrieve the cue ball when you scratch.

⊙   Concede easy shots on the game ball if the rules permit.

⊙   Let your game do the talking.

Playing by the rules and observing the accepted code of behavior gives you and your opponent the chance to get the most out of your encounter. When either of you bucks tradition, you are cheated out of having a positive and memorable experience.

Post match behavior—Once the match is over, both the winner and especially the loser are given the acid test of sportsmanship.

One of the toughest things to do immediately after a loss is to summon your "A" personality long enough to shake your opponents hand and to sincerely congratulate him for a well played match. This kind of sportsmanship can provide you with several rewards. You will feel good for paying a compliment to your adversary. Your reputation as a good sport will increase your stature in the pool world. And most importantly of all, it's simply the right thing to do. Acting graciously in defeat goes a long ways toward adding an element of class to competitive pool.

When you win, good sportsmanship dictates that you seek out your opponent. Shake hands and offer a sincere expression of how you feel about them or their game. Try to say something that's appropriate given the nature of the match. After all, there will be many occasions when a win could just as easily have been a loss. One bad roll, one missed shot and it could have been your opponent consoling you about the outcome. Some of the standard expressions for the winner include "good shooting," "great match," "I enjoyed playing with you" or "I was very fortunate to win."

Respect for Your Opponent

Although you are in an adversarial position during a match, it may do you some good to lighten up a little on your view toward your opponent. This will enable you to focus even more on your game. You also won't get as upset when they win their share, which they most certainly will.

All serious players have a common bond that comes from sharing the same experiences. If your opponent is a reasonably nice person, you might be at least a little happy for their success. There's nothing wrong with showing the same respect for your opponent's game that you would like for them to demonstrate toward yours.

CAPELLE'S LAWS for POOL

Pool is such a great sport that it's devoted participants should settle for nothing short of the best.

Your reputation speaks before you enter a pool room. Make sure it has something good to say.

Life is too short to waste valuable pool time playing jerks.

Life is not so short but that there is always time for courtesy.
— **Ralph Waldo Emerson**

One man practicing sportsmanship is far better than 50 preaching it.
—**Knute K. Rockne**

Part Three
Your Journey

Chapter 18
Your Journey

"A long life may not be good enough, but a good life is long enough."

— Benjamin Franklin

Your Life in Pool

If you like to keep doing the things you love forever, then pool's your game. Pool can provide you with the ultimate blend of physical and mental activity that will keep you fascinated for decades. It's possible, if you start playing young enough, that your journey could last from ages 9 to 90.

The intellectual nature of pool is such that your growth as a pool player can mirror your progress in other areas of your life. The lessons you learn on a pool table can help you with your real life, and vice versa.

A pool player does not reach full maturity until an age when participants in more physically demanding sports have long since retired. In fact, you can retain a very significant portion of physical skill clear into your 50s and beyond. When physical skill combines with knowledge and maturity, the results can be a very strong player. As a case in point, Buddy Hall was named the Professional Billiard Tours (PBT's) player of the year at age 50. You won't find that happening in tennis, golf or any other sport.

Your journey can take many shapes as both a player and a participant. In your early years you will probably be focused on playing and improving your game. As you grow older, other pool related activities will assume an important role in your life. And in your later years you will have a treasure chest of memories to look back on and that will provide you with stories to swap with your buddies in the pool room.

Your journey will take you to many fascinating places and pool rooms where you will play many memorable matches. Along the way you will meet many wonderful people who share your love of pool and who help to make the game what it is today. At some point you may realize that you remain a part of the sport as much for the friendship of your fellow pool nuts as you do for the game itself.

Your journey could span several decades and be comprised of untold numbers of experiences, insights and observations. Many will be worth remembering. You might wish to start a journal of your most valued experiences. When a fascinating story unfolds or you discover a new secret, take a couple of minutes to jot them down. A couple of lines or a paragraph should do. Be sure to write enough details so you can recall the highlights when you read your entry many years later. But don't make such a big deal about writing that you soon quit the practice altogether.

At some point your journey in pool will reach an end. When you look back, what would you like to see? I'm hoping it's many, many years of fun, friendship, learning and contributing to this great sport of pool. Whatever your vision that you've pictured for yourself, why not start today to make that dream a reality. Then you can look back when your journey's near an end with a smile of contentment because you know it was all that you could have hoped that it would be.

 CAPELLE'S LAWS for POOL

Your journey may start down one path and end up on an altogether different one, but that's just fine as long as you are enjoying the ride.

Pool is the ultimate combination of physical and mental skills for those who wish to play the same game from ages 9 to 90.

You can trust your memory with your most important experiences, thoughts and discoveries. But why take a chance when keeping a journal can eliminate the risk of forgetting.

Let us endeavor so to live that when we come to die even the undertaker will be sorry.
— Mark Twain

The journey is the reward.
— Tao saying

There are only two ways to live your life. One is as though nothing is a miracle. The other is as though everything is a miracle.
— Albert Einstein

You're only here for a short visit. Don't hurry. Don't worry. And be sure to smell the flowers along the way.
— Walter Hagen

The palest ink is better than the best memory.
— Chinese proverb

The most beautiful thing we can experience is the mysterious. It is the source of all true art and science.
— Albert Einstein

Questions to Improve Your Journey

You can proceed along your journey on automatic pilot once you've established your pool-related routine. A certain group of activities may satisfy your needs, at least for awhile. Still it doesn't hurt to occasionally spend a few moments reflecting on the quality of your journey. This will ensure that you don't completely miss out on a new activity or approach to playing that could add measurably to the pleasure you receive from pool.

Your self-appraisal consists of asking the right questions. You may already know the answers and the questions could serve to draw your true feelings out into the open. If the answer to a question doesn't come right away, don't worry. Your subconscious will go to work on the question and an answer will appear soon enough.

Your answers will confirm those things that you enjoy about pool. Your responses will also alert you to the things that you are not happy about. Now you are ready to make the necessary changes so that you can again be totally enthusiastic about your involvement in pool. If you know about an area of discontentment and choose to do nothing differently, then you only have yourself to blame for not enjoying pool as much as you possibly can.

Your answers to the questions that follow should give you a fairly accurate indication as to the quality of your journey. You will probably come up with several more on your own.

Questions About Your Journey

- ☑ How have you been playing lately?
- ☑ Has your game been improving, staying the same or regressing?
- ☑ Are you continuing to learn new strategies and techniques?
- ☑ Are you playing with great enthusiasm or are you simply going through the motions?
- ☑ What games do you like best? Are you playing them regularly?
- ☑ Do you enjoy the company of the people that you play with regularly?
- ☑ Are you happy with your home room or is the time for a change?
- ☑ Do you enjoy your current level of competition?
- ☑ Do you enjoy the tournaments or leagues that you're competing in regularly?
- ☑ Are you involved with any non-playing activities such as teaching or running a tournament? If not, would you like to be?
- ☑ Do you like to travel to new pool rooms and new cities to play pool? Have you done so lately?

You can have a good time playing pool by following the same routine year after year because pool is such an awesome game. By evaluating your journey from time to time, however, you could windup with some mid-course adjustments. Any changes could help keep pool as much fun as those heady days when you first started playing and couldn't wait to get to the pool room.

CAPELLE'S LAWS for POOL

When you ask questions about your game, you'll be taking a big step towards improving the quality of your journey in pool.

He who asks questions cannot avoid the answers.
> — **Cameroonian Proverb**

I keep six honest serving men
They taught me all I know;
Their names are What and Why and When
And How and Where and Who.
> — **Rudyard Kipling**

No man really becomes a fool until he stops asking questions.
> — **Charles P. Steinmetz**

A prudent question is one-half of wisdom.
> — **Francis Bacon**

One who never asks either knows everything or nothing.
> — **Malcolm Forbes**

Every Day's a New Day

When you're a pool player everyday is indeed a winding road. One day you're in dead stroke and the next you cannot make a ball. The luck factor can also gyrate out of control. One day you can't buy a roll and the next time your opponent leaves you a road map run-out every time they miss. It's no wonder the game can make a head case out of the stoutest of souls.

Because you are a person and not a machine your game will change day by day. Some of the most noticeable deviations in skill show up in your break, speed control and in your ability to locate the pocket. Once your game is fairly well established, these day-to-day fluctuations should stay within a relatively narrow range. The differences may amount to anywhere between 2 and 20 percent depending on your consistency and level of skill. This is enough to make sure that each new day retains an element of adventure. If you played poorly one day, you could bounce back to your "A" game the next time out. And if you played particularly well one day, perhaps you'll even exceed this level of play next time or possibly fall flat on your face.

The luck factor, also known as the rolls, can be especially frustrating when it's working against you. Though the rolls even out over the long run, it never seems that way to most players. Your lens of perception can cloud your vision of the rolls. Like most players you probably anguish over your bad rolls (or your opponent's good fortune) and pay little attention to your good breaks. This bias toward your cause also shows up when you're rooting for your favorite team in football, basketball or whatever sports you follow.

 Over the course of your career you will play hundreds of thousands of good shots and tens of thousands of lousy shots. You'll get thousands of good rolls and bad rolls. Once you learn to accept that the game changes from day-to-day and that you will get your share of the good days, then you will no longer feel so angry or frustrated when things don't always work out your way. You can't control Lady luck, nor can you totally control the day by day fluctuations in your skill. So why not enjoy the good days and shrug off the bad? In the long run you'll certainly make your journey a much more enjoyable one.

 CAPELLE'S LAWS for POOL

Every time you play you bring to the table possibly 98 percent of your game from the previous session. It's the other 2 percent that makes each day such an adventure.

Regarding your level of play, the only constant is change.

Over the long course of your career, you're going to play hundreds of thousands of good shots and tens of thousands of poor shots. Expect some bad shots and don't let them destroy your enjoyment of the game.

Everything is the same as yesterday except that it's today instead of yesterday.

If matters go badly now, they will not always be so.
— Horace

> *Tomorrow will be a new day.*
>
> — Cervantes
>
> *Some days you tame the tiger, and some days the tiger has you for lunch.*
>
> — Tug McGraw

Drafting Your Laws of Pool

When you start on your pool playing journey there are a world of experiences awaiting you - most of them good, but some not so pleasant. Experience will teach you what you enjoy and what episodes you would just as soon not repeat.

 Over time your various adventures into the wonderful world of pool will help you in formulating your personal laws for enjoying pool. Your laws will also give you a nose for trouble. Some of my laws are listed below. They may be useful in helping you to develop your code for your journey in pool.

- ⊙ Don't play drunks for fun or profit.
- ⊙ Don't bother playing obnoxious shark artists for money.
- ⊙ Don't sneak into tournaments were you're head and shoulders above the competition.
- ⊙ Compete in tournaments and money games where both you and your opponent have a reasonable shot at winning.
- ⊙ Play in places you enjoy and with people whose company you enjoy.
- ⊙ Respect the tradition of the game. Observe proper etiquette.
- ⊙ Respect the rights of your opponent.
- ⊙ Always give each match your best effort.

Some of these laws may be part of your code of action. Possibly you have come up with some of your own. Now take a moment to recall any incidents when you acted against your personal set of laws. Did you give in to the urge that said it would be different this time? Have you failed to heed your inner guidance system that is designed to shield you from unpleasant experiences? Chances are you often paid some kind of price when you failed to follow your better judgment.

Your laws of pool are not supposed to eliminate your sense of adventure or to take the mystery out of your journey. Instead they are designed to ensure that the memories you make will be the kind you can look back on with a smile on your face.

 CAPELLE'S LAWS for POOL

In life there are so many decisions that can affect your happiness. You can simplify the process and enjoy the game even more by sticking to your personal laws of pool. Your character and your experiences will reveal them to you.

The laws that govern your game and your life reveal your character. Choose them wisely.

A precedent embodies a principal.

— **Benjamin Disraeli**

Our principles are the springs of our actions; our actions the springs of our happiness or misery. Too much care, therefore, cannot be taken in forming our principles.

— **Philip Skelton**

The wisest men follow their own direction.

— **Euripides**

Choosing Your Home Room

 Your pool playing time will be divided up between your home room and everywhere else that you play. Therefore it makes good sense to research the local scene before selecting your home room. The selection process is not completely unlike house hunting. You can speed up the search and ensure that you find the ideal room by drafting a list of criteria that meets your special needs. Pool rooms have a very addictive quality to them, so before you become hooked on one, make sure that it's the room for you. The items below should be helpful in your search.

- ☑ Is the room reasonably close to where you live?
- ☑ Is the room open the hours that you like to play?
- ☑ Do your friends go there?
- ☑ Does the equipment meet your standards?
- ☑ Are tables generally available when you like to play?
- ☑ Do they sponsor leagues?
- ☑ Does the room hold tournaments?

☑ Is their action to watch or to get involved in?

☑ Do they have a member's program or discounted practice rates?

☑ How is the people watching?

☑ Is a room comfortable to be an, or is it noisy and crowded?

☑ Is it important that they feature televised sports?

☑ Do they have a good sound system? Do you like the music on the CD player?

☑ Do they serve food and beverages that are to your liking?

☑ Do you feel at home in the room?

☑ Do you feel safe going to and from the room?

☑ Is the atmosphere (decor) to your liking?

☑ Are the employees friendly and courteous?

☑ Are there any special amenities such as cue lockers that are important to you?

☑ Do they have a pro shop that does repairs?

☑ Do they have an instructor in house?

When you find a pool room that meets most of these criteria, including the few that you can't do without, then you have found your own piece of heaven on earth. And yes, rooms like this to exist. I've been lucky enough to have had a few home rooms that featured nearly every one of these items. Happy hunting!

 CAPELLE'S LAWS for POOL

Your home room should be a home away from home where you are welcomed when you walk in the door.

The acid test for your home room is how you feel while you're there.

Home is a place where, when you have to go there, they have to take you in.

— **Robert Frost**

Paradise is where I am.

— **Voltaire**

Please accept my resignation. I don't want to belong to any club that will accept me as a member.

— **Groucho Marx**

> *A man travels the world over in search of what he needs and returns home to find it.*
>
> — George Moore

Out on the Road

The lure of the road has been irresistible to pool players for possibly as long as the game has been played. The big drawing cards have always been a change of scenery, new faces and the promise of action. Road trips were a way of life for players and hustlers who made their living at the game. There are still some players who travel in search of action, but a more modern definition of a road trip is now in order.

Nowadays pool players mostly go on road trips to play in tournaments. The change is due largely to the substantial growth in league play and to the number of local and regional tours now in operation. Those who play pool professionally make more money than ever before from a combination of tournament winnings, lessons, appearances and business ventures. These new sources of income have lessened their reliance on road trips for money games

 A road trip can be loosely defined as an excursion out-of-town lasting a couple of days to several weeks or longer. You can expand this definition to include those evenings you spend driving around town in search of a new and rewarding experience. Calling these local ventures road trips has the effect of raising your sense of adventure.

Selecting Your Road Stops

Your road trips can take you from a crowded one table tavern to a convention room filled with over a hundred tables. You can experience the entire spectrum of society as your travels can range from a dingy back alley bar to the most posh of settings in one of the thousands of upscale rooms that have opened in recent years. Some of your possible choices include:

⦿ traditional neighborhood pool rooms

⦿ comfortable taverns

⦿ upscale palaces that may include dancing/nightclubs

⦿ beautiful new rooms that cater to serious players

⦿ sports bars

⦿ action bars

- ⊙ pool rooms in a bowling center
- ⊙ all-purpose rooms that include several other games

You may enjoy spending time in many of the different settings or you may prefer a certain kind of room. Very serious players, for example, only go to places where they can find meaningful competition. A road trip can be to a big tournament. Your travel plans could also include those regions or cities that are bona fide hot beds of pool. Some of the comments you'll hear describing various Mecca's of pool are "it's a real good pool town," "tons of leagues" and "lots of action." A big part of the excitement of visiting a hotbed is the prospect of being around hordes of pool nuts like yourself.

Your time must be spent wisely to gain maximum enjoyment from your road trips. So whether you are traveling around town, to the next county or across the country, don't waste time in places that simply don't trip your trigger. I recommend you adopt the time-honored system that's been used to rate hotels, resorts, golf courses and restaurants. The system rates those places from one to five stars, five stars being the best. Our system uses cue balls. You're in charge of the rating for each place you visit. Your rating should naturally lead to the appropriate course of action.

How to Rate a Pool Room

OOOOO — Where the pool gods play.

OOOO — Excellent, worth putting on your regular road trips.

OOO — Good, worth an occasional visit to see what's going on.

OO — Make the best of your visit if you must stay, but you probably won't be back.

O — In and out, instant veto. Wrong crowd, no action, lousy tables, or whatever. You'll never return.

Developing Your Agenda

Road players have developed black books filled with the lowdown on who to play, where to play, when to play and other choice bits of information on gamblers and high-stakes players across the country. These players have made a practice of sharing information with each other. Today there is a more up-to-date system that can put you in touch with tournament action. When you are planning a pool playing vacation or road trip, you can use you're pool intelligence system to select what cities to visit and where to go when there.

The major pool publications list tournament results from all over the country. The rooms that host these events are almost always the kind that hold regular weekly events as well. The publications also give you a list of upcoming events that may be worth your consideration as either a player or spectator.

Upon arriving in a new city you should consult the ads and listings in the Yellow Pages for rooms worth checking out. Give the rooms a call and ask if they are holding any tournaments while you're in town, or if there are some games worth watching. If nothing is going on, ask them what other pool rooms are worth a try. You can even use this approach before leaving home by consulting the Yellow Pages at your local library or over the Internet.

Your road trips will lead to many new places and people that can combine to provide you with a memorable experience. To help ensure that you have as good a time is possible, you may wish to consider some of the items on the checklist.

Planning a Road Trip

☑ What kind of pool room(s) or tavern(s) are you looking for? Action spots? Fun? Tournaments?

☑ What level of competition are you looking for?

☑ Do you want to watch some great pool?

☑ Would you like to play against semi-pros or pros for the experience in a regional event?

☑ Do you want to just travel without a plan and see what you run into?

☑ Are there any pool rooms you have read or heard about that you particularly want to visit?

☑ What pool people would you like to see on your travels? Any special pool playing friends on your agenda?

☑ Do you plan to play for money?

☑ Are you knowledgeable about the rules of the road: learn the local rules to Eight-Ball; don't bet high with strangers; stay out of the wrong kind of places.

In summary, there are no limits to the richness and variety of your road trips. So when you've had it with the same old same old, it's time to hit the road. Spend a little time to plan your itinerary, crank up your sense of adventure and prepare to embark on every pool player's dream—a road trip in which the pool gods ride on your shoulder every mile of the way.

CAPELLE'S LAWS for POOL

No two pool rooms are exactly alike. Each should be valued for what it adds to your pool playing experiences.

Wherever you travel to play, your game goes with you.

After you've gained some experience, your instincts will quickly tell you whether a room or tavern is your kind of place.

The first thing to do when playing Eight-Ball in a new tavern is to learn the house rules.

For my part, I travel not to go anywhere, but to go. I travel for travels sake. The great affair is to move.
—Robert Louis Stevenson

Travel is fatal to prejudice.
— Mark Twain

Traveling may be one of the two things - an experience we shall always remember, or an experience which, alas, we shall never forget.
— Rabbi Julius Gordon

When the whistle blew and the call stretched thin across the night, one had to believe that any journey could be sweet to the soul.
— Charles Turner

Pool Ages You Gracefully

Father Time eventually wields his influence on every player's game. You may lose your ability to see the edge of the balls sharply and your muscles can tighten, causing you to lose some of the power in your break. In addition, your nerves may not hold up as well under pressure. That's the bad news. The good news is that the decline in your physical skills is usually long and very gradual. You will hardly notice the slippage until years after your peak. And due to the nature of the game, your peak years could last for a long time. As a pool player, you also don't have to worry too much about an injury reducing or eliminating your participation in the sport.

The pool gods were thinking ahead to the needs of its senior citizens when they invented the game. They, in their infinite wisdom, decreed that knowledge would play a huge role in the game. At the time a pool player starts to notice a decline in their physical game, they will begin to fully realize how much knowledge they have at their disposal.

Pool rewards those who stay with it and who have a penchant for learning. Once a player discovers that they must use their smarts to win, they also discover that they have a plethora of tricks and strategies at their disposal. An aging pool player is really like a baseball pitcher who has lost some zip off his fastball and who now relies on his knowledge of the hitters and selection of pitches to win games.

The pool gods invented several games that could be played by people of all ages. They created Nine-Ball on a 4 1/2' X 9' to be the most physically demanding pool game. Youngsters who can destroy a rack with a sledgehammer break and who can cut the paint off the balls do enjoy a slight advantage. Still, it's been proven that players clear into their 50s can compete successfully with the younger set.

Once a player decides, however, that he's lost his edge at big table Nine-Ball to the point where he no longer enjoys the game, he is far from finished with pool. He can simply shift his emphasis to a number of games that place a greater premium on knowledge. One-Pocket on a big table and both Eight-Ball and Nine-Ball on a bar table are all games that can be played very well up into your 70s or beyond.

When you finally arrive at the point where playing doesn't interest you much anymore but you still love the game, then it's time to enjoy possibly the most rewarding experience of all: passing your knowledge on to others. Yes, the pool gods seemed to have it all arranged so that a pool player can age gracefully clear through to the end.

 CAPELLE'S LAWS for POOL

When the long green shots start to intimidate you, then it's time to take up One-Pocket in earnest.

How much One-Pocket you should play largely depends on your ability to switch back and forth between it and your other games without suffering a drop in your level of play.

When you can no longer win by out shooting your opponents, then it's time to win by outsmarting them.

When you feel you can no longer play your game, then it's time to help others learn to improve their game.

He who is of calm and happy nature will hardly feel the pressure of age.

— Plato

No man love's life like him that's growing old.

— Sophocles

Education is the best provision for old age.

— Aristotle

Growing old isn't so bad when you consider the alternative.

— Maurice Chevalier

The best tunes are played on the oldest fiddles.

— Sigmund Z. Engel

None are so old as those who have outlived enthusiasm.

—Henry David Thoreau

Chapter 19
Enjoying Pool

"All the world's a stage and all the men and women merely players.."

—**Shakespeare**

Why it's So Easy to Love Pool

It's easy enough to understand why people that catch the pool bug stay entranced by the game for life. The sheer beauty and variety of the game offer so much. On top of this there are a whole host of other reasons that make pool the game of choice.

Whenever your enthusiasm runs a little low, the list below can serve as your reminder of why it's so great to be a pool player in the first place.

◉ The never-ending challenge of the game.

◉ The thrill of competition.

◉ You can practice by yourself.

◉ There are so many games you can play.

◉ A fine looking table that plays true.

◉ The beautiful works of art by the master cue makers.

◉ A pool room is a refuge from the concerns of everyday life.

◉ Pool rooms offer an oasis from bad weather.

◉ Pool rooms are open most of the day and night.

◉ Pool gives you a great excuse for a two-hour lunch.

◉ You can play a few racks on your way home from work.

◉ You can play for a few minutes up to several hours.

◉ Pool rooms are a great place to socialize.

◉ You can enjoy a meal and a beverage while playing.

◉ Pool rooms are a fine place to listen to music.

◉ There are a wide variety of settings in which to play pool.

 CAPELLE'S LAWS for POOL

There is so much to love about pool that it's simply foolish to waste any time on the negatives.

We are shaped and fashioned by what we love.
— **Johann Wolfgang von Goethe**

Anything will give up its secrets if you love it enough.
— **George Washington Carver**

> *The balls used in top class games are generally smaller than those used in other games.*
>
> — **Paul Fussell**

All of the Pool Room is a Stage

People watching in a pool room can be as entertaining as live theater, perhaps even more so, because of the disparate cast of characters, the totally spontaneous performances and the close proximity to the action.

On a busy night a well-rounded poolroom may provide the stage for the following cast of characters as they each play out their role.

⊙ Singles

⊙ Couples

⊙ Fun players

⊙ Wannabies

⊙ Old-timers

⊙ Good players

⊙ Serious pool addicts

⊙ Champions

⊙ Stakehorses

⊙ Regulars

⊙ Houseman

⊙ Waiters and waitresses

⊙ Tournament directors

⊙ League players

⊙ Cool players

⊙ Dorks

⊙ Hustlers

There are many dramas and comedies being acted out by the performers. Among the most common:

⊙ Couples playing for fun.

⊙ Non-players going through the motions while appearing very cool or completely bored.

⊙ Serious money games between two good players.

⊙ Tournament action.

⊙ League play and the reactions of each player.

⊙ Good shots and misses—how various players around the room respond to each.

⊙ Guys "teaching" their girlfriends how to "shoot pool".

⊙ Men scamming on women or vice versa.

⊙ Parties and groups that are having and especially good time.

⊙ Watching average players play for money.

One of the more intriguing spectacles is the changing face of a pool room. A pool room can be completely dead at 6:30. Then the actors start to file in, each with their hopes for the evenings play. It's fun to watch them arrive with their cases slung over their shoulders. It's a fascinating guessing game trying to make an instant assessment of their caliber before they've even played a shot based solely on their appearance and mannerisms.

 While you're hanging out there are a number of strategies you can employ that will entertain you and that will build your awareness and appreciation of the surroundings. They include:

- ⊙ Talking pool with your friends or your mentor.
- ⊙ Playing your favorite tunes.
- ⊙ Partaking of the rooms cuisine and beverages.
- ⊙ Observing and critiquing the decor in great detail.
- ⊙ Checking out the tables, balls and lighting.
- ⊙ Evaluating the color and texture of the cloth.
- ⊙ Checking out members of the opposite sex.
- ⊙ Observing the arrangement of the seating and the pool tables.
- ⊙ Evaluating the different players strokes and styles of play.
- ⊙ How are the customers dressed? Any fashion statements? Rebels? Conformists?
- ⊙ Learning all about the room and the regulars.

 CAPELLE'S LAWS for POOL

It's well worth being a pool player if for no other reason than it's the greatest people watching game.

It takes all sorts of people to make a world.
                              —Douglas William Jerrold

No pleasure endures unseasoned by variety.
                              — Publilius Syrus

We are as much as we see. Faith is sight and knowledge.
                              — Henry David Thoreau

Talking a Great Game

Part of a player's education includes developing a working knowledge of the game's colorful jargon. Command of the pool players vernacular can help you converse fluently with a fellow player when making a game or discussing the action. Pool talk can also intimidate and impress those who are less well schooled in the art of pool conversation.

Like any other facet of the game, it takes time to learn the lingo and how to use it correctly. Your education naturally should begin with such basics as draw, english, foot rail, rolls, speed control, stripes and cut shots. In time you'll be able to talk pool with the best of hustlers. The following passage is designed to test your knowledge of the language of pool.

"I got *locked up* by a *nut artist* who *robbed* me because I *spotted* him the *world*. He *dogged* a *hanger* on the *cheese* on the *double-hill* game but got a *roll* and left me *corner hooked*. I *kicked* off the *side-rail* with *running english* but barely missed a *hit* and *scratched*. My *stake-horse* lost his *case barrel* and went *tap city*.

Translation:

I played in a match in which I was not the favorite because I was out negotiated. My opponent beat me because I gave him a substantial handicap. He missed an easy shot on the nine-ball with the score tied with one game to go. He got a fortunate break when the cue ball stopped behind the edge of the corner pocket. I shot the cue ball off the cushion with sidespin on the cue ball but failed to contact the object ball. The cue ball disappeared into a pocket. My financier lost all of his funds.

CAPELLE'S LAWS for POOL

If you can talk a great game, you'll never lack for an audience of eager listeners.

The better a player talks the game, the tighter you should hold onto your wallet.

You can stroke people with words.
— **F. Scott Fitzgerald**

Words form the thread on which we string our experiences.
— **Aldous Huxley**

> *Half the world is composed of people who have something to say and can't and the other half who have nothing to say and keep on saying it.*
> — **Robert Frost**
>
> *One always speaks badly when one has nothing to say.*
> — **Voltaire**

Listing Your Pool Pleasures

Lists are fun and easy to do because they involve one of your favorite subjects about which you're an expert, that being you. You can quickly discover or recall what you like or dislike about the game from your list. With this information you can then tailor your activities so that you gain maximum enjoyment from pool. You can also eliminate the items you dislike from your schedule.

A list may verify that you're making the most of your pool experience. It may also remind you of things that you have been neglecting that have brought you pleasure in the past.

Below are some ideas to get you started. You'll probably come up with several more selections on your own. As time passes you will want to amend your list by adding new items and by deleting things that no longer apply.

- Your favorite pool games, in order of preference.
- Pool rooms you particularly enjoy.
- Your favorite playing partners.
- Your favorite tournaments.
- The best lessons you've learned.
- Your best matches.
- Your most memorable shots.
- Your favorite music to get in stroke by.
- Cues you'd like to own.
- Your favorite books on pool.
- The reasons why you love pool.
- Your favorite shots.
- Your best practice routines.

CAPELLE'S LAWS for POOL

When you commit what you like about the game to paper, you're more likely to experience those things.

> *The world is so full of a number of things,*
> *I'm sure we should all be as happy as kings.*
> **—Robert Louis Stevenson**
>
> *Method will teach you to win time.*
> **— Johann Wolfgang von Goethe**
>
> *Good order is the foundation of all good things.*
> **— Edmund Burke**

Your Definition of Fun

Your journey should be as enjoyable as you can possibly make it. The game itself, the friendships that you develop and the places in which you play should all combine into making pool a total blast.

In the broadest sense, it is important to discover which kind of fun you wish to experience from playing pool: fun fun or serious fun.

Fun fun—When you play strictly for fun, your goal is simply to enjoy playing pool. You're not playing for money or trophies but rather for the excitement of watching the balls do crazy things and for the possibility of running a table from time to time. You like to laugh, kid around, try impossible shots and show off a little. There's nothing wrong with this approach to pool if fun and relaxation are what you're after.

Serious fun—Playing competitive pool can give you a real sense of satisfaction when you play particularly well. When you are playing for serious fun, that doesn't mean that you're not enjoying yourself just because you're not laughing and grinning all of the time. Serious fun comes quietly from the process of playing each shot as well as possible and from the thrill of competition.

To enjoy playing pool as much as possible, you need to clarify you're objectives. You will then be at peace with your game and your approach to the game. It certainly doesn't make sense to get uptight about your lack of results if you play strictly for fun. You also should not take a frivolous attitude towards the game if your true desire is to whip the competition.

CAPELLE'S LAWS for POOL

When it comes to your pool game, your definition of fun is yours and yours alone.

Enjoy pleasures, but let them be your own, and then you will taste them.
> — **Lord Chesterfield**

I've taken my fun where I've found it.
> — **Rudyard Kipling**

Are we having fun yet?
> — **Bill Griffith**

Of all days, the day on which one has not laughter is surely the most wasted.
> — **Chamfort**

Freewheeling

When children play a game, they usually cut loose with reckless abandon. They play for fun. They freewheel. Children don't waste time overanalyzing every shot or situation. To them, pool is a game and not a matter of life-and-death.

To be played at its best, pool requires a disciplined and thoughtful approach. Still there are occasions when taking a carefree attitude to the game may work to your advantage. The next time you are playing for fun or in practice, try adopting the attitude of a child. Don't make a big deal about every shot. Loosen up and truly enjoy stroking the cue ball without caring so much what happens. Within a short while you may find yourself in dead stroke almost as if by accident.

CAPELLE'S LAWS for POOL

We all act like children once in awhile so we might as well try occasionally playing pool like one.

Children seem to have so much fun when playing pool no matter what their level of skill. Perhaps they know something we don't or that we have forgotten.

The great man is he who does not lose his childlike heart.
> — **Mencius**

> *I could solve my most complex problems in physics if I had not given up the way of thinking common to children at play.*
>
> — J. Robert Oppenheimer

Happiness is Your Pool Game

A big part of the learning curve in pool involves discovering more and more ways to increase your enjoyment of this great game. You can help the process by adopting certain thoughts and attitudes about the game that increase your sense of wonder and that raise your level of awareness about all of the good things that make up your game. The ideas below should be useful in spurring the process.

- ⦿ Start to enjoy the game you have right now, not the one you're going to own six months or a year from now.

- ⦿ Look at every pool game as an adventure into the great unknown where fabulous shots, blunders, fantastic rolls, spectacular victories and gut wrenching defeats lie in wait.

- ⦿ Focus more on what's right with your game rather than stressing out about what's wrong.

- ⦿ Allow pool to be a means of you're self-expression. Let it show what you, as an individual, are all about.

- ⦿ Enjoy all that your life as a pool player encompasses.

- ⦿ Appreciate the good rolls and laugh at the bad ones.

- ⦿ Love to compete against a worthy opponent as you try to play each shot as well as possible.

- ⦿ Appreciate everything that goes into your playing your best pool.

 CAPELLE'S LAWS for POOL

Your journey in pool is a long one, so you might as well take the time to discover what it takes for you to enjoy the game to the utmost.

> *If happiness is activity in accordance with excellence, it is reasonable that it should be in accordance with the highest excellence.*
>
> — **Aristotle**
>
> *There is no duty we so much underrate as the duty of being happy.*
>
> — **Robert Louis Stevenson**

> *All we need to make us really happy is something to be enthusiastic about.*
> — Charles Kingsley
>
> *Human felicity is produced not so much by great pieces of good fortune that seldom happen, as by little advantages that occur every day.*
> — Benjamin Franklin
>
> *Laughter is wine for the soul. Once we can laugh, we can live.*
> — Sean O 'Casey

Eliminate the Negatives—Now

To enjoy pool to the maximum you must eliminate those factors that take away from your pleasure. You can start your analysis by asking yourself if you are having as much fun playing pool as you would like to? If not, why not? The questions below can help you pinpoint the reasons for your discontent. The next step is to take active measures to eliminate the negatives and to replace them with the things that bring your pleasure from playing pool.

- ☑ Do you play in a room out of habit that you're really not too thrilled about?

- ☑ Do you play obnoxious people just for the money?

- ☑ Are you playing in a weekly tournament that's unfairly handi-capped?

- ☑ Is your league team comprised of spoilsports?

- ☑ Are you bored from playing the same crowd over and over again?

- ☑ Is your game stagnating from lack of a plan for improvement?

- ☑ Has your game changed but you're still playing with a cue that's no longer right for your game?

- ☑ Why do you play pool in the first place?

- ☑ Have any compromises in your life caused your game to fall off?

CAPELLE'S LAWS for POOL

Pool should be lots of fun, serious or otherwise. When it's not fun, you really only have yourself to blame.

> *If you are distressed by anything external, the pain and is not due to the thing itself but to your own estimate of it; and this you have the power to revoke at any moment.*
> **— Marcus Aurelius**
>
> *And hour of pain is as long as a day of pleasure.*
> **— English proverb**

Music Can Elevate Your Play

Studies have shown that music can wield great power over your moods and your mind. The right kind of music can:

⊙ Energize you and prepare you for maximum performance.

⊙ Relax you and help you to remain patient in a game that requires much patience.

⊙ Focus your mind on the task at hand and raise your IQ to facilitate learning.

Classical music can be particularly useful for improving your game. If you have a pool table at home, you have a distinct advantage as you can pop a Mozart Symphony into your CD player while your competitors at the pool hall may have to settle for rock and roll. Certain types of classical music seem to be especially useful in opening your mind to new techniques that can elevate your game.

At the pool room, the music does not stop for a big money game or even during the finals of many important tournaments. Since the music will play, you might as well use it to set a pace and mood that is ideal for your game. This could give a winning edge when the competition is particularly keen. It's a good idea to write down the numbers of your favorites on your home rooms CD player. During an important match, you can set the mood by controlling the music. The right song at the right time could help to raise your spirits when they need it most.

It could be worth a few moments of your time to examine some of your personal preferences. Some items to consider include:

☑ Do you like background music or do you really like to hear and feel the music?

☑ Do you like the music loud, soft or somewhere in between?

☑ Do you like rock and roll (what kinds), blues, country, jazz or classical?

☑ Do you like to have music relax you or to give you extra energy?

When I need a dose of motivation, I like to hear "Money" by Pink Floyd or "Keep on Chooglin" by Creedence Clearwater. My all-time favorite background music is Miles Davis' "Kind of Blue." The music is particularly soothing and it has a way of transporting you back to the era of great players in serious action in the old-style pool halls of the '50s and '60s.

CAPELLE'S LAWS for POOL

If a small investment in the CD player can give you the winning edge, then let the music play.

Studies have shown that certain types of music can raise your IQ and facilitate learning, which of course can improve your pool game.

Music provides a kind of pleasure which human nature cannot do without.
— **Confucius**

Generally music feedith that disposition of the spirits which it findeth.
— **Francis Bacon**

Music is my weapon. I believe in music, in its spirituality, its exaltation, its ecstatic nobility, its humor, its power to penetrate to the basic fineness of every human being.
— **Henry Cowel**

Your Gallery of Memorable Shots

As the years pass, perhaps nothing in your pool playing experience will stand out as vividly as your most memorable shots. Your great shots will cause you to break out in big smile as you recall heroic deeds of yesteryear.

Because of the very nature of pool, even very ordinary players can, on occasion, execute spectacular shots that top pros would be very proud of. You may never whack a fastball 450 feet or dunk a basketball. It is quite possible that you could fan in an 80 degree cut shot or split the pocket with a table length combination.

Just for fun, why not take a few minutes to search back to those special moments when you pocketed an unbelievably difficult shot, played amazing position or came through in the clutch to win an important match. Describe your big shots in rich detail.

☑   What was the shot?

☑   How did it look and sound?

☑   Did the spectators explode in applause?

☑   Did you celebrate by shaking your fist or some other gesture?

☑   Who was your opponent?

☑   Did the shot win an important match or launch a comeback?

☑   Did the shot help to bolster your confidence and to
     permanently elevate your game?

☑   Did you learn something important about the game from the shot?

A perfectly played match or run-out are very noteworthy, but there's something extra special about a big shot that makes some standout as the years pass and your memory starts to dim. You may want to start recording your most memorable shots on a blank diagram of a pool table. Make your observations as detailed as possible. When your game needs a lift, or when you want to relive a special moment, you will have your notebook of great shots to assist you.

No set of memories would be complete without your most prominent disasters, so you might also wish to record these in your pool diary. Some key questions to ask about your greatest mistakes would be: what went wrong?; how did you feel?; what did you learn from the mishap?

 CAPELLE'S LAWS for POOL

The memory of a great shot can bring you pleasure for many years to come, so do what you can to preserve them for future reference.

> *To be able to enjoy one's past life is to live twice.*
>
> — **Marcus Valarius Martialis**
>
> *Forgetfulness transforms every occurrence into a nonoccurrence.*
>
> — **Plutarch**

Time Management

A host of activities go into making up your experiences in pool. They can range from playing to teaching to captaining a league team and much more. It's up to you to determine which activities give you pleasure and to divide your time so you can do the things you like as much as you like. This approach will add balance and richness to your journey, and it will ensure that your most precious resource, time, is being used wisely.

It's never too late to reallocate your time in a way that maximizes your participation in pool. Find out what you like best and make sure you devote ample time to those activities. This will keep you from waking up one day years later and saying to yourself that you wished you'd spent more time playing in tournaments or teaching your children to play.

One method for analyzing your allocation of time is the pie chart. The complete circle represents the time you have for pool related activities. The circle is divided into your areas of participation in proportion to the time you spend on each one. Add up the hours you spend every week (or month) on each activity and create your chart. Then consider what changes are in order and create a new chart. Compare the two. Ask yourself what it would take to reallocate your time so that the second chart becomes a reality.

The example below demonstrates a reasonably well rounded approach to pool. How does yours compare?

TIME MANAGEMENT

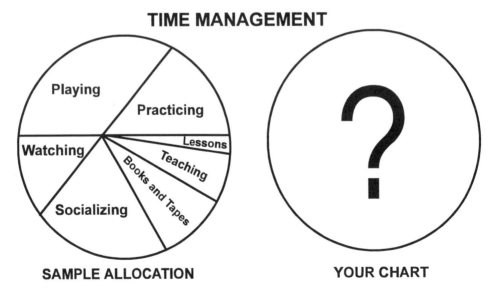

SAMPLE ALLOCATION   YOUR CHART

CAPELLE'S LAWS for POOL

The richness of your journey in pool will be enhanced by balancing your time among the activities that give you pleasure in the proper proportions.

> *Dost thou love life? Then do not squander time; for that's the stuff life is made of.*
> — Benjamin Franklin
>
> *Our costliest expenditure is time.*
> — Theophrastus
>
> *Never before have we had so little time to do so much.*
> — Franklin D. Roosevelt
>
> *Those who make the worst use of their time are the first to complain of its brevity.*
> — Jean de la Bruyere

The Games that You Play

You've gone to a restaurant and been both pleased and somewhat perplexed at the wide variety of mouth watering items to choose from. Pool is much the same. You can choose league Eight-Ball on a bar table, or perhaps a Nine-Ball tournament on a big table is more to your liking. When you stop to consider the table sizes, games and competitive formats, your options can easily run into the teens and beyond. You should take time to discover which mix of options (format, game, and table size) you prefer and allocate your pool playing time accordingly.

Your Pool Menu

	League		Tournaments		Money	
	3 1/2x 7	4 1/2x 9	3 1/2x 7	4 1/2x 9	3 1/2x 7	4 1/2x 9
Eight-Ball	A	A	A	A	A	B
Nine-Ball	A	A	A	A	A	A
One-Pocket	——	B	——	B	——	A
Straight Pool	——	B	——	B	——	A
Bank Pool	——	——	——	B	B	A

The table above lists the five most popular pool games. Some are commonly played on a bar table, while all are regularly played on a big table. The "A" indicates that the combination of variables is widely encountered relative to the number of people who play that game. Eight-Ball tournaments on a bar table are very common, so this combination rates an "A." Straight Pool tournaments take place on a big table, but not very often, so they are rated a "B." Bank pool leagues on a bar table are unheard of.

The table's value is in showing you the availability of your favorite forms of competition. If you really enjoy one of the combinations rated " B," then you will probably want to jump on the chance to play it whenever it becomes available.

There are a few approaches to creating your menu of pool games. One method is to try several games under a number of formats until you have discovered your niche. You may discover that you truly enjoy league Eight-Ball on a bar table. As a second choice you may enjoy playing Nine-Ball for low stakes on a bar table. The vast majority of your pool will be confined to these two selections. You may discover you're a pool player for all seasons. You could enjoy playing on both a big table and a bar table and you could be just as thrilled to be playing league Eight-Ball as you are playing Straight Pool for a few bucks.

 Confining your menu to a couple of items can help you to excel at a particular game. Playing a wide variety of games under a number of conditions can help you develop a well-rounded game. Taking this approach can also help keep you from burning out on pool. The downside is that you could lack the focus to really excel at any one game.

 When to add additional games and formats to your pool menu is largely related to how rapidly your game develops. If and when you expand your menu is also a matter of personal preference. The most logical progression for learning the four most popular pool games is Eight-Ball, Straight Pool, Nine-Ball and then One-Pocket.

It takes years of steady play to even come close to mastering any pool game, much less all of the games and formats. Much of what you learn from any game, however, can be applied to the others. As your skills grow, you sort of spin in a circle from game to game as you pick up elements from each game that can strengthen another game. In essence, the different games feed off each other. That's a big part of the reason why some of the great champions can play so many games so very well.

The differing skills required for each pool game leads to a rather unique phenomenon: you can often beat someone regularly at Eight-Ball and your opponent may in turn be able to trounce you at Nine-Ball.

Those who stick with one game often believe that it's the only game for real players. You'll often hear a specialist proudly proclaim that "I'm a Nine-Ball player" or "I only play One-Pocket." Players are often closely associated with their specialty, so much so in fact that most observers believe that their specialty is the only game they play, which may be entirely true.

CAPELLE'S LAWS for POOL

There is perhaps no greater joy than discovering which of the many great pool games is your game.

The variety of pool games ensures that the sport should never be boring to you.

When you learn a new game, you will improve your other games at the same time.

Your journey is on the right path when you have discovered what really turns you on about the game.

Adding new games to your repertoire can increase your enjoyment and knowledge exponentially.

You should make time to play your favorite game, even if it is not commonly played in your area.

The same man cannot be skilled in everything; each has his special excellence.

— **Euripides**

There are two things to aim at in life: first to get what you want; and after that, to enjoy it. Only the wisest of mankind achieves the second.

— **Logan Pearsall Smith**

Retaining Your Zest for Pool

When your flame of desire is burning hot you'll naturally find yourself in the pool room. Occasionally, however, your zest for the game may drop. To ensure that you retain your enthusiasm for pool it's important that you pace yourself. When you are merely going through the motions, it's often better to get away from the game for awhile. A break will allow you to recharge your batteries and have you itching to play once again.

The worst case scenario is that you play so much pool that you completely burn out on the game. This could lead to a several year hiatus from pool or even cause you to quit pool forever, which is, of course, unthinkable.

A number of players solve the problem of burnout by making pool a seasonal sport. In colder climates many players follow a schedule of 6 months on, 6 months off. If you can't bring yourself to stay away from the game that long (and I certainly don't recommend it), then you must create your own sense of pace. Perhaps you'll be most excited about pool if you play steadily for one to three months. Then take a one to three-week break. If you become a full-time pool addict like myself, then you'll find yourself playing five or six days a week, 48 weeks out of the year. I've pretty much followed this schedule for nearly 30 years and have lost absolutely none of my enthusiasm for the game.

The big question is how to retain your love of the game so you keep playing year after year without ever completely giving up pool. The following tips should prove helpful.

How to Stay Enthusiastic About Pool

⊙ Play enough to keep your game sharp.

⊙ Stay hungry by not over doing it.

⊙ Play only when you feel you can give it your best effort (not necessarily your best level of play).

⊙ Don't play so much that you feel guilty about the time you spend on pool.

⊙ Your goals for elevating your game play a big part in determining how much pool is enough.

⊙ Finding new things to incorporate into your game.

⊙ Choose carefully who you play, where you play and what to play.

⊙ During a break, occasionally take a few moments to reflect on your game. A revelation could propel you back into the pool room.

⊙ During a prolonged slump, it may help to get away from pool for a while.

Taking a break is a balancing act. You need to play competitively to keep you're stroke razor sharp. You also need to be away from pool or you'll lose your zest for the game. The trick is to establish a pattern of play and rest that keeps your interest high and that enables you to play at a level that you're very satisfied with.

CAPELLE'S LAWS for POOL

You can ensure your enthusiasm for pool by always playing just a little less pool than you'd really like to. That will always keep you looking forward to your next match.

A break should be long enough to restore your zest for pool, but short enough so that you don't lose much of your game.

Breaks are your best insurance against totally burning out on pool.

---

*Every now and then go away, have a little relaxation,
 for when you come back to your work
 your judgment will be surer.*

— **Leonardo da Vinci**

Can we ever have too much of a good thing?

— **Cervantes**

Enthusiasm is the most important thing in life.

— **Tennessee Williams**

What the Game Means to You

Many of you who start playing pool at a relatively young age harbor the notion that you will become a champion player, maybe even a touring professional. Then the realities of making a living in the real world and/or coming to terms with your less than world class potential short circuits your dreams of stardom. Those of you who continue in the game of may still enjoy playing, but you may also discover other activities that give you great joy from pool.

Next to playing a great game, what's one other thing that you really enjoy about pool? Chances are whatever first came to mind is the thing that continues to excite you about being a part of the sport. This activity may now represent the essence of the game to you. Some possible choices would include:

⊙ Teaching others to play.

⊙ Captaining a league team.

⊙ Running tournaments.

⊙ Studying the game's history.

⊙ Owning a pool room or supply store.

⊙ Practicing and learning about the game.

⊙   Collecting cues.

⊙   Collecting pool memorabilia.

⊙   Building your library of pool books and tapes.

⊙   Playing pool with your family at home.

⊙   Watching excellent players.

⊙   Talking pool with your fellow pool nuts.

CAPELLE'S LAWS for POOL

There is so much to enjoy about pool that you don't have to become a great player to have a great time.

I know the way of all things by what is within me.
— **Lao-tzu**

You often find your destiny on the path you take to avoid it.
— **Chinese Proverb**

Moments of Pool Magic

Knowledge is a big key to enjoying watching pool. The more you know, the more you can appreciate the game when you see the basics and the fine points being skillfully executed. And the more you appreciate the game, the more you will want to watch and learn even more. As a dedicated student and spectator of the game, you can set in motion a cycle that continually raises your enjoyment of the sport.

To the well trained eye, there is so much going on that you should never become bored watching good pool. Even routine shots are enjoyable when you are paying attention to the players style, where the cue ball comes to rest, and how it got there. It is also fun to evaluate how you would have played the shot. The items below can raise your appreciation of pool and stimulate your thinking about other techniques for enjoying pool watching.

Watching Pool

⊙ The fury and passion of a powerful Nine-Ball break. Watching the players jump up, twist, motion with their cue and plead for the balls to drop.

⊙ Tough shots such as banks, thin cuts and combos.

⊙ Draw shots where the cue ball spins in its tracks before shooting back.

⊙ Safeties that put a player in jail.

⊙ Three-rail position through traffic.

⊙ The flight of the cue ball on a jump shot.

⊙ Watching the cue ball as english takes off the rail.

⊙ The arc of the cue ball on a draw-cut shot.

⊙ Frozen 90 degree cut shots that seemingly defy physics.

⊙ The cue ball's white blur on firmly struck shots.

⊙ A great position play to a small shape zone.

⊙ The fundamentals and shooting style of each player.

⊙ The players "game face" and their reactions to good shots and bad shots.

In addition to the beautiful and extraordinary exploits of the players, you may also wish to keep an eye out for their mistakes and blunders. Look for how a player recovers from missed position or what mechanical flaw may have led to missing a shot. As a spectator, you can learn not only what to do but also the most common mistakes to be avoided.

CAPELLE'S LAWS for POOL

Your enjoyment from watching pool is directly related to your knowledge of the game.

The more you watch and learn, the more you will enjoy the game. And the more you enjoy the game, the more you will want to watch and learn even more.

Every good shot has a bit of magic to it. To the well-trained eye this continuously radiates the beauty of the game.

> *Wherever life takes us, there are always moments of wonder.*
> — **Jimmy Carter**
>
> *In small proportions we just beauties see,*
> *And in short measures life may perfect be.*
> — **Ben Johnson**
>
> *They have mouths, but they speak not; eyes have they, but they see not.*
> — **Psalms 115: 5-6**

The Sounds of Spheres in Motion

A symphony of sounds emanate from within the confines of a typical pool room. A course in pool appreciation is not complete without gaining a heightened sense of awareness of the broad array of sounds that are music to the ears of a true pool aficionado.

The crack of a powerful break shot makes a distinctly loud bang that can easily be heard throughout the room. An unusually powerful Nine-Ball break can propel the cue ball into the rack at upwards of 25 to 30 mphs. There is a more uniform tap and click on routine shots and the plopping sound as a softly hit object ball gently topples into the pocket. And naturally all players have come to despise the sound that echoes when a ball repeatedly strikes the jaws of the pocket.

When several tables are filled with players, there is the nonstop sound of cues striking cue balls, cue balls colliding with object balls and with balls slapping into the backs of pockets. Together the sounds create a kind of free-form jazz that is beautiful music to any hardcore pool enthusiast.

At times the sounds of the balls may turn into background music. A couple of dozen conversations may fill the air which may, in turn, be punctuated by sudden outbursts of anguish or applause. When a large group is present, conversations tend to escalate as everyone raises their voice to be heard. At some point, the level of noise falls to a low-level and begins to climb again as the cycle repeats itself. This ebb and flow provides a fascinating study in group psychology.

 You can enhance your appreciation of the sounds of a pool room by employing this tip: close your eyes for a few minutes and take special notice of all that you hear. Try switching your attention from one sound to another much in the same way as you might focus on the lead guitarist and then the drummer in a band.

CAPELLE'S LAWS for POOL

The symphony of balls clicking nonstop throughout the room is fine music to the ears of the most dedicated pool enthusiast.

The more that you involve each of you're senses in a shot, the greater will be your awareness and appreciation of the game.

Music from the spheres.
> — Shakespeare

For there is a music wherever there is a harmony, order, or proportion; and thus far we may maintain the music of the spheres.
> — Sir Thomas Browne

Sweet is every sound.
> — Lord Tennyson

Seeing, hearing, feeling, are miracles, and each part and tag of me is a miracle.
> — Walt Whitman

Pool is a Book Lover's Dream

There has been an explosive growth in the number of books on pool in recent years. The new and existing titles offer a bonanza for aspiring players and fans as well as for collectors of billiards memorabilia.

The number of books in print that are readily available from a variety of sources ensures that you can build a pretty impressive library in no time flat. You'll of course find numerous books that can help you improve all facets of your game. If you are looking for a new cue, there are books that cover the subject from inexpensive production cues clear through to the most expensive works of art. There are books that profile leading players, tell colorful stories of road players and novels that capture the spirit of the game. An absolute must for all players is the BCA Rule Book. In short, there's something for everybody.

To help you get started on building your pool library I've compiled a list of some of my personal favorites. They are broken down into very specific categories so that you can pinpoint titles in your area of interest. Naturally I've included my own books, as an author is entitled to be biased towards their work.

The retail price for our 24 library essentials, for the budget conscious, checks in at a mere $650.00.

Building Your Library

Instruction

- *Play Your Best Pool,* Philip Capelle.
- *Play Your Best Straight Pool,* Philip Capelle.
- *The Science of Pocket Billiards*, Jack Koehler.
- *Byrne's New Standard Book of Pool and Billiards,* Robert Byrne.
- *Precision Pool & Billiards*, Gerard D. Kanov and Shari J. Stauch.
- *Advanced Pool,* George Fels.
- *Shots, Moves and Strategies* (One-Pocket), Eddie Robin.

Introduction to Pool and Instruction on Basics

- *The Complete Idiot's Guide to Pool & Billiards,* Ewa Mataya Laurence and Thomas C. Shaw
- *Steve Mizerak's Complete Book of Pool,* Steve Mizerak and Mike Panozzo

The Mental Game

- *A Mind for Pool,* Philip Capelle
- *Smart Pool,* John Delaveau

Training Manual

- *The Pro Book*, Bob Henning

Cues

- *Blue Book of Cues*, Brad Simpson

Rules

- *The Billiard Congress of America Official Rules and Records Book*

Player Profiles

- *Buddy Hall: Rags to Rifleman, Then What?*, W.W. Woody
- *Willie's Game,* Willie Mosconi and Stanley Cohen
- *Cornbread Red*, Bob Henning

Stories and Novels

- *The Hustler,* Walter Tevis
- *Playing Off the Rail*, David McCumber

- *Byrne's Book of Great Pool Stories,* Edited by Robert Byrne

Trick Shots

- *Byrne's Treasury of Trick Shots in Pool and Billiards,*
  Robert Byrne

Pool Appreciation and History

- *Billiard Encyclopedia,* Victor Stein and Paul Rubino
- *Pool,* Mike Shamos
- *Shooting Pool,* Mike Shamos and George Bennett

 CAPELLE'S LAWS for POOL

No matter what your area and level of interest, you'll find something of value among the numerous excellent books on pool.

A classic...something that everybody wants to have read and nbody wants to read.
— **Mark Twain**

The fact of knowing how to read is nothing, the while point is knowing what to read.
— **Jacques Ellul**

There are worse crimes than burning books. One of them is not reading them.
— **Joseph Brodsky**

Just the knowledge that a good book is awaiting one at the end of a long day makes that day happier.
— **Kathleen Norris**

Pool on the Silver Screen

No course in pool appreciation would be complete without at least a viewing or two of "The Hustler", which came out in 1961. The movie is my choice for the No. 1 film of all time, due in part, I suppose, to my bias for pool. Paul Newman received an Oscar nomination for his role as Fast Eddy Felson. While Eddy does pull off a successful hustle at the beginning of the movie, the majority of the story revolves around his overwhelming desire to become the best player. Standing in his way is the legendary Minnesota Fats. Fats was played by Jackie Gleason, who was a very accomplished player in his own right. Gleason was also nominated for an Oscar. Rounding out the major players were George C. Scott (Eddy's stakehorse) and Piper Laurie (Eddy's girlfriend). Both were also nominated for Oscars. In sum, "The Hustler" won two Oscars and was nominated for seven more.

Although I recommend the movie highly, I'm not advocating that you take up hustling pool. In fact, the movie would turn off just about anybody to the lifestyle of a hustler. What the movie does show so well is how pool relates to real-life and how the game, at its best, is an exercise in building one's character. It also shows and describes so well what it's like to be in dead stroke. The movie was shot in black and white, which really allows you to focus in on each character.

"The Baltimore Bullet," which came out in 1980, has become pool's "B" movie cult classic, to put it kindly. The story is about hustling on the road, predictably enough. The movie had a very respectable cast that included James Coburn, Omar Sharif and Bruce Boxleitner. Die hard pool nuts will get a kick out of the cameo performances of ten of the world's best players.

Paul Newman resurrected his role of Fast Eddy in "The Color of Money" (1986), for which he won an Oscar. The movie was also nominated for three additional Oscars. Tom Cruise starred as Newman's youthful protégé. Mary Elizabeth Mastrantonio received an Oscar nomination for her role as Cruise's girlfriend while Helen Shaver portrayed Newman's significant other.

"The Color of Money" is a fast-paced frolic through the world of pool on the road, with equal parts of fiction and fact. For example, nobody who could ever run a rack would be caught dead twirling their cue as Cruise does in taunting his foes. Serious pool players are probably the movie's hardest critics. Less knowledgeable fans will probably get a big kick out of the films sometimes offbeat look at pool. In sum, I enjoyed the movie very much, but "The Hustler" spots it the six-ball and steals the cash. Since there is no continuing story line of major significance, I suggest that you watch " The Color of Money" first and then "The Hustler."

To give you an idea of what the critics think of pool at the movies, I consulted the four major movie guides. I calculated the percentage of "stars" won to possible "stars." "The Hustler" scored a perfect 100 percent. "The Color of Money" checked in at a very respectable 80.6 percent, while "The Baltimore Bullet" registered a very "B" movie like 50.5 percent

Movies and the Pool Business

"The Hustler" and "The Color of Money" have each spurred booms in the pool business immediately upon their release. It's simply amazing what two hours plus on film can do to wake up the consciousness of the masses to this most wonderful of games. The impact of these movies on pool also makes you wonder what the sport would be like if live big money tournaments were featured regularly on TV.

One of the great ironies of the pool business is that two films, which portrayed some of the less flattering aspects of the sport, could be so good for business. The industry has, at the same time, fought so hard to clean up the game's image in the hopes of attracting new participants and corporate sponsorship.

To put the movies in their proper perspective, you can find the good or bad in anything with just a little effort. The good news is that the two leading pool movies were both first-rate productions that featured top Hollywood talent. The movies featured real people in roles that captured the imagination of the viewers. Both films also showed what exposure can do for pool. The bad news is that the sport has had to rely on these movies in the first place to pull itself out of the doldrums.

 CAPELLE'S LAWS for POOL

No course in pool appreciation is complete without a viewing of "The Hustler."

We despise no source that can pay us a pleasing attention.
— Mark Twain

For me, the cinema is not a slice of life, but a piece of cake.
— Alfred Hitchcock

There is only one thing that can kill the Movies and that is education.
— Will Rogers

For I am nothing if not critical.
— Shakespeare

The cinema has thawed out people's brains.
— Jean Cocteau

Chapter 20
Pool People

"Lives of great men all remind us
We can make our lies sublime
And departing, leave behind us
Footprints on the sands of time."
— Henry Wadsworth Longfellow

Great Players

A great player can mean that the player meets any of several definitions. A great player can excel at Nine-Ball, Straight Pool or One-Pocket. A great player may shine in tournaments or money games. A great player can be revered for their skills in phases of the game such as position play or bank shots. The more categories in which a player excels, the higher will be his status in the pool world.

In the final analysis, tournament results must carry the most weight because that's where permanent records are written. The BCA Rule Book lists scores of great champions stating back to the 1800s. Champions named Taberski, Greenleaf, Mosconi, Lassiter, Crane, Mizerak, Sigel and Varner among the men and Balukas, Jones, and Fisher among the women are all household names to most every serious pool player with even a passing interest in the game's history.

The changing nature of the pro tours and the games that the pros play make it impossible to compare the champions of the past with today's stars. Straight Pool, which used to be the championship game, has been replaced by Nine-Ball. Other significant championships are also contested in One-Pocket and Eight-Ball.

Because you can't easily compare players from different eras based on tournament results alone, the pool world has developed its own "system" for rating players. To fully grasp the magnitude of pool's superstars, past and present, you must do some reading and talk with knowledgeable fans of the sport. Your research will fill in the gaps that are a residue of the lack of a consistent series of pro tournaments over the long-run.

Tournament Champions

The greatest prestige falls on those who have won multiple world titles in the game or games that were commonly played in a given era. It takes much skill and a dose of luck to win even one world title. If a player wins two or more titles, then the skill factor dominates over the possibility that the player won a single title due to a preponderance of good rolls.

The U.S. Open is one of the most coveted titles in pool, especially now that it has over 20 years of history behind it. A virtual Who's Who of today's current stars show up each year. This makes the U.S. Open the most hotly contested event in professional pool. The winner must successfully grind his way through a field of approximately 200 players to be crowned U.S. Open champion.

Players can also meet the criteria for greatness by winning a number of regular tour stops. You'll find that most of the truly great players will have that one special year when they were at the pinnacle of their game, the pool gods were on their side, and they won an inordinate number of championships. In 1989, for example, Hall of Famer Nick Varner captured eight titles, which would be an excellent career for any player.

Little Known Champions

The mantle of greatness can be awarded for a player's skills and accomplishments that do not show up in the record books. Pool's historians and biographers have done a fine job of making sure that many of pools unsung greats receive their rightful place in history. Of particular note is Tom Shaw's "Legends of the Road" series that appears regularly in *Pool and Billiard Magazine*.

The unknown greats of the game shunned the spotlight of tournament play so they could play in big money games. This approach was understandable since they could not hope to make a living from playing solely in tournaments. These greats built their reputations by excelling at various facets of the game and for their ability to play their best when big money was on the line.

What Makes a Champion

In some sports, the players need only master a select set of skills. A baseball pitcher doesn't need to hit, and a lineman doesn't have to catch or throw the football. To be a great pool player, however, you must achieve mastery in several areas of the game and near mastery in the rest. If your development is not complete, you will lose out to those who have the total package, plain and simple.

 A great player must combine mastery of the game with a measure of emotional control and mental toughness that far exceeds the requirements of nearly any other sport. A pool player has no teammates to cover for his lapses in play. He must maintain exquisite control of his muscles when his mind and a rush of adrenaline could easily sabotage his efforts. And at those times when a great player has lost the edge, he must be able to "grind away" and give it his best effort until his top game reappears. Great players are also great competitors.

Champions in Action

When you watch great players, there are many things to look for in addition to their position and shotmaking. Some of the conclusions which you may draw from watching the greats are that they:

- ⊙ Play with great confidence.
- ⊙ Make a very difficult game often look ridiculously easy.
- ⊙ Seem to have a purpose for every shot.
- ⊙ Can take their game up a notch when necessary.
- ⊙ Can pull off the big shots.
- ⊙ Show us what is possible on a pool table.
- ⊙ Exhibit their unique style.
- ⊙ Play the game as it was intended to be played.
- ⊙ Show relentless determination.

Watching the greats will give you a greater appreciation for what they do and a greater understanding of what's possible. You'll get charged up for playing because they make the game look so easy. You may even feel as if their level of play is within your reach. As icing on the cake, your game, through osmosis, will almost surely show improvement on your very next outing.

CAPELLE'S LAWS for POOL

Professional pool players truly love the game because they are certainly not in it to get rich.

Great players are the sum total of a wide variety of hard earned skills, each honed to a razor sharp edge.

Pool players have more heart than most other sportsmen, simply because the very nature the game demands it.

At the top, it's not just about how well you play, but how well you can play when the heat is on.

Top players are to be admired for their exceptional games and for their ability to bring their best game to the table against formidable opposition.

The best effort of fine persons is felt after we have left their presence.
— **Ralph Waldo Emerson**

Imagination is more important than knowledge.
— **Albert Einstein**

The great man does not think beforehand of his words that they may be sincere, nor of is actions that they maybe resolute—he simply speaks and does what is right.
— **Mencius**

> *Bigness comes from doing many small things well...individually, they are not very dramatic transactions. Together, though, they add up.*
>
> — **Edward S. Finkelstein**

Geniuses of Pool

Your pool IQ has nothing to do with the tests you took in school. A pool player's IQ is measured instead by how well he can play in competition. Champions such as Buddy Hall, Efren Reyes, Earl Strickland, and Johnny Archer, to name a few, are true geniuses at what they do. Their mastery of the game should not, however, be confused with the skill of teaching pool, which is a completely separate matter.

The genius which can be ascribed to the great players is largely a result of a more enlightened view of intelligence. It's now recognized that each and every one of us has our special area or areas of expertise. These special talents are partly God given and partly acquired through hard work.

Some people are good with numbers, some can paint while others have great people skills. Top pool players have their own form of intelligence that is a combination of several skills in which they are highly proficient.

Pool players possess a high degree of physical intelligence. This enables them to match the movement of their arm and hand to what they see on the table. Champions have great memories for a wide variety of complex data. They can quickly read the table and make smart decisions on the best course of action. On a typical shot a player must factor in the cut angle, throw and deflection, the size of the pocket, how english takes off the rail, where to hit the cue ball, what force is required, where he wants the cue ball to go and how it's going to get there! Sounds impossible, doesn't it? The pros, however, make it look like child's play.

The package of talents described above is capped by a player's emotional makeup and mental abilities. These enable him to apply his skills to the utmost when the pressure is on. By viewing great pool players as true geniuses of the green cloth, you can gain an even greater appreciation for the magic they perform at the table.

Like the pros, you may have a special aptitude for pool that enables you to play a very respectable game. You may even have the makings of a champion. Regardless of your innate talent for pool, you can nevertheless raise your pool IQ by applying yourself to the game in as intelligent a manner as possible. In doing so, you will enable yourself to get the absolute most from what you've got.

 CAPELLE'S LAWS for POOL

A champion may not necessarily be a great teacher, but they sure as heck know what they are doing.

Rocket scientists are not professional pool players and vice versa. But if you are pool smart you're smart.

Genius does what is must, and talent does what it can.
— **Edward Robert Bulwer-lytton**

Genius must be born, and never can be taught.
— **John Dryden**

Eccentricities of genius.
— **Charles Dickens**

Hats off, gentlemen—A genius!
— **Robert Schumann**

Old-Timers

My favorite "old-timer" was a grizzled veteran named Tower Bill who graced the San Diego pool seen in the early '70s. While sweating the action at College Billiards he would pass judgment on each player's skills. The majority of the time he would conclude by saying " Oh, George, (or whatever the players name was) why heee can't play." This used to amuse the onlookers, myself included. What was just as amusing is that he probably said the same thing about me when I was playing. No matter, I loved talking with Bill because, as the pool players would say, he was the nuts.

 Old-timers like Bill are a treasured part of the landscape of any pool room. These are pure pool people with a long history in the game. They may go back 30-40 years or longer. You can just imagine the many colorful people and adventures they've experienced along their journey in pool.

Old-timers can provide you with hours filled with amusing tales of their exploits. They enjoy being themselves around their fellow pool nuts as they no longer have anything left to prove. They love to talk pool and they will generally warm-up to anyone with a genuine interest in pool and a love for the game.

Nearly every old-timer will tell you how great they played when they were young. If you are interested in their words of wisdom on how to play, you should first test their credentials. Consider the following:

- ☑ Does he still play well enough to indicate that he could have played really well in his prime?

- ☑ Does he talk a good game when it comes to technique and strategy?

- ☑ Are there other pool people who can verify his status as a player?

The answers to the questions above will help you assign your old-timer/ mentor candidate to one of two broad categories: those that really could play and those who can talk like they could play but who really couldn't.

 CAPELLE'S LAWS for POOL

Treat old-timers with respect because you'll be in their place someday.

Everybody used to play 50 percent better than they really did long ago when they don't have to prove it on the table anymore.

An old-timer who was once a fine player has forgotten half of what he knew, but he still knows twice as much as somebody half his age.

The trick is growing up without growing old.
— Casey Stengel

Things ain't what they used to be and probably never was.
— Will Rogers

Time goes by: reputation increases, ability declines.
—Dag Hammarskjold

If the young and only knew; if the old only could.
— French saying

Friends and Acquaintances

If you like people, then you'll love pool, because it's the ultimate people game. When competing, it's just you and your opponent. You get to know other players in a way that's not possible in team sports. The competitive atmosphere also fosters a sense of brotherhood among pool players. The nature of a pool room leads to much interaction among players when they are not competing. There is ample time between matches for discussing the in and outs of a game that particularly lends itself to intellectualization.

You can develop as many friendships in pool as you wish because most pool people are very pleasant and outgoing. What you receive from your relationships in pool will mirror what you put into them. Your pool playing friends will share with you a burning desire to talk pool. Your pool friends desperately want to tell you their tales of heroic shots and their bummer rolls that unjustly robbed them of victory. And, of course, you will want to reciprocate with your stories of triumph and heartbreak.

How to be a Pool Friend

The common denominator of a healthy and well-balanced pool friendship is a willingness to listen to each other. Because you will spend much time listening, in also helps if your pool friends are good storytellers.

You and your closest pool playing friends can play a number of important roles. These roles can help you each get more from the game. The key is a willingness to do the little things for your friends that you would want them to do for you. This is sort of a golden rule among pool players.

Some of the key roles include:

⊙ well wisher
⊙ instructor
⊙ psychologist
⊙ critic
⊙ road partner
⊙ comedian
⊙ go-fer
⊙ financial consultant
⊙ agent

Nicknames

One of the most obvious signs of affection and belonging in pool is when you are given a nickname. Your nickname can be an adaptation of your name or it could describe your physical characteristics. "Minnesota Fats" is pool's best-known nickname. Notice how it incorporates the player's supposed place of origin.

Nicknames can be based on your style of play, your mental makeup, your likeness to some animal, your occupation, your knowledge of pool or any other description that seems appropriate. Some of the best nicknames rightfully belong to some of pool's greatest champions. Perhaps you and your friends can come up with some ideas for nicknaming each other from the examples below.

Nicknames of Famous Players

Minnesota Fats	Rudolph Wanderone
The Magician	Efren Reyes
Machine Gun	Lou Butera
King James	Jim Rempe
Cool Cat	Ray Martin
Tennessee Tarzan	Mike Massey
Wimpy	Luther Lassiter
Knoxville Bear	Eddie Taylor
Cowboy	Jimmy Moore
The Professor	Grady Matthews
Cornbread Red	Bill Burge
The Deacon	Irving Crane
Captain Hook	Mike Sigel
Rifleman	Buddy Hall
The Pearl	Earl Strickland
The Meatman	Joe Balsis
Red Raider	Jack Breit
Young Hoppe	Allen Hopkins
Champagne Eddie	Ed Kelly

CAPELLE'S LAWS for POOL

If the game you tell your friends about is even 70% as good as you describe, then you're probably a wonderful player.

CAPELLE'S LAWS for POOL

Some of the most highly skilled and underpaid psychologists hang out in pool rooms.

You're a great listener if you listen 50% as hard to your friends pool stories as you hope they are listening to yours.

Every pool player you meet has the potential to add something meaningful to your journey and vice versa.

You shouldn't waste too much energy worrying about the people in pool because without them there wouldn't be a sport.

I genuinely like most pool players but even if I don't like someone, I love them all the same because we're all in this crazy, beautiful, wonderful, demanding, frustrating and glorious game together.

Without friends no one would choose to live, though he had all other goods.
> — Aristotle

The only way to have a friend is to be one.
> — Ralph Waldo Emerson

Be slow in choosing a friend, slower in changing.
> —Benjamin Franklin

What's in a name? That which we call a rose
By any other word would smell as sweet.
> — Shakespeare

The most called-upon prerequisite of a friend is an accessible ear.
> — Maya Angelou

There can be no friendship without confidence, and no confidence without integrity.
> — Samuel Johnson

The more the merrier.
> — John Heywood

Junior Pool Builds Character

Pool has so much to offer that I would encourage any parent to introduce their child or children to the game. For starters, pool levels the playing field for all participants. Your child does not have to fit the stereotype of the naturally gifted athlete to play pool. Pool teaches youngsters many valuable lessons that can be applied to everyday life. The game also represents a near perfect blend of physical and mental skills. This allows your child to simultaneously develop their mind and their hand-eye coordination. By introducing your child to pool now you will be giving them a gift that can last a lifetime, because pool, unlike so many other sports, can be played clear into your 80's or even beyond.

Every child can use some help in maturing into a responsible and well-behaved young adult. Pool can be a big help. When the game is properly taught in the ideal environment, then your child becomes the beneficiary of a whole host of character building activities.

Positive Lessons From Pool

Self-confidence	Competitive spirit
Hand-eye coordination	Respect for others
Problem solving	Etiquette
Patience	Goal setting
Self-control	Decision making
Self-reliance	Sharing
Concentration	Honesty
Sportsmanship	Humor
Overcoming adversity	Acceptance

After reflecting upon the above list, I'm sure any parent can see the many benefits of having their child or children participate in this wonderful sport. The more that you as parents are willing to put into it, like any other activity, then the more you can expect to receive back from pool. I suggest that you encourage your child to focus not just on the game but on the terrific life enhancing benefits that were listed above. Support their efforts without pushing or pressuring them. Give them a good head start with qualified instruction on the fundamentals and with a grounding in the game's etiquette. And always remember that pool is a game that can be enjoyed together and that can strengthen your relationship.

If I could wave a magic wand and make a wish come true, then pool would be an accepted sport at every high school and college. Unfortunately, this is beyond my power. It is, therefore, up to parents to take the initiative in their community to create a regular series of competitions between aspiring junior players.

Juniors who show a special aptitude for the game now have the opportunity to compete for national championships that are held annually by both the Billiard Congress of America and the Valley

National Eight-Ball Association. You can find out how to contact each organization in the appendix.

CAPELLE'S LAWS for POOL

When pool is properly taught and played in an ideal environment, it can bring a child much joy and personal growth.

Train a child in the way he should go, and when he is old he will not depart from it.
— **Proverbs 12:4**

Your children need your presence more than your presents.
— **Jesse Jackson**

Children have more need of models than critics.
— **Joseph Joubert**

If a child is to keep alive his inborn sense of wonder without any such gift from the fairies, he needs the championship of at least one adult who can share it, rediscovering with him the joy, excitement and mystery of the world we live in.
— **Rachel Carson**

It is a wise father that knows his own child.
— **Shakespeare**

Every adult needs a child to teach; it's the way adults learn.
— **Frank A. Clark**

The Rogues of Pool

A big part of pool's colorful history is the cast of characters who oftentimes have crossed over the boundary of socially acceptable behavior. The rogues of pool entertain us and at times infuriate us, like the characters you see on "pro" wrestling. Rogues also act as reverse role models by showing us what we don't want to become ourselves.

Have ever wondered about your behavior? Perhaps its time to find out if you resemble pool's more outlandish characters. You can start by asking a couple of your friends about your conduct. If you have no one you can question, it's possible you already have your answer. One other approach is to take the rogues self-test. If you discover that your "normal" behavior is in accordance with any of the items below, you qualify as a rogue. Even one yes makes you a candidate to be 86'ed from any self-respecting establishment.

Rogues Self Quiz

☑ Do you hustle helpless victims and drunks out of large sums of money?

☑ Can you "do business" and still sleep at night?

☑ Do you make derogatory comments about your opponent or shark them unmercifully?

☑ Is winning your only goal no matter what means are required?

☑ Do you sneak into tournaments that would bar you from competing if they knew your true speed?

☑ Do you curse loudly and/or slam racks and balls around when you get angry?

☑ Do you get drunk regularly and act in a totally obnoxious manner?

Your answers to these questions should tell you if you are a member of the rogue's gallery. Those of you who qualify may, in fact, relish your role. The reasons for your behavior probably date back to your childhood. While it's never too late to change your stripes you may get some comfort from knowing that you serve several useful purposes.

The True Value of Pool's Rogues Gallery

⊙ Their exploits make for great storytelling.

⊙ They create a buzz in a pool room.

⊙ Their antics can be entertaining as long as you are not the victim of their shenanigans.

⊙ They make us appreciate good behavior.

⊙ They serve as excellent role models in reverse.

 Pool is a game meant to be played by real people, not by colorless robots. Within certain limits, people must be allowed to be themselves. Besides, most people get a kick out of other peoples somewhat nutty and eccentric behavior. How else can you explain the popularity of the trash talk shows, tabloids and the evening news?

CAPELLE'S LAWS for POOL

Enjoy being entertained by the rogues of pool but always try to keep them at arm's-length.

There will always be rogues in every sporting activity, pool most definitely included. Without them, the game would lose much of its color.

Rogues behavior make the rest of us look better than we probably really are.

I do desire we may be better strangers.
— Shakespeare

You can fool some of the people some of the time, and some of the people all of the time, but you cannot fool all of the people all of the time.
— Abraham Lincoln

God bears with the wicked, but not forever.
— Cervantes

Don't mistake personality for character.
— Wilma Askinas

Dishonor will not trouble me, once I am dead.
— Euripides

Our deeds determine us, as much as we determine our deeds.
— George Eliot

APPENDIX

Periodicals

The publications listed below give you stories, features, playing tips and reviews on books and tapes as well as other products of interest to the pool enthusiast. Most offer complete coverage of pro events and, in some cases, extensive coverage of regional events. They also provide you with schedules of upcoming events that may interest you as either a player or spectator.

Although there is obviously some overlap between the publications, each one nevertheless offers enough original material to make their modest annual cost well worth it to the serious player. The tab for all six is about $150 a year. Each publication comes out monthly.

All About Pool
Academy Plaza
717 South Main Street
Bradford, MA 01835

PH: 978-469-9311

www.bca-pool.com/allaboutpool

American Cueist Magazine
8020 Carr Street
Dallas, TX 75227

PH: 214-388-3632

cust.iamerica.net/cueist/

Billards Digest
122 South Michigan Avenue
Suite 1506
Chicago, IL 60603

PH: 312-341-1110

www.billardsdigest.com

The National Billard News
P.O. Box 807
Northville, MI 48167

PH: 248-348-0053

News & Cues
66 Greenview Drive
Suite 603
Kingston, Ontario K7M 7L5
Canada

PH: 613-545-9737

www.aracnet.net

Pool & Billiard Magazine
810 Travelers Blvd., Suite D
Summerville, SC 29485

PH: 843-875-5115

www.poolmag.com

League Pool

There are several National league associations that offer a very satisfying form of competition to players of all levels of skill. In many areas you will have a choice between leagues. And you may wish to play on more than one team if "League Night" is different for each association in your area. In many regions your choice may be limited as each association's penetration nationwide is highly fragmented. If you are very serious about league pool and your area lacks the association of your choosing, you are a candidate to bring their organization to your area.

Each of the major associations is profiled below. You can start your selection process by visiting their web sites and by calling them to find out if their association is established in your area. You can also discover what's available in your area by visiting your favorite pool room or tavern. By applying a little thought to your selection process you can ensure that your league experience is as completely satisfying as possible.

American Poolplayers Association (APA)

1000 Lake Saint Louis Blvd., Suite 325
Lake Saint Louis, MO 63367

Phone: **314-625-8611 or 800-3-RACKEM**
Internet: **www.poolplayers.com**
Franchise Opportunity: **dhubbart@poolplayers.com**

Overview: The APA is the Nation's largest association with over 165,000 members. The league's handicap system allows beginners to compete alongside advanced players. There is an emphasis on the better players teaching newcomers to play. The APA is very well organized and it does a great job communicating with its members.

- Games Played: Eight-Ball, Nine-Ball
- Coed. 76 percent Men, 24 percent Women.
- Three Seasons Annually. 14-16 weeks long.
- Format:
    First Team to Win 3 matches. One on one.
    Handicapped—self correcting
    Average of 7 players per team
- Mostly bar table, but some big tables

National Championship held annually in Las Vegas
$800,000 Prize Money
5,000 + Participants
Qualifying: Must play in spring season
Earn entry to Nationals in local qualifying tournaments

Billiard Congress of America (BCA)
910 23rd Avenue
Coralville, IA 52241-1221

Phone: **319-351-2112**
Internet: **www.bca-pool.com**
Email: **bca@netins.net**;web:**http:11**

Overview: The BCA is the most flexible of the major associations. It provides sanctioning for leagues that prefer to establish their own format. As a result, some leagues are handicapped, some not. On balance, the BCA is for players with several years' experience although that certainly does not exclude newer players from participation. There are 41,000 members, making it the nation's third largest league.

- Games Played: Eight Ball, Nine-Ball, and some Straight Pool
- Seasons Last 8-32 weeks
- Format:
    Up to league's discretion
    Some handicapped, some not
    3-5 persons per team
    Bar table and big table

National Championships held annually in Las Vegas
$550,000 Prize Money
6,000 + Participants
Qualifying: Meet minimum standards of participation by playing in 8 matches over 8 weeks

Valley National 8-Ball Association (VNEA)
333 Morton Street
Bay City, MI 48706

Phone: **800-544-1346**
Internet: **www.vnea.com**

Overview: The VNEA is the second largest amateur league with over 70,000 members. The league is very flexible in its format. All play on tavern size tables. The VNEA works hard to ensure the progress of its members by offering a Certified Instructor Program. All members receive a very comprehensive quarterly magazine.

- Games Played: Eight-Ball and Nine-Ball
- Coed. 80 percent Men, 20 percent Women
- Three Seasons Annually

- Format: Varies
  Tavern sized tables
  National Championships, held annually in Las Vegas
  $500,000 Prize Money
  5,000+ Participants
  Qualifying: Play a minimum of 12 weeks

The Association For P.O.O.L., Inc.
720 Jackson Street, Suite 205
Herndon, VA 22070

Phone: **800-984-7665**
Internet: **www.pool-net.com**

Overview: The Association for P.O.O.L. is a 10,000–20,000 member league with affiliates in the Midwest and Eastern Seaboard, but that seeks a national presence. The league features a proprietary handicapping system, and it encourages better players to help teammates with their game.

- Games Played: Eight-Ball and Nine-Ball
- Coed. 75 percent Men, 25 percent Women
- Three Seasons Annually. 16 weeks long
- Format:
  Five Matches One on one
  Handicapped
  Six to seven players each

Six Regional Championships held throughout the year.
$10,000 in prizes at each event.

Pot O' Gold Pool & Dart Leagues
456 Grove Street
Worchester, MA 01605

Phone: **888-554-6530**
Internet: **www.potogoldleagues.com**

Overview: Pot O' Gold uses a proprietary handicap system to promote equal competition. The league has 3,000 members in 25 states. Pot O' Gold features high payouts. A winner's choice league enables participants to play both Eight-Ball and Nine-Ball on the same night.

- Games Played: Eight-Ball and Nine-Ball
- Coed
- League Seasons can start anytime. They last about 12-20 weeks.

- Format: 5 Players- 5 Games Each
  Play on all size tables

National Championships, held in Las Vegas.
Qualifying: 1 in 12 teams from regional qualifying goes to the Nationals.

Pro, Semi-Pro and Regional Events

The tours in this section are open to all players. As a result, you'll often find some of the best players competing along side amateurs of "average" ability. The entry fees are rather modest, which allows any player to taste the rigors of top-flight competition. The tours are an excellent training ground for the aspiring player. They also feature many excellent players who have chosen to limit their competition primarily to regional events.

Most tournaments run two or three days. They typically offer prizes of a few thousand dollars to as much as twenty thousand dollars or more for their championship events. All are very well run by organizations with years of experience in tournament pool.

BCA All-American Tour   **PH: 319-351-2112**
910 23rd Avenue
Coralville, IA 52241-1221   **Internet: www.bca-pool.com**
Contact: Jeff Wallace

The Florida Tour   **PH: 561-743-9501**
201 North U.S. Hwy 1, D-6
Jupiter, FL 33477
Contact: Paul Johnson

Joss Northeast 9- Ball Tour   **PH: 518-356-7163**
1206 Fort Hunter Road
Rotterdam, NY 12303
Contact: Mike Zuglan

National Nine Ball Tour   **PH: 972-712-8687**
P.O. Box 700814   **Internet: www.texasexpress.com**
Dallas, TX 75370   **www.national9balltour.com**
Contact: John McChesney

The Viking Cue 9-Ball Tour   **PH: 800-200-7665**
Mike Janis Productions
P.O. Box 111135
Cleveland, OH 44111
Contact: Mike Janis

Women's Regional Tours

The Ladies Florida Tour   PH: 407-676-9977
Attn: Tracey McCreary
271 E. Haven Drive
W. Melbourne, FL 32904

Ladies Amateur Southeastern Region   PH: 770-451-3351
Attn: Joe Watson
P.O. Box 47222
Doraville, GA 30362

Southeastern Amateur Ladies Tour   PH: 770-513-6563
Attn: Joe Watson
415 Alcovy Hills Dr.
Lawrenceville, GA 30045

Northeastern Women's Tour   PH: 508-998-3330
Attn: Candy Rego
2901 Acushnet Ave.
New Bedford, MA 02745   **Internet: www.op.net/~lobo**

Arizona Women's Billiard Tour   PH: 602-927-1680
Attn: Nicole McCue
P.O. Box 10241
Scottsdale, AZ 85271

Western Women's Regional Tour   PH: 702-882-8997
Attn: Julie Hunter
C/O Cue-Phoria Billiards
55 East Winnie Lane
Carson, NV

**Association of Cue Sports for
   Women, Inc. (ACW)**
Attn: Linda Carter
5235 16th Ave., SW
Seattle, WA 98106   **Internet: www.acwtour.com**

Hunter Tour   PH: 210-846-9244
Attn: Shayla Neris
P. O. Box 81254
Aistin, TX 78709-1254

Wheelchair Pool

National Wheelchair Poolplayers   **PH:**   **734-422-2124**
    Association (NWPA)
Attn: Bob Calderon
30872 Puritan Street
Livonia, MI 48154

Professional Tours

The pro tours listed below feature the very best players in the world. In most of the men's events, entry is limited to top ranked pros or to those who have won a spot in a qualifying tournament. In some events, such as the U.S. Open, you can pay the entry and step to the table against the very best. The Women's Professional Billiard Association (WPBA) is limited only to ranking players and a handful of players who earn spots in qualifying tournaments. The WPBA sponsors the Ladies National Amateur Championship annually. Each organization can provide you with the details on how you can "Turn Pro."

Camel Pro Billiard Tour   **PH:**   **800-372-2536**
Contact: Larry Kieger

Professional Cue Sports Association   **Internet: www.cuesports.com**

Pro Billiards Tour   **Internet: www.propool.com**

Steve Mizerak Senior Tour   **PH:**   **561-840-0048**
Steve Mizerak Promotions, Inc.
1243 52nd Street, Suite 1
Mangonia Park, FL 33407
Contact: Steve Mizerak
(For pros and semi-pros over 50)

Women's Professional
   Billiard Association   **PH:**   **901-380-1102**
5676 Summer Avenue   **Internet: www.wpba.com**
Memphis, TN 38134
Contact: Steve Tipton

About the Author

Mr. Capelle took up pool in 1969 while attending U.C. Berkeley where he earned a degree in business. He spent 18 years in the financial services industry as a newsletter editor, stockbroker, financial analyst and as a columnist for the *Orange County Business Journal*. His first book, *Investing in Growth*, was published by Probus in 1992.

Mr. Capelle has spent the last 30 years studying, playing, watching and teaching pool. He has directed several tournaments including the 1993 Orange County Bar Table 9-Ball Championship. He has won numerous local tournaments and a major Southern California 8-Ball Championship. Mr. Capelle is a Certified Instructor with the Billard Congress of America and he is an instructional columnist for *Pool & Billiard Magazine*.

In 1995 Mr. Capelle formed Billiard Press. He has since written *Play Your Best Pool, A Mind for Pool* and *Play Your Best Straight Pool*.

Reader Comments

I would like to hear your comments on the book and suggestions for future editions. You can write to me at:

BILLIARD PRESS
P. O. Box 400
Midway City, CA 92655